Happy #60 Barb,
You wear it so well!
Hope this inspires you
as it has me ♡
Enjoy!
Love, Ellen
5-15-12

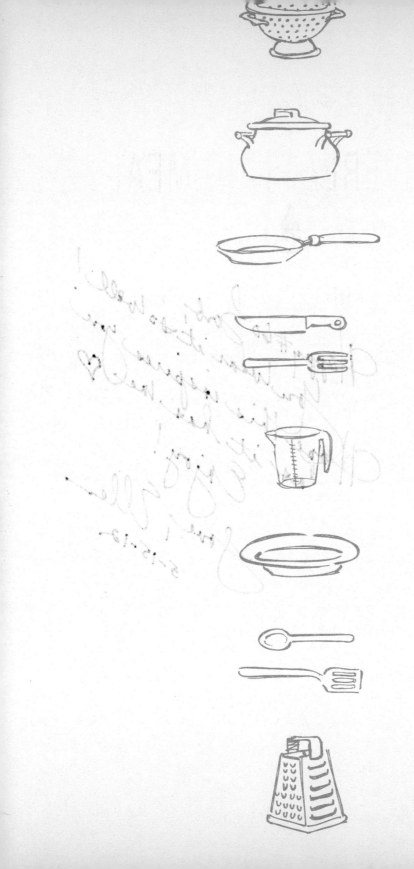

AN EVERLASTING MEAL

Cooking with Economy and Grace

TAMAR ADLER

SCRIBNER
New York London Toronto Sydney New Delhi

For my mother, my brother, and my father,
and all amateur cooks

There, then, is the role of the amateur: to look the world
back to grace.

— Robert Farrar Capon, *The Supper of the Lamb*

Contents

~

Foreword *by Alice Waters*   *xi*

Introduction: How to Begin   *1*

1. How to Boil Water   *5*
2. How to Teach an Egg to Fly   *19*
3. How to Stride Ahead   *35*
4. How to Catch Your Tail   *57*
5. How to Paint Without Brushes   *63*
6. How to Light a Room   *69*
7. How to Have Balance   *79*
8. How to Season a Salad   *93*
9. How to Live Well   *105*
10. How to Make Peace   *117*
11. How to Feel Powerful   *129*
12. How to Build a Ship   *141*
13. How to Find Fortune   *147*
14. How to Be Tender   *155*
15. How to Fry the Littlest Fish   *175*
16. How to Snatch Victory from the Jaws of Defeat   *187*
17. How to Weather a Storm   *199*
18. How to Have Your Day   *207*
19. How to Drink to Saints   *215*
20. How to End   *221*

Appendix: Further Fixes   *229*

Acknowledgments   *239*

Index   *241*

Foreword

~

Alice Waters

I met Tamar Adler in 2007 when she first came to work in the Chez Panisse kitchen and wove herself into the fabric of the restaurant with easy grace. She was only twenty-nine at the time, and I was instantly struck by her preternatural poise and presence. Tamar had never had formal culinary training, but she grew up cooking all the time, opened a restaurant in Georgia with friends, and came to Chez Panisse from there: she made a profession of her amateur cooking.

Tamar has an instinctive gift for cooking, an almost effortless way of creating meals—and as I quickly learned, she is an extraordinary writer: tremendously talented, with an unswerving commitment to the philosophy of honest food.

What is remarkable about *An Everlasting Meal* is how true it is to Tamar's spirit. The book is beautifully intimate, approaching cooking as a narrative that begins not with a list of ingredients or a tutorial on cutting an onion but with a way of thinking. How rare and wonderful it is to have a book grounded in instinct, prompting the reader to examine the world around him- or herself differently, allowing cooking to become a continuous, integrative process that flows from meal to meal.

In this way, the book is profoundly economical; it is predicated upon the idea that nothing should be wasted, that cooking well is built upon a deep, preservative impulse. Tamar knows that when you cook you are left with scraps that, instead of being discarded, can make the perfect beginnings of another meal: the skins and tops of onions for soups and beans, bones for stock, orange peels for marmalade.

Rather than a heady, lofty affair full of absolutes and inflexible recipes, the book is resolutely practical, a celebration of the malleability of cooking. Tamar champions the amateur cook, empowering readers to embrace the process, including the mistakes along the way. In her wonderful chapter "How to Snatch Victory from the Jaws of Defeat," she deals with just that: overcooked meat becomes a Thai meat and toasted rice salad (*laarb*), or crispy lardons, or meat and vegetable hash; burned zucchini becomes a delicious variation on a smoky baba ghanoush. She sees the frustrations and challenges that home cooks face every day, and then shows them how to meet these challenges smilingly. She is teaching people not just how to cook but how to *love* to cook.

Tamar is one of the great writers I know—her prose is exquisitely crafted, beautiful and clear-eyed and open, in the thoughtful spirit of M. F. K. Fisher.

This is a book to sink into and read deeply, relishing the quiet way Tamar fits profundity into the smallest of moments. On the subject of salt: "The noodle or tender spring pea would be narcissistic to imagine it already contained within its cell walls all the perfection it would ever need. We seem, too, to fear that we are failures at being tender and springy if we need to be seasoned. It's not so: it doesn't reflect badly on pea or person that either needs help to be most itself." On the subject of eggs: "Eggs should be laid by chickens that have as much of a say in it as any of us about our egg laying does." Or on the subject of using leftovers (from the chapter "How to Catch Your Tail"): "When we leave our tails trailing behind us we lose what is left of the thought we put into eating well today. Then we slither along, straight, linear things that we can be, wondering what we will make for dinner tomorrow." With sentences like these, this is so much more than a cookbook, or even a book about food; *An Everlasting Meal* is an important work about living fully, responsibly, and well, and gently reveals Tamar's philosophy that what we eat and how we eat it is inextricably linked to our happiness.

AN EVERLASTING MEAL

Introduction

~

How to Begin

In 1942, M. F. K. Fisher wrote a book called *How to Cook a Wolf*. *How to Cook a Wolf* is not a cookbook or a memoir or a story about one person or one thing. It is a book about cooking defiantly, amid the mess of war and the pains of bare pantries. Because food was rationed, it is about living well in spite of lack, which made a book "devoted to food and its preparation" as the *New York Times* described it, spiritually restorative.

The essays it contains make it seem practical to consider one's appetite. It advocated cooking with gusto not only for vanquishing hardship with pleasure but for "weeding out what you yourself like best to do, so that you can live most agreeably in a world full of an increasing number of disagreeable surprises."

I love that book. I have modeled this one on it.

This is not a cookbook or a memoir or a story about one person or one thing. It is a book about eating affordably, responsibly, and well, and because doing so relies on cooking, it is mostly about that.

Cooking is both simpler and more necessary than we imagine. It has in recent years come to seem a complication to juggle against other complications, instead of what it can be—a clear path through them.

If we are to weed, today, through all the advice for how to eat better, and choose what we ourselves feel most able and like best to do, we must regain our faith that cooking can be advantageous, something that helps eating well make sense.

Resources for simple cooking often do more harm than good. A fast-and-easy cooking magazine I picked up recently seemed contrived to scare its readers off. The magazine advertised recipes for "boil-and-toss pastas" and "last-minute omelets" amid other tips for getting meals to the table quickly. It pretended to make cooking easier, but complicated it instead.

All pasta is "boil and toss." A lot of perfectly wonderful meals are "boil" alone. You don't need a shortcut for either, but to reserve the three dollars you might have spent on the magazine and use it for buying salt and decent olive oil.

There's plain deceit in hawking "last-minute" omelets. Omelets happen almost instantly, no matter what you do to speed them up or slow them down. Suggesting there are special "last-minute" ones is akin to selling tips for breathing air more rapidly—if you have an egg, you have a meal that needs but a quick tap to be cracked open.

This book contains what I know of boiling and cooking eggs. It contains my strategies for cooking vegetables and meat, which rely on the fortuitous truth that both are best bought whole and cooked ahead, and the ways I have of making each earn its keep.

It doesn't contain "perfect" or "professional" ways to do anything, because we don't need to be professionals to cook well, any more than we need to be doctors to treat bruises and scrapes: we don't need to shop like chefs or cook like chefs; we need to shop and cook like people learning to cook, like what we are—people who are hungry.

We're so often told cooking is an obstacle that we miss this. When we cook things, we transform them. And any small acts of transformation are among the most human things we do. Whether it's nudging dried leaves around a patch of cement, or salting a tomato, we feel, when we exert tiny bits of our human preference in the universe, more alive.

Luckily we don't have far to go. Great meals rarely start at points that all look like beginnings. They usually pick up where something else leaves off. This is how most of the best things are made—imagine if the world had to begin from scratch each dawn: a tree would never grow, nor would we ever get to see the etchings of gentle rings on a clamshell.

I have spare but sturdy recommendations for beginnings, and lots for picking up loose ends. Stale slices of bread should be ground into breadcrumbs, which make a delicious topping for pasta, and add crunch to a salad. Or they must be toasted and broken apart for croutons or brittle crackers, which ask to be smeared with olive paste.

Meals' ingredients must be allowed to topple into one another like dominos. Broccoli stems, their florets perfectly boiled in salty water, must be simmered with olive oil and eaten with shaved Parmesan on toast; their leftover cooking liquid kept for the base for soup, studded with other vegetables, drizzled with good olive oil, with the rind of the Parmesan added for heartiness.

This continuity is the heart and soul of cooking. If we decide our meals will be good, remanded kale stems, quickly pickled or cooked in olive oil and garlic, will be taken advantage of to garnish eggs, or tossed with pasta. Beet and turnip greens, so often discarded, will be washed well and sautéed in olive oil and filled into an omelet, or served on warm, garlicky crostini. The omelets or little toasts will have cost no more than eggs and stale bread, and both will have been more gratifying to eater and cook.

In her first book, *Serve It Forth,* M. F. K. Fisher wrote that its recipes would be there "like birds in a tree—if there is a comfortable branch."

I hope that the recipes in this book are only there because branches offered themselves. I have been economical with them. I have always found that recipes make food preparation seem staccato: they begin where their writers are, asking that you collect the ingredients their writers have, and end with the instruction: "Serve hot," or less often "Serve cold."

But cooking is best approached from wherever you find yourself when you are hungry, and should extend long past the end of the page. There should be serving, and also eating, and storing away what's left; there should be looking at meals' remainders with interest and imagining all the good things they will become. I have tried to include more of that and fewer teaspoons and tablespoons and cups.

This is my attempt to hand over what I think matters. Then, whether you are hungry or anxious or curious, you can at least weed through and decide what seems right. I only mean to show what cooking is: an act of gathering in and meting out, a coherent story that starts with the lighting of a burner, the filling of a pot, and keeps going as long as we like. So, our end I think is clear. If our meal will be ongoing, then our only task is to begin.

One

How to Boil Water

— · —————————————————— · —

When is water boiling? When, indeed, is water water?
— M. F. K. Fisher, *How to Cook a Wolf*

There is a prevailing theory that we need to know much more than we do in order to feed ourselves well. It isn't true. Most of us already have water, a pot to put it in, and a way to light a fire. This gives us boiling water, in which we can do more good cooking than we know.

Our culture frowns on cooking in water. A pot and water are both simple and homely. It is hard to improve on the technology of the pot, or of the boil, leaving nothing for the cookware industry to sell.

The pot was invented 10,000 years ago, and a simmering one has been a symbol of a well-tended hearth ever since. I don't mean to suggest that now that you have been reminded of the age and goodness of a pot of water, you start boiling everything in your kitchen— but that instead of trying to figure out what to do about dinner, you put a big pot of water on the stove, light the burner under it, and only when it's on its way to getting good and hot start looking for things to put in it.

In that act, you will have plopped yourself smack in the middle of cooking a meal. And there you'll be, having retrieved a pot, filled it, and lit a burner, jostled by your own will a few steps farther down the path toward dinner.

There are as many ideas about how to best boil water as there are about how to cure hiccups. Some people say you must use cold water, explaining that hot water sits in the pipes, daring bacteria to inoculate it; others say to use hot, arguing that only a fool wouldn't get a head start. Debates rage as to whether olive oil added to water serves any purpose. (It only does if you are planning to serve the water as soup, which you may, but it makes sense to wait to add the oil until you decide.)

Potatoes should be started in cold water, as should eggs. But sometimes I find myself distractedly adding them to water that's already boiling, and both turn out fine. Green and leafy vegetables should be dropped at the last second into a bubble as big as your fist. Pasta, similarly, should only be added when a pot is rollicking, and stirred once or twice.

Ecclesiastical writers on the subject point out that in the beginning there was water, all life proceeded from water, there was water in Eden, water when we fell, then the slate got cleaned with it. Water breaks, and out we come.

The point, as far as I can tell, is that water has been at it, oblivious to our observations, for longer than we know.

I recommend heating up a great deal of it, covered if you're in a rush, because it will boil faster that way, or uncovered if you need time to figure out what you want to boil. As long as it's a big pot and the water in it gets hot, whichever technique you choose and however you time your addition of ingredients, the world, which began by some assessments with a lot of water at a rolling boil, will not come to an end.

Julia Child instructs tasting water periodically as it climbs toward 212 degrees to get used to its temperature at each stage. Her advice might be overzealous, but it teaches an invaluable lesson, not about boiling, but about learning to cook: if there is anything that you can learn from what is happening, learn it. You don't *need* to know how the properties of water differ at 100 degrees and at 180, but by tasting it at those temperatures you may learn something about your pot or your stove, or the spoon you like best for tasting.

Once your water reaches a boil, salt it well. The best comparison I can make is to pleasant seawater. The water needs to be this salty whether it's going to have pasta cooked in it or the most tender spring peas. It must be salted until it tastes good because what you're doing isn't just boiling an ingredient, but cooking one thing that tastes good in another, which requires that they both taste like something.

All ingredients need salt. The noodle or tender spring pea would be narcissistic to imagine it already contained within its cell walls all the perfection it would ever need. We seem, too, to fear that we are failures at being tender and springy if we need to be seasoned. It's not so: it doesn't reflect badly on pea or person that either needs help to be most itself.

Add salt by hand so that you start to get a feel for how much it takes, and as you do, taste the water repeatedly. This may at first feel ridiculous, and then it will start to seem so useful you'll stand by the pot feeling quite ingenious. Even though the water is boiling you can test it with your finger. If it's well seasoned, just tapping the surface will leave enough on your skin for you to taste.

When you find yourself tasting your water, you are doing the most important thing you ever can as a cook: the only way to make anything you're cooking taste good, whether it's water or something more substantial, is to make sure all its parts taste good along the way. There are moments in cooking when common sense dictates not to taste—biting into a dirty beet or raw potato—but taste anything else from a few minutes after you start cooking it until it's done. You don't need to know what it's supposed to taste like: what anything is supposed to taste like, at any point in its cooking, is good. This is as true for water as for other ingredients.

Boiling has a bad name and steaming a good one, but I categorically prefer boiling.

We think we're being bullish with vegetables by putting them in water when we're actually being gentle. There may be nothing better than the first tiny spring potatoes and turnips, their pert greens still attached, or the first baby cabbages, thickly wedged, all boiled.

Salted water seasons the vegetable, which means that by the time it comes out, it is already partially sauced. Additionally, boiling a vegetable improves the water as much as it does the vegetable. Water you've cooked cabbage in is better for making cabbage soup than plain water would be, and it's easier than making chicken stock.

The best vegetables to boil will be the ones in season. They will also be the ones with the most leaves, most stalks, longest stems. Knowing that you can simply boil the expensive, leafier vegetables at the farmers' market should help justify your buying them. All you have to do is cut them up and drop them in water, and you can drop *all* of them in water.

When you go hunting for vegetables for your boiling pot, don't be deterred by those stems and leaves. Though it's easy to forget, leaves and stalks are parts of a vegetable, not obstacles to it. The same is true for the fat and bones of animals, but I'm happy to leave that for now. You can cook them all.

We most regularly boil broccoli. If you do so obligatorily, I want to defend it. If you don't do it, because you've always held boiling in contempt, I suggest you buy a head of broccoli that is dark jade green, stalky, and bold; and while you're at it, one of cauliflower, whole, with light, leafy greens still attached; and boil each on its own. If only withered, mummified versions of either are available, they can be improved by slow stewing with olive oil, garlic, and lemon peel, but for boiling, only the best will do.

To boil broccoli or cauliflower, cut off the big, thick, main stem, or core. Cut the remainder of the heads into long pieces that are more like batons than florets, including stem and leaves on as many of them as you can. Cut the stem or core you've removed into equivalent-sized pieces and include them in your boiling, or save them to turn into the pesto of cores and stems on page 43.

Bring a big pot of water to boil, add salt, and taste. Drop the vegetables into the water and then let them cook, stirring once or twice. This does not, contrary to a lot of cooking advice, take only a minute. You don't need to stand over the pot, because your vegetables don't need to be "crisp" or "crisp-tender" when they come out.

For boiled vegetables to taste really delicious, they need to be cooked. Most of ours aren't. Undercooking is a justifiable reaction to the 1950s tendency to cook vegetables to collapse. But the pendulum has swung too far. When not fully cooked, any vegetable seems starchy and indifferent: it hasn't retained the virtues of being recently picked nor benefited from the development of sugars that comes with time and heat. There's not much I dislike more than biting into a perfectly lovely vegetable and hearing it squeak.

Vegetables are done when a sharp knife easily pierces a piece of one. If you're cooking broccoli or cauliflower, test the densest part of each piece, which is the stem. Remove the cooked vegetables from the water with a slotted spoon directly to a bowl and drizzle them with olive oil. If there are so many that they'll make a great mountain on each other, with the ones on top prevailing and the ones at the bottom of the bowl turning to sludge, spoon them onto a baking sheet so they can cool a little, and then transfer them to a bowl.

There seems to be pressure these days to "shock" vegetables by submerging them in ice water to stop their cooking. The argument in favor of shocking vegetables is that it keeps them from changing color. If you drop cooked broccoli into ice water, it will stay as green as it ever was.

As a rule, I try not to shock anything. I also don't think keeping a vegetable from looking cooked when it *is* cooked is worth the fuss.

A British chef named Fergus Henderson gently reprimands new cooks who want to plunge perfectly warm boiled vegetables into ice baths and tells them that fresh vegetables can be just as beautiful when they're pale and faded. Nature isn't persistently bright; it wears and ages. At Mr. Henderson's restaurant St. John, the two most popular side dishes on the menu are boiled potatoes and cabbage boiled "to the other side of green," and happy patrons, after a few bites of either damp, cooked-looking vegetable, order two or three servings with any meal.

A plate of boiled vegetables can be dinner, with soup and thickly cut toast rubbed with garlic and drizzled with olive oil. If you boil a few different vegetables, cook each separately. Dress each of them like you do broccoli, with olive oil, and if they're roots or tubers, like turnips or potatoes, add a splash of white wine vinegar or lemon while they're hot.

Once you have a vegetable cooked, you can cook a pound of pasta in the same water and use the boiled vegetable to make a wonderfully sedate, dignified sauce by adding a little of the pasta water, good olive oil, and freshly grated cheese.

Boiled broccoli and cauliflower both take particularly well to this.

Put two cups of either vegetable, boiled until completely tender and still warm, in a big bowl and leave it near the stove. Bring its water back to a boil and adjust its seasoning. If the water is too salty, add a bit of fresh water. When the water returns to a boil, add a pound of short pasta, like penne, orecchiette, or fusilli.

While the pasta is cooking, smash your vegetable a little with a wooden spoon and grate a cup of Parmesan or Pecorino cheese into the bowl.

Taste a piece of the pasta by scooping it out with a slotted spoon. When the pasta is nearly done, remove a glass of the pot's murky water. This will help unite pasta, vegetable, and cheese. If you think you've pulled the water out before it's as starchy and salty as it can be, pour it back and return for saltier, starchier water a minute or two later.

Scoop the pasta out with a big, handheld sieve or drain it through a colander and add it to the bowl with the vegetable and cheese, along with a quarter cup of pasta water, and mix well somewhere warm. This is always a good idea when you combine ingredients. Heat is a vital broker between separate things: warm ingredients added to warm ingredients are already in a process of transforming. They're open to change. Even small amounts of heat, released from the sides of a pot while it simmers away, or by the warmed surface of a heated oven, help. Whenever I'm mixing things that aren't going to cook together, I look around for odds and ends of heat.

This pasta is good as is, but is improved by a big handful of chopped raw parsley or toasted breadcrumbs.

I often push the limits of a single pot of water's utility, boiling broccoli or cauliflower, then pasta, and then potatoes, all in succession, and then use the water to make beans. As long as you move from less starchy ingredients to more starchy ingredients, one pot of water can get you pretty far.

It almost always makes sense, if you've bought a slew of vegetables, to cook more than you need for a given meal. If you can muster it, you should go ahead and cook vegetables you're not even planning to use that night. The chapter "How to Stride Ahead" explains how and why to cook a lot of vegetables at once, then transform them into meals on subsequent days. In it, I recommend roasting because you can fit a lot in your oven at one time and then go do other things. But while you have a pot of water boiling and are standing near it, let it do you proud.

The simplicity of boiling vegetables might be maligned in our country, but the idea of boiled meat is pure anathema. Meals of boiled meat, though, are cornerstones of the world's great food cultures.

In each of the really good ones, the elements of the boiling pot are served separately. This means that you either get a very elaborate meal from one pot or the building blocks for a number of them.

In France, pot-au-feu, a traditional meal of boiled meat and vegetables, is served in stages: first comes a bowl of rich broth with a thin toast and a marrow-filled bone with a silver spoon for scooping, then a plate of the meat and vegetables themselves. In northern Italy, region of truffles and cream, the broth of bollito misto is served similarly, on its own, adorned with little tortellini. Once they've finished their broth, diners select the pieces of meat they want from gilded carts.

We are probably most familiar with the English boiled dinner, which has none of that pomp about it, and a bad reputation. To be fair, only some of boiled meats' bad reputation owes to the British. The rest owes to it so regularly being boiled badly. There's a misleading laxity to the terminology of boiling. In neither pot-au-feu nor bollito misto—nor the English version, for that matter—is the meat actually boiled: the term refers more to ingredients being cooked in a pot of water than to the violent rumble of a real boil. Pasta and plain vegetables are the only things you *truly* boil; everything else would get bounced around too much, ending up tough or just worn out.

Boiling meat must mean, in addition to cooking it in water, a commitment to stewarding it through a process of enriching both meat and cooking medium, and being careful not to deplete either. The nuance of this commitment is most poetically illustrated by the centuries-old debate in French cooking about whether, when you cook beef and vegetables in water to make pot-au-feu, you're cooking the meat (called the *bouille*) or the broth. It doesn't need resolution: it's the Zen koan of boiling.

The best instructions I've read for how to make good boiled meat come, in fine, predictable irony, from the nineteenth-century cookbook *The Cook's Oracle* by the British physician William Kitchiner: "Take care of the liquor you have boiled your meat in; for in these times, no good housewife has any pretensions to rational economy, who boils a joint without making some sort of soup. If the liquor be too salt, only use half the quantity, and the rest water . . . boil or rather stew the meat slowly, instead of fast, and . . . take it up when it is done enough."

Those are the fundamentals: cook your meat until it's done, not a minute longer. If your broth tastes too thin, let it go on cooking; if it's too salty, water it down.

Dr. Kitchiner goes on to give detailed instructions for boiling mutton leg, neck, lamb, beef, veal, calf's head, pork, tongue, rabbit, and tripe. Mutton and calves' heads are good for special occasions, but for developing a practice, I recommend boiling a chicken.

Chicken is already a mainstay of American diets. Roasted chicken is wonderful and produces great drippings, but a chicken cooked in a pot of water leaves you with several dinners, lunches, and extra broth, and is an appropriate and honest way to do a lot with a little.

Buy a whole chicken at a farmers' market if you can. They're much more expensive—up to three times as expensive—as chickens raised in factories, which most, even the ones labeled "free range," are. The two are completely different animals. As soon as you boil a chicken that was raised outdoors, pecking at grubs, you'll notice that its stock is thick, golden, and flavorful. When it cools, it will thicken. Chickens that've led chicken-y lives develop strong, gelatinous bones, which contribute to the soup you get from them and to how good they are for you. If you're getting more meals out of your chicken, and more nutrition out of those meals, spending the extra money makes sense.

If your chicken comes with its feet on, cut them off at the knee joint. This is easy, if unsettling the first time you do it. If you end up with chicken feet, freeze them in a plastic bag for making chicken stock, for which there are directions on page 166.

I salt chicken for boiling or any cooking a day ahead, if I've planned that far. It gives the seasoning time to take and ensures you don't end up with underseasoned meat and salty broth. If you forget, salt the chicken more heavily and three hours ahead, and leave it sitting at room temperature, which will help the meat absorb the salt.

If you buy your chicken from a local farmer, there's a good chance it will come with its giblets (liver, heart, and gizzard) inside, though not attached. I've included a recipe for chicken liver pâté on pages 172–73.

If it has been salted overnight, let the chicken come to room temperature before you cook it. The water won't have to spend as much time heating the meat through, and it will cook before getting tough.

There are two ways to deal with vegetables for a boiled chicken meal. Neither is better than the other. If you've got time for an extra step, for a four-pound chicken, put the ends—not tops—of three carrots (or all of one), half an onion, a stalk of celery, any strange leek-looking thing you find, a bunch of parsley stems, a few whole stems of thyme, a bay leaf, and a whole clove of garlic in your pot underneath the chicken and cover it all by three inches of water. The carcass will hold them down, and you won't have to knock them away when you skim the pot. You could truss the chicken for more even cooking, but I don't. Set aside whole vegetables to cook separately in the finished broth once the chicken is cooked.

If you don't have time for extra cooking, add big chunks of carrot, celery, and fennel directly to your chicken pot. Cook them at the same time as the chicken, with the intention of serving them alongside. Potatoes, which will make the broth murky, can be added toward the end of the chicken's cooking.

This might be blasphemy, but I usually add a whole or half piece of star anise to my cooking water. Star anise is a ubiquitous spice in Asian and Middle Eastern poultry dishes, and the two ingredients have an affinity for each other. I occasionally also add a stick of cinnamon for about five minutes. The combination adds a little extra richness to the broth that's quite magical.

Let the pot come to a boil, then lower it to a simmer. Skim the gray scum that rises to the top of the pot and collects around its sides. You will have to skim it periodically. It doesn't mean anything is wrong with your chicken. There is scum in the finest of them, as in any meat or bean.

Cook the chicken at just below a simmer, starting to check for doneness after thirty minutes, and then retrieving each part as it's cooked. The vegetables might be done before the chicken. If they are, remove them. If the chicken's done first, which you'll know by when a leg, wiggled, begins to come loose, remove it.

I cook chickens leg side down because legs take longer to cook. This can make for messy testing for doneness, but I clumsily make do.

If wiggling doesn't feel reassuring, cut into a piece of leg when you think its time might be up. You will lose some juices, but you're only losing them into broth, which you're going to eat anyway. Regardless, that always seems an illogical argument for not testing the temperature of meat. Better to lose a few juices than to over- or undercook an entire piece of meat.

Remove the chicken. Taste the broth. If it doesn't taste delicious, let it go on cooking.

If you're going to eat it immediately, let the broth settle, then use a ladle to skim any fat off the top of the liquid by making a little whirlpool with your ladle and lightly skimming what rises to the top of the ladle. This takes practice. If you can wait, put the broth in the refrigerator. Tomorrow there will be a thin layer of fat over the top of the broth, which you can skim off with a spoon and save for sautéing vegetables or spreading on toast.

If I'm making a to-do of it, I serve some of the broth as a first course. In that case, I cook a few vegetables or pasta that are as small and beautiful as I can manage and serve a spoonful of them in each bowl of broth.

If it's summer, dice a little zucchini and onion and cook them in butter in a pan. If it's spring, pull a little of the broth aside and cook English peas in a combination of broth and butter. If it's autumn, little cubes of butternut squash and rice are good. If it's winter, cook tiny pasta shells or heartier pasta, like tortellini.

Warm enough broth for everyone, then warm the vegetables, grains, or pasta in the broth, and ladle it out in bowls with spoonfuls of each in each.

If it's a second or third or fourth day soup I'm making, I pick off whatever meat is left on the carcass, heat up my broth, and cook noodles in it, omitting vegetables entirely and using enough noodles that the resulting soup is a golden broth, flush with swollen noodles and little bits of chicken. I like twisted pasta like fusilli and gemelli for this.

For a soup that's equally delicious but more rustic, toast thick slices of stale bread, put a slice at the bottom of individual soup bowls, and grate Parmesan cheese on them. Ladle hot broth over the toasts and top with lots of freshly cracked black pepper, a little more cheese, and olive oil. Make sure that the pepper is freshly cracked. When you've got only five ingredients and pepper's one of them—and two of the others are bread and broth—the small amounts of attention you put into each is not only tasteable, but where the meaning in the meal resides.

Generally on whatever day I cook it—which is often Sunday— I serve my chicken, cut into pieces, and some of the vegetables I've cooked with it. To cut a whole chicken into pieces, look for its joints and apply pressure to them in the direction opposite from the one in which they want to go. They will show you where to separate them. The breast can be cut down the middle with a heavy knife, and just above the ribs on both sides, or its meat can be carved off the breastbone by your pressing a knife blade against it and lifting the meat off the bone.

I cut each half of a breast into a few pieces because it makes the same amount of meat last longer. A half breast of a four-pound boiling bird is a lot of chicken if you're eating it accompanied by vegetables and a piquant sauce, like *salsa verde*.

Salsa verde is what's served with Italian boiled meals. It's the best accompaniment to boiled meat, and among the best accompaniments to anything.

This is a simple one.

Salsa verde

~

1 shallot, finely chopped
½ teaspoon salt
red or white wine vinegar
1 bunch parsley, leaves picked from stems
    and roughly chopped
½ clove garlic, chopped and pounded to a
    paste with a tiny bit of salt in a mortar
    with a pestle or on a cutting board
1 anchovy fillet, finely chopped
1 teaspoon capers, finely chopped
½ cup olive oil

Put the shallot in a small mixing bowl. Add the salt and then enough vinegar to cover. Let it sit for 10 to 15 minutes. Drain the shallot of its vinegar, reserving it for a future vinaigrette. Mix the shallot and the rest of the ingredients together.

Make *salsa verde* whenever you boil meat, or anything. Once you have it, you'll start spooning it on everything in sight. That is how boiling works, truly, because you will find yourself with *salsa verde* and nothing boiled to put it on. It will be time to put on a pot of water to boil, then put something in the pot, and there you will be, cooking, without wondering what to do, because you'll have already begun.

Two

How to Teach an Egg to Fly

———————————•——————————————————————•———————————

It may be hard for an egg to turn into a bird: it would be
a jolly sight harder for it to learn to fly while remaining
an egg.

— C. S. Lewis, *Mere Christianity*

Everyone has something to say on the subject of eggs. M. F. K. Fisher is the best: "Probably one of the most private things in the world is an egg until it is broken." The egg industry drones that eggs are incredible and edible. The French philosopher Diderot noted that all the world's theologies could be toppled by one.

I am going to be as practical as I can be because most people know how to "make eggs." But "making eggs" sounds dull and habitual, and too much like "making do," and we and eggs deserve better.

I have three things to say.

First, an egg is not an egg is not an egg. I don't know what to call the things that are produced by hens crowded into dirty cages, their beaks snipped, tricked into laying constantly. Whatever they are, they are only edible in the sense that we can cram anything down if we need to; their secrets merit airing, but not eating.

Eggs should be laid by chickens that have as much of a say in it as any of us about our egg laying does. Their yolks should, depending on the time of year, range from buttercup yellow to marigold. They

19

should come from as nearby as possible. We don't all live near cattle ranches, but most of us live surprisingly close to someone raising chickens for eggs. If you find lively eggs from local chickens, buy them. They will be a good deal more than edible.

Second, at sixty cents each, which is about what one costs, a good egg is only worth it if you know all it's good for. Whether or not they ever take off, eggs possess in them some of the mystical energy of flight. A cookbook from the 1930s lists, in a catalog of eggs' uses: "albumen water [*egg whites*] for invalids," "for exhaustion," "emergency dressing for a burn," and "antidote to poisoning." I haven't used them to treat poisoning, but if the need arose I would.

Good eggs are worth it, as long as your stance egg in hand isn't automatic. As long as you stop before cracking it and think: "I am going to softly scramble this egg," or "A bowl of yesterday's rice would be delicious topped with this one."

Here Diderot stumbles. A gently but sincerely cooked egg tells us all we need to know about divinity. It hinges not on the question of how the egg began, but how the egg will end. A good egg, cooked deliberately, gives us a glimpse of the greater forces at play.

Third is the stance of a man I met in eastern Africa. He was a reedy, white-blond Berliner named Gregor. Gregor had spent five years driving trucks up and down the coast from Mombasa to Capetown. He had seen a lot of backcountry meals over that time, and whenever he was served one, he reacted in one of two ways. If the plate of food he was handed included an egg, he would look happy and eat. If it didn't, he'd look mournfully up at whoever had delivered it and ask, always as though for the first time: "What about egg?"

For my taste, meals still qualify as meals if they are eggless. But an egg can turn anything into a meal and is never so pleased as when it is allowed to.

I.

Boiled eggs are almost as underappreciated as boiling water. The egg's being unappreciated is its own story, but boiling them needs a moment of consideration.

I don't know why we make it so difficult. Perhaps we can't bear the simplicity of it.

I boil eggs by putting them in a pot of cold water, bringing the pot to a boil, then, as soon as I see the first bubble, turning the burner off. I let the eggs sit in the water for about four minutes, meanwhile setting up a bowl of water with ice in it nearby.

When four minutes are up I remove one egg, drop it into the ice water, crack the shell a little, peel some off, and check for doneness by pressing on the white. I think the perfect boiled egg has a firm white and a yolk that's just cooked enough to hold together when the egg's cut in two. If the white's not firm when I check, I leave the eggs in the water for another twenty seconds or so, then scoop them all out into the ice water and peel them. I still call them boiled eggs, soft and hard, because though it's not what they are, it's what they're called.

There have been reams of paper devoted to problems with removing boiled eggs' shells. Conventional wisdom dictates that shells stick to their closeted membranes when eggs are too fresh to boil, and that it's best to boil eggs that have been sitting around for a few days to a few weeks. Hervé This, a molecular gastronomer, has committed significant resources in his Parisian lab to the age-old question. He has concluded that the best way to ensure shells' easy removal is to soak boiled eggs in vinegar for a few hours, and then to neutralize their surface with an alkali, like baking soda, to rid them of their bad flavor.

I am perhaps less particular, but I find that after a few minutes in an ice bath, once water gets under shells and loosens them, they come off fairly easily.

It's true that there's nothing like the momentary elation of getting a shell off in one fell swoop, but if you're having trouble, try peeling eggs under running water. If it doesn't work, chip shells off in little pieces. I always lose some white when I do this and try to remember not to blame myself or my pot or the hen, but the freshness of the egg.

II.

Poached eggs love to be drizzled with good olive oil and grated with hard cheese, like Parmesan or Pecorino, then a lot of freshly cracked black pepper, and topped with fresh herbs. Poached eggs like contrasts, and are especially good at turning what looks like two-thirds of a meal into a whole one.

Warm polenta or rice are suitable fractions because you can make egg-sized wells at their middles. So is any vegetable that will accommodate an egg in some way. Grilled asparagus or scallions are good, because they can be curled into a nest. Less nestlike vegetables should be smashed up so that a yolk, once broken, will have something into which to seep.

Lettuce is delicious with a poached egg on top. The yolk becomes a part of its dressing. Dress salads to which you're adding eggs lightly and drizzle a little vinaigrette directly onto the egg. The vinaigrette, salt, and egg will mix themselves up happily.

If you want to have your poached egg on toast, and at a meal other than breakfast, cut your bread especially thick, toast it, rub it with raw garlic, then top it with an egg, salt it, drizzle it with oil, and grate it with cheese and freshly cracked black pepper.

I've heard of a lot of perfect ways to poach an egg. I'm sure they work. The problem with them is that to poach eggs is to understand egg cooking as you can't when you cook them any other way. A boiled egg stays secret until it's cooked, and a frying egg sizzles in fat, too hot to touch. But poached eggs are cracked out of their shells and cooked directly in barely simmering liquid, which means you can literally feel them as they cook. The trouble with setting a timer, covering a pan, and walking away is that you end up bound to your trick, lost without a timer, stuck without a lid.

An egg takes about three minutes to poach. Begin by bringing a pan of water at least four inches deep to a boil. You will need just enough room around each egg to move it in and out of the pan. Lower the water to a simmer and add an unmeasured teaspoon of vinegar. The vinegar helps the whites seize up around the yolks. If you're at the start of your egg-poaching career, be liberal with the vinegar. It will make the whites especially resilient. Then, as you start to feel comfortable, add less vinegar for a softer white.

Lower the heat to just below a simmer before adding your eggs. Crack each egg into a shallow cup with a sharp rim, like a teacup. If the yolk breaks you can save it to turn into scrambled eggs tomorrow.

Slide the eggs quickly into the barely simmering water, as close in time to each other as possible so you don't need to keep track of which went in first. If loose strands of egg white start drifting away from the yolks, gather them back in with a spoon.

After a minute and a half, each will have begun to *look* like a poached egg. Once it does, use a slotted spoon to lift it out of its liquid and prod it very lightly with your finger. When the egg is cooked, its white will be firm, its yolk will still have give.

Once each egg is cooked, lift it out of the water and let it drain for a moment in the spoon. If you are poaching eggs for a crowd, poach them in advance in batches. Put a bowl of ice water next to your poaching pan and remove the eggs directly from the hot water into it. Leave them in the ice water in the refrigerator until you are ready to eat, then lower them into barely simmering water to reheat for a few seconds just before you serve them. This is a good trick if you don't want spectators watching while you poach.

Always salt an egg directly. This is something every good egg cook does. Do it when it's hot. It makes all the difference in the world. Also drizzle your eggs lightly with olive oil, even if they're going to get another drizzle when they get put on top of something else. The same salting rule holds for soft-boiled eggs, halved or quartered. Salt each one, especially its yolk.

Poach eggs directly in stews. In the Middle East there is a wonderful egg-in-stew dish called *shakshouka,* traditionally eaten in late morning. It is made by stewing onion, garlic, sliced peppers, and whole tomatoes in a lot of olive oil, then poaching eggs directly in the rich, oily sauce. It is a glorious food. Make a version using any tomato sauce you have. If it's store-bought, cook fresh onions, garlic, and peppers in a lot of olive oil before adding the sauce. Serve it very hot, drizzled with more oil, with a lot of bread.

The French dish called *oeufs en restes,* literally "eggs in leftovers," has as its only two requisite ingredients eggs and leftovers. Recipes instruct to heat any leftover, like boiled or roasted meat, or vegetables, or beans, in a pan with a little broth, crack and slide the eggs onto the warm *restes,* salt the eggs, cover the pan, and cook on medium-low heat until the eggs are cooked through. This is a delicious and very adaptable meal. As long as the *restes* are hot, the eggs should be able to resist the temptation to meander toward the bottom of the pan. If they yield to temptation, use a soft spatula to scramble them into the *restes* instead.

Try poaching eggs directly in chicken broth. This is delicious if philosophically perplexing. Sauté a little garlic in olive oil in a pot, add chicken broth to it, then when it's hot, crack an egg or two into a cup each, and slide them into the broth. While the eggs are cooking, put a piece of toasted stale bread into the bottom of a bowl, then ladle egg and broth on top.

III.

When we make eggs, we usually fry or scramble them.

"Frying" and "scrambling" imply too much aggression. I soft-fry and I soft-scramble. Fried eggs should be cooked at a gentle sizzle, which keeps their whites from toughening, and scrambling should just be a series of persistent nudges.

Fried eggs do a good job on spaghetti. There is a slightly harrowing Tuscan pasta sauce called *carbonara* for which raw eggs are beaten with Parmesan and then tossed with hot noodles. It isn't difficult, but there is always the looming chance that the eggs will start scrambling before they are convinced to become sauce. Frying an egg sunny-side up and putting it on *top* of olive-oiled and cheesed pasta takes the guesswork out of it and allows you to experience the rightness of the combination.

Fry eggs for pasta as I learned to in Spain. Cook them slowly in a half inch of just warm olive oil, constantly spooning the oil over the top of the eggs, to lightly poach each part of them in oil.

Toss freshly cooked pasta with a little pasta water, olive oil, and butter, add a handful of fresh parsley, divide it into bowls, then top each bowl with an olive-oil fried egg and grate it all with Parmesan cheese.

Don't worry too much about the timing of the egg frying and pasta cooking. The eggs, however, are better at waiting than the pasta.

Frying eggs to put on pasta is an especially good use of eggs you feel proud of. I recently did it with duck eggs, which I didn't want to poach because I wanted for their huge, orange yolks to make themselves immediately *known*.

Scrambled eggs make a delicious sandwich. I first tried a scrambled egg sandwich in Laos, where a big mound of softly scrambled eggs with strange little mushrooms was stuffed inside a warm, soft roll. It was perfectly creamy and the mushrooms were earthy and just barely browned, and it was a revelation. I make a similar one with wild mushrooms or simply with good butter and fresh herbs.

Or scramble eggs so that they're still very soft in bacon fat or olive oil and spoon them, while still warm, over a salad.

IV.

Omelets can take a thousand forms. They can't, though, very well be made with a single egg: they are good made with two eggs, and at their very best made with three. Two eggs in the morning is a hearty breakfast, but three is an orgy. I usually save eggs for when I'm awake enough to put thought into them, but if you like yours with your coffee, boil or poach, or gently fry or nudge and save omelets for later in the day.

Omelets are a near relation of scrambled eggs, with less *doing* to them. A friend recently expressed disdain at the idea that people don't know the difference between making one and making the other. I don't know the difference. I make omelets and scrambled eggs the same way. I find it easiest to think of omelets as scrambled eggs I stop pushing around and add a spoonful of something wonderful to.

Probably the best scrambling or omelet medium is clarified butter. Make clarified butter by heating butter over very low heat, then skimming off the foam that forms on top. When all you have left is golden liquid, pour it off slowly, leaving behind the solids at the bottom. Store clarified butter in the refrigerator, and it will keep and keep and keep.

I cook omelets in olive oil because I forget that it is easy to clarify butter, or run out, and like eggs and olive oil together nearly as much. It doesn't burn as quickly as fresh butter. If you want to use butter instead, melt it in a tiny bit of oil, which decreases the chances of burning.

Beat two or three eggs in a bowl, adding a pinch of salt and a teaspoon of heavy cream if you want. This is not a trick, but an expression of the fact that things taste good with cream added.

Heat a tablespoon of clarified butter or olive oil in a small nonstick pan over medium heat. Lower the heat slightly before adding the eggs. Give them about three seconds to set. Once they have, use a rubber spatula to move everything toward one side of the pan, then tip the still unset eggs into the empty space. Lower the heat if things seem to be coming together too quickly. Do the same thing again at a more measured pace in small ways, pulling some egg that looks like it's beginning to get firm toward the middle of the pan, and pushing more liquid to fill its empty place.

The instant the bottom of an omelet is coherent, and before any of it has browned, remove the pan from heat. If the top still seems too wobbly to be quite described as creamy, smooth whatever still wobbles toward the pan's margins, where it should finish cooking. Let the inside of the omelet still have softness to it. Whatever you put in an omelet will like having something to grab on to.

The omelet, though exempt from "making eggs," gets stuck in the automatism of "making omelets." Once we are making omelets we reach for fillings as though under duress: the blandest cheese, whole leaves of spinach, uncooked peppers, as though omelet making meant finding something, anything, with which to fill an omelet.

An omelet is an egg's comeuppance. There shouldn't be anything plain or predictable about omelet fillings. The person who understands this best is a beautiful bulldog named Gabrielle Hamilton, chef of the restaurant Prune, in New York City's East Village, who cooks omelets like she's there on the eggs' behalf, to make sure their comeuppance is paid on time and in full.

An omelet that you make should be something like one of hers. Let it have, as one of Gabrielle's omelets does, three deep-fried oysters and a heavy smear of cold rémoulade sauce. If you don't have oysters, there is still something luxurious about thick, cold, creamy filling in the same bite as warm eggs.

My favorite cold filling for an omelet is garlicky yogurt, which I make by pounding a little garlic to a paste with salt and mixing it with the thickest yogurt I can find. This will begin to seep and run as soon as you get your omelet out of the pan, so I serve mine in shallow bowls.

Or make an omelet like another of Gabrielle's, filled with poached beef tongue awash in garlicky *salsa verde*. I make a faster, less perfect version whenever I have boiled meat around by roughly chopping it and mixing a quick relish of chopped pickles, olives, capers, and an anchovy, or using leftover *salsa verde*. This omelet is a meal that makes complete sense of everything else you're doing in your kitchen. After the first bite you think, *This is why I've boiled meat; this is why I've bought good eggs; this is why I've taken time to cook; this is why I eat.*

Vegetables can be fine omelet fillings, but they must be exciting. In Provence omelets are made with turnips cooked in herbs and butter, and in Thailand with *cha om,* a sweet, soapy grass that makes your mouth tingle. The only interesting vegetable that does not make a good omelet is avocado, which tastes flabby. Avocado with soft-boiled eggs, on the other hand, is as it is with anything— very good.

Spoon your filling over the half-moon of the omelet closest to you. Tilting the whole pan up toward you, fold the farther side, with a combination of gravity, your spatula, and optimism, over the filled half. Slide it out of the pan onto a plate.

Or make an omelet but leave it unfilled and unfolded. Flat, round omelets are quiet, and a little serious. I like to eat them with bread or cut into wide ribbons and placed on hot rice, sprinkled with vinegar and a few pickled chiles. I recently learned a trick for making plain, flat omelets taste dressier: whisk in a teaspoon of white wine per three eggs before adding them to the pan.

To make a flat omelet, use a little more olive oil than you would for scrambled eggs or a filled omelet—the extra oil helps the top cook as well as the bottom—and cook it on higher heat, moving it only a few times.

Flat omelets are as good cold or at room temperature as they are hot. Make one in the morning, let it cool, and then eat it, hours later, squeezed with lemon and drizzled with olive oil, in a fresh baguette.

V.

There is no reason that eggs must always be hot. A cold fried egg can be a cheerless thing. Cold scrambled eggs are all right with some lemon and, if you have gulps of wine or beer, better than all right. If you can get over the idea that eggs *need* to be hot, though, cooking them can be quite liberating. They never take long, and there's no rush to serve them. I have always liked soft-boiled eggs cold, and often cook more than I want, then leave a few unpeeled. I usually have at least one nicely cold soft-boiled egg on hand to lure my thoughts away from eating lunch out.

Frittatas in Italian, *tortillas* in Spanish, and "egg pies" in English need to be made ahead and are best served at room temperature. No one has ever eaten a frittata hot and not been scolded for it. They must cool for hours or days because they are better that way.

Once you have a frittata made, it can be any part of the day's eating. At dinnertime you only need a salad and bread or a few simply cooked vegetables. At breakfast or lunch, a slice is your breakfast or lunch.

In Spain, the most common one, called *tortilla española,* is made of potatoes, onion, and eggs. Like everything in Spain, it's made unabashedly oily. I recommend following suit.

Tortilla española

~

> 2 small potatoes
> 1 onion
> a lot of olive oil
> salt
> 3 eggs, beaten

Heat the oven to 375 degrees. Peel and thinly slice the potatoes and onion. Cook them together in a deep sauté pan with a committed ½ inch olive oil. Layer a combination of potatoes and onion in the pan, salting each layer. Cook them over low heat, letting them poach in the oil and the liquid they emit. When they're soft, drain them in a colander over a bowl; save the starchy oil to cook vegetables in later in the week. Let the potatoes cool.

Heat new olive oil in an eight- or nine-inch pan. Mix the potatoes, onion, a quarter of their oil, and beaten eggs to cover them, in a bowl, and pour the mixture into the pan. As soon as the eggs are set, put the pan in the oven to finish cooking for 10 to 15 minutes, until the top is set and just firm to the touch. Put a plate on the pan and flip the pan over. Serve at room temperature.

My favorite frittata is made from leftover pasta. Pasta for a frittata can be any kind of pasta with any kind of sauce. I have made delicious ones from linguine with wild mushrooms, penne with zucchini, rigatoni with sausage ragú, fusilli with pesto. Other than the perfect solitary sybaritic breakfast of pasta eaten directly out of a cold bowl, in bewilderment and utter presence, this is the best use, I believe, of leftover pasta. Glory be.

Mix two or three cups of pasta with three beaten eggs. Salt it lightly. If you have Parmesan cheese, grate a little directly into the pasta-egg mixture. Add as many herbs as you have, up to a half cup. Any are good. Celery leaves or the celery-like herb, lovage, give pasta frittatas a particularly pleasant bite. Cook the frittata as you do *tortilla española*. When you can lift the sides of the pie up and peek under it, put it in the oven to finish cooking.

After making any frittata, leave it out of the refrigerator if you're serving it within three hours. Otherwise chill it and let it come back to room temperature before eating.

VI.

Spring is the best time of year for eggs. Hens get cold in the winter and lay irregularly. Spring is when they start warming up, seeing the sun, pecking at green things, laying darker-yolked eggs, and laying more of them. It is when I find myself making whole meals based around the notional and actual egg.

The eggiest thing you can make is mayonnaise. The degrading of mayonnaise from a wonderful condiment for cooked vegetables or sandwiches to an indistinguishable layer of fat has been radical and violent.

Mayonnaise is a food best made at home and almost *never* made at home. This has robbed us of something that is both healthy and an absolute joy to eat with gusto.

Mayonnaise deserves to be the focus and main attraction of any meal that contains it. A good mayonnaise helps foods stay their course. To serve a big bowl of bright yellow homemade mayonnaise alongside vegetables, raw or cooked, is not to disguise or dilute their health-giving properties, but to advise your visceral self to eat them.

Mayonnaise is egg yolk bound in oil, and oil bound in egg yolk. Both should be the best possible quality. Put "homemade mayonnaise" in the column of reasons to spend resources there.

Mayonnaise and aioli are cousins, the second the first's bolder relation. *Aioli* is Provençal for garlic mayonnaise. If cheese is milk's leap toward immortality, aioli is garlic and egg's collective shot at the firmament.

Aioli is also the name of the festive Provençal meal that is organized around big bowls of it, for dipping, spreading, smothering, spooning. There are different-sized "aioli" meals ranging from *petite,* which can contain just little boiled potatoes, boiled eggs, bread, and garlic mayonnaise; to *grande,* which includes salt cod, green beans, carrots, and chickpeas, or any other arrangement of spring or summer vegetables; to an *aioli monstre,* which goes all-out, with bowls of aioli accompanied by at least all of those and baby artichokes, little snails, and squid stew.

Make an aioli of whatever size your appetite and refrigerator allow. All of the ingredients above are good. Some can be raw, some cooked. Substitute any fish for salt cod or squid stew. Boiled leeks are a wonderful addition, while they're in season. If it's summer, ripe tomatoes, cut into thick wedges, are perfect.

Mayonnaise and aioli are begun the same way: by cracking and separating eggs, putting yolks into a bowl, and whisking one cup olive oil per one yolk into mayonnaise.

I start with room-temperature eggs. There are scientific disagreements about whether this is good sense or superstition. I do not care what anyone says, my mayonnaise stays together better that way.

Serve this in a bowl, with its accompaniments and a lot of warm bread. In Provence, an aioli without rosé is a nameless thing, and I'm not sure anyone would begin eating if there were none to pour.

Mayonnaise and aioli

~

2 egg yolks
¾ teaspoon salt
⅛ teaspoon Dijon mustard
2 cups best olive oil around, plus more if the
    mayonnaise is not too wobbly when you're done
¼ to ½ teaspoon room-temperature water
¾ teaspoon (a squeeze) fresh lemon juice
1 drop red wine vinegar

For aioli: 2 cloves garlic, pounded to a paste with salt
    in a mortar with a pestle or on a cutting board

Dampen a dish towel, form it into a ring on the kitchen table, then set a bowl in the ring. This will steady it while you whisk. Whisk the egg yolks, salt, and mustard. When the yolks are a uniform yellow, about 5 seconds into whisking, begin to add the oil in a very slow stream, only drop by drop to start. This matters, and there's no voodoo or trick or way *of getting around it. Once the mayonnaise thickens, start adding the oil more quickly. When it becomes hard to whisk, add the water and lemon juice. Then whisk in the remaining oil. Taste for salt. Salt will take time to disperse throughout the mayonnaise because it's not dissolved by heat or vinegar. If you're not serving it for hours, keep the seasoning light and refrigerate it until just before you're ready to eat, then taste it again for salt.*

If you want to make aioli, whisk in the garlic at the end. If it doesn't seem garlicky enough, wait, again, until just before you eat to decide, then add more. Garlic, too, takes time to disperse. A single drop of red wine vinegar brings all the qualities of egg, olive oil, and garlic out, but if it tastes perfect and delicious without the vinegar, leave it be.

This should all be done by hand. Good olive oil gets bitter when it's broken by blades. Making mayonnaise by hand is tiring, hurts a little, and is particularly worth it once you've stopped sweating. If you want to use a blender or food processor, or handheld mixer, use vegetable oil instead of olive oil for one-half to three-quarters of the total amount, then whisk in the best olive oil you have for the remaining half cup to one cup by hand. It will taste less divine, but still good, and it's a reasonable compromise.

If mayonnaise or aioli breaks into liquid and solid, save it by separating an egg. Save the white for scrambling with whole eggs tomorrow. Put the new egg yolk in a clean bowl. Whisk the new yolk, then slowly add the broken mayonnaise to the bowl as you would olive oil. The resulting mixture should be thick and stable. Whisk in a little straight olive oil at the end to make up for the extra egg. If it breaks again, do the same thing a second time.

If it breaks after you've whisked it back together twice, save the broken mayonnaise to use as pasta sauce (there is a recipe on page 238), and begin with fresh eggs and fresh oil.

I keep mayonnaise and aioli for two or three days in the refrigerator even though they contain raw eggs. I trust the freshness of my eggs, and the cleanliness of the lives of the hens that lay them. If your eggs don't come from a source you know or if you are worried, make less and keep it for a shorter time.

Just eggs, softly boiled, halved, served with bread and mayonnaise, can stir something in us.

The food writer Amanda Hesser wrote an article about having lunch with Julia Child in which the grande dame of French cooking ordered *oeufs mayonnaise* off a bar menu and ate it with joy comparable to euphoria.

I think it is in part their serenity, and the reassuring fact that so much privacy, cracked open, isn't a fragile thing at all but ready for gusto, incubating euphoria.

And they are fortifying. My brother, now an accomplished chef, likes to recount a meal I made him one night before he went to cook in Italy for the first time. He was terrified, and we sat up late doing not much but trying to be less scared. The meal was two halved soft-boiled eggs served with a blob of tarragon mayonnaise he remembers my lovingly whisking to a grassy gloss.

I did not make the mayonnaise from scratch. I wasn't practiced at it yet. I served him store-bought mayonnaise to which I'd added a little good olive oil and finely chopped tarragon and lemon juice in hopes of improving it.

If you have store-bought mayonnaise, spruce it up with chopped herbs, an extra drizzle of olive oil, and a squeeze of lemon, and serve it with good eggs.

Three

How to Stride Ahead

O me, while I stride ahead, material, visible,
imperious as ever!
—Walt Whitman, *Leaves of Grass*

Our desire to eat fresh vegetables has left us with an idea that vegetables are only good if they're cooked just before being eaten. But many of the best vegetable dishes are created over time. This is true of a lot of dishes, but particularly of ones made from vegetables, those unwieldy things that take more *doing* than anything else in the kitchen does before they're even close to done.

Here is what I do, and I think it works well:

Each week I buy whole bunches of the leafiest, stemmiest vegetables I can find. Then I scrub off their dirt, trim off their leaves, cut off their stems, peel what needs peeling, and cook them all at once.

By the time I've finished, I've drawn a map of the week's meals and created the beginnings of a succession of them.

Then each day I pick up where I left off. On Monday night, I decide to neatly make a vinaigrette, plump a few raisins in warm vinegar, and have a roasted vegetable salad. Or I warm some vegetables up with a sprig of thyme, a little broth, and a splash of cream and have soup. On Tuesday, I choose to eat the salad as is, or turn what is left into a frittata, or I decide to eat soup and spend my time making little garlic-rubbed toasts to accompany it. On Wednesday, I add freshly chopped mint and vinegared onions to roasted beets, or perhaps press garlicky cooked kale into sandwiches, or toss the kale with a béchamel sauce and spread it in a buttered dish to make a warm, bubbling gratin.

This ensures my vegetables don't go bad—crisper drawers must be some of the most inaptly named things in history: I have never seen anything get crisper in one—it also means that I eat vegetables at most meals: turned into cooked ingredients, mine are as convenient as canned beans.

I like to roast vegetables. I can fill my oven once and create a week's worth of healthy, delicious ingredients. Roasted vegetables are also particularly good when they have had a few days to settle into themselves.

I recommend buying two heads of cauliflower or broccoli or one of each. Both are celestial cooked in a hot oven. They're also two-in-one vegetables: cauliflower's pale leaves and solemn core and the leaves and stem of broccoli can be eaten.

I buy one or two whole bunches of beets. Beets love to be roasted, are better cold than hot, and wait, without losing their pluck, to be turned into different dishes all week long.

Look for beets with their dark green leaves attached, then salvage them from their delicious roots and sauté them with garlic and olive oil, along with the rest of the greens you buy. Other vegetables also have pleasantly peppery tops. If you ever have to buy beets or turnips or kohlrabi already shorn of their leaves, ask whoever is minding the farm stand or stocking vegetables about them. You'll likely be given what they just sheared.

If it is autumn or winter, buy one butternut squash, or any combination of carrots, parsnips, celery root, and turnips. Simply roasted, these are one of the great pleasures in life. I grew up eating them hot at dinner, turned into salads at lunch, and cold as an after-school snack. There's nothing wrong with a snack of granola, but there is something unarguably right with one of roasted vegetables.

I usually buy a few sweet potatoes as well. They are delicious in dozens of arrangements. They also store the best in their dark jackets and have such an unfriendly habit of goo-ing everywhere if you cut them before cooking that they're best cooked whole regardless of your plans for them. This means that it takes no more effort to cook three or four than one.

And always a few bunches of dark, leafy greens. This will seem very pious. Once greens are cooked as they should be, though: hot and lustily, with garlic, in a good amount of olive oil, they lose their moral urgency and become one of the most likable ingredients in your kitchen.

Greens must be bought whole. The balance of the universe dictates that one man's head is another man's tail. In Provence, warm baked Swiss chard tarts, studded with raisins, are made *only* with stems. There, Swiss chard leaves are cast-offs, sometimes used for bean and vegetable soups, more often fed to the chickens.

Here, we sauté leaves of Swiss chard and throw their good stems away. More often we buy greens precut in bags, relinquishing their stems to the companies that hack greens up, only to then buy them back in frozen tamales and canned minestrone soup. A more efficient approach is to buy and use both ingredients, since they come conveniently attached to each other.

I start cooking as soon as possible after shopping, when the memory of the market's sun and cheerful tents are still in mind. If you can't get to it immediately, though, put everything but the greens in a big bowl on your kitchen table instead of refrigerating it. In plain sight, your vegetables will chide you to cook them, and it feels pleasantly frivolous to spend a few moments fussing cauliflower, beets, and squash into a tableau.

⸜◈⸝

A hot oven is the rightful domain of a capable cook. It is what makes the roasted vegetables we eat at restaurants, where ovens are set to much higher temperatures than ours are at home, so plainly, unremittingly *good*.

Roast vegetables at 400 degrees, or 450 if your oven is full of them. This can be cathartic. Santayana said that to knock a thing down, especially if it was placed at an arrogant angle, was a deep delight of the soul. I can't picture the philosopher gloating over cubes of roasting squash, but after digging the slippery seeds out from inside one, I have felt, as I put a tray of it in a blazing oven, the frisson of retribution.

After lighting your oven, do your preparations in an order from longest to shortest cooking, thinking of them as taking the shape of brightly colored Russian nesting dolls, with each bout of trimming and oiling taking place within the time frame of another vegetable's cooking.

All vegetables other than the squash and roots prefer to be roasted separately. Each has a slightly different makeup and cooking time and is easiest to cook correctly if you can know that once a piece or two of it tastes good and done, the whole tray of it is ready. Although botanically squashes and root vegetables aren't more closely related than cactus and elm, culinarily they're kin. They cook well mixed together, and the ratios of one to the other don't matter.

If you need vegetables to share a roasting pan, choose ones that have grown in similar ways. This rule helps when you want to know which vegetables can stand in for which in recipes as well. Substitute any vegetable that grows with its leafy head aboveground for another: a flower for a flower, a root for a root, shoot for shoot, stem for stem, tuber for tuber. (No rules apply to beets. Beets have their own way of cooking and their own way of being.)

Prepare cauliflower and broccoli first by removing their outer leaves with a small knife. Store the leaves in a bowl to await other leaves and cores and stems.

Cut the cauliflower in half, top to bottom, then cut out its core. Add the core to the same bowl as the leaves. Turn the cauliflower's two flat surfaces onto your cutting board and cut it into slices of even thickness, about a quarter inch each, imagining it's a loaf of bread.

Cut broccoli off the bottom third of its stem. If the stem is tender and easy to cut, include it with the broccoli itself. Add anything that seems tough to the bowl with the leaves and core. Cut the rest into batons as for boiling.

Toss the vegetables with olive oil and season them with salt, imagining that you're seasoning half the surface of everything, lightly. A faster and messier way to do this is to pour olive oil over vegetables in their pans. It requires that you get your hands oily, but you save washing a bowl. Lay them in shallow pans or trays in single layers. Cookie sheets are useful. If the pieces start to pile up on one pan, use a second one. Eke an extra ingredient out of the roasting by dropping a few whole cloves of unpeeled garlic among the vegetables. You can also add a few whole dried chiles or chile flakes. If you do, add them in the middle of roasting to keep them from burning.

Then prepare the beets. Cut the roots off their greens all at once. Leaving their little, fibrous tails attached, fit the beets snugly in a single layer in a shallow pan and wash them under hard running water, directly in the pan, keeping it tipped to the side.

When the water runs clear, let a good amount pool in the corner of the pan; better too much than too little. Once the beets are cooked, their skins will rub off easily, taking with them stem remains, tails, and leftover dirt, so they don't have to be perfectly clean. Add a drizzle of olive oil and cover the pan very tightly with aluminum foil so that the beets steam through while they roast. Place in the oven.

Fill the basin of your sink with cold water and put the beet greens in. You'll add your cooking greens to the same water, and wash everyone together.

Next, cut the butternut squash's narrow neck from its base to make cubing it easier. Peel both parts, cut each in half, and scoop the seeds out of the bulb with a big spoon. Peel any carrots and parsnips and turnips and rutabagas. Celery root's terrible skin is too fearsome, and I always cut it off with a knife. Cut everything into rough cubes about an inch around. They only need to be about the same volume so that they cook in the same time.

Toss the squash and root vegetables together in a mixing bowl with olive oil and salt, and pour them onto roasting pans in a single layer, making sure not to pile them on top of each other. Add any whole stalks of rosemary or thyme you have. Whole cloves of garlic are also good nestled among everything.

You can skip all peeling, scooping, and cutting if you want to cook your squash alone. Stick the whole squash directly in the oven unoiled and untouched and cook it until its skin is darkened, papery, and easy to pierce with a knife. Let it cool overnight. Tomorrow, the flesh will have shrunk away from the skin, and it will be as easy to peel as a banana.

Finally, wash sweet potatoes under running water, then prick them in a few places to keep them from bursting, and put them in the oven whole in a roasting pan or on pieces of aluminum foil.

Start checking everything but beets for doneness after half an hour. You may still be scrubbing and washing or peeling. By your fourth or fifth (or tenth) week you will be wiping down your cutting board. By your twentieth, your greens will be nicely washed and cooking in their sauté pans on the stove. For now, stop wherever you are in your preparations and check.

If when you open your oven you notice vegetables browning very quickly but they still seem uncooked inside, use a spatula to crowd them together on one side of the pan so that they steam a bit. The reverse also works: if the vegetables seem to be getting soft without browning, move some onto another tray to spread them out.

All roasted vegetables are most delicious when they're completely, completely tender. Test the doneness of cauliflower and squash and root vegetables by tasting them. When you don't wonder, but reach to eat another, they're done.

Remove them from the oven and let them cool on the counter. I like to squeeze a little lemon juice directly onto newly roasted cauliflower and broccoli. Remove brittle herb branches from the trays of squash and root vegetables, but let the herb leaves stay settled on the vegetables. Squeeze any garlic you've roasted with either out of its skin and store it with the vegetables. Tomorrow you can eat it as is or spread it on a sandwich.

Sweet potatoes are ready when they are soft to the touch and look like they've withdrawn from their skins. Remove each one as it is.

Beets are best checked with a paring knife. Check them forty minutes after they've gone into the oven by removing their pan, lifting a corner of the foil carefully so that you can refasten it, and sliding a sharp little knife into each beet. They're cooked when the knife slides through easily. If you're not sure if they're done, they're not.

Beets are almost always all different sizes. One might be ready and another raw. Remove any that are done, re-cover the rest tightly, and let them go on cooking. The foil must remain well sealed. If you notice a little puncture or tear in your foil, surrender and replace it.

Once the beets are cool enough to touch, use one towel to hold and another to rub and rub off the skins. If you hit difficult spots, cut them out with a knife. Cut the beets across into thick rounds or down their axes into wedges. Put them in a mixing bowl. Sprinkle the cut beets with a little red wine vinegar and some salt. Vinegar seems to bring out the very essence of the beet. It doesn't make theoretical sense that they'd taste more like themselves after being dressed with vinegar, but this is not theoretical. Let them absorb both for a minute before tasting them. Drizzle any you plan to eat immediately with olive oil.

If your kitchen is running like a finely tuned engine, you will get to washing greens before the roasting is done. Some days mine hums along beautifully and the Russian nesting dolls all fit together perfectly. Others it sputters and I don't get to the greens until I've finished all the other cooking.

Stem cooking greens by pulling leaves away from their stems in the opposite direction, and drop them into the water in your sink, where the beet greens await them. Beet leaves' stems are tender enough to leave connected to their leaves. If other stems are slim and seem to want to stay where they are, let them.

Swish the leaves around in the cold water, then move them to a cutting board in batches and cut them roughly, once or twice. Cut the stems of beet leaves into smaller pieces when you get down toward their bottoms. It's easier to do any finer cutting than this after they are cooked and cooled and won't shake water everywhere.

Don't worry about drying them. The water that clings to the cooking greens' leaves is your best friend in sautéing them. They will cook better if they're damp when you begin.

Cook your greens in batches. Put the two biggest deep pans or widest pots you have on the stove. Heat a tablespoon of oil in each. Add greens directly to the pans, letting the leaves pile up a little. Salt each batch lightly when you start cooking it, knowing that the greens will cook down significantly. Add a smashed or chopped garlic clove just after the greens and let it sizzle in the warm oil for a few seconds before mixing it through.

Stir the greens with a big spoon, and lower the heat if they seem to be getting burned without getting cooked. If the pan seems dry, add a spoonful of water. A nice occasional addition is an infinitesimally small scrape of cinnamon, nutmeg, or ginger.

Taste the greens as they cook by removing one, moving it to a cutting board, and slicing a piece off with a sharp knife. If the knife cuts through easily and the green tastes good, the batch is done. Lift the cooked greens out and put them onto a baking tray to cool. Wipe the pans out with a cloth towel. If there is liquid left, pour it into a jar and save it. Keep cooking the greens in batches, beginning again with olive oil and so on, until all of the greens are cooked.

If you can summon the energy, upturn your bowl of leaves, stems, and cores, chop them, scrape them into a pot, and make this pesto. Otherwise make it later in the week.

Garlicky leaf, stem, and core pesto

⁓

4 to 5 cups stems, leaves, and cores of cauliflower, broccoli, kale, collard greens, Swiss chard, cabbage, sliced or diced into ½-inch pieces	3 cloves garlic ½ cup olive oil ½ teaspoon salt water

Put everything in a pot just big enough to hold it and add water to cover by half. Cook it at below a simmer until anything you prod with a wooden spoon is smashable. Keep just enough water in the pot to make sure the bottom's not burning, adding a little water as you need it. When everything is soft, purée it quickly in a blender or food processor, or simply smash it with a wooden spoon until you get tired, leaving moments of appealing, irregular texture.

This is delicious dolloped on toast and grated with Parmesan, or treated as a side dish and served with fish or meat, or, with a cup of Parmesan cheese added, mixed with hot pasta.

While your oven is lit, use its heat thoroughly. When a pan of vegetables comes out, replace it with a toaster tray of walnuts or almonds. They will be perfectly toasted after ten minutes or so and can be stored in the refrigerator for months and used in vegetable salads, added to pesto, or snacked on. Or scatter stale bread in a little pan, drizzle it with olive oil, and make toasted breadcrumbs or croutons.

If you can't find anything to fit into the spaces vacated by roasting vegetables, use the oven's heat once everything is out. Let it warm your dinner plates, or the meal's bread. Use its ambient heat for loosening vinaigrette that's hardened in the refrigerator, softening a stick of butter, or mixing pasta with cheese.

I once lived with a man who grew up in a very Spartan household. If his breath hung visible and cold above the breakfast table, he would be admonished to put on a sweater. He taught me to leave the oven door open when I was finished cooking. It is troublesome to step around, but a warm empty oven heats a cold kitchen well.

When everything you've cooked is cool, put it away in clear containers. I use quart- and half-quart-sized heavy glass canning jars and other glass jars reclaimed once their original contents have been used. Pour hot water over jars you're going to re-purpose to remove their original labels, or put them in the dishwasher and hope for the best.

I.

Hot vegetables is a doctrine every bit as encumbering to good vegetable eating as pressure to leave them raw until right before dinner. Room temperature is the temperature at which most vegetables taste best. When we eat antipasti at Italian restaurants, they are gloriously oiled and vinegared and perfectly tepid. So, often, are Spanish tapas.

When you don't taste heat first but instead the sweetness of cauliflower or beet, the prickliness of vinegar, or tingle of good olive oil, it is flavor, not temperature, you experience.

No bacterial treachery lurks in vegetables once they have spent time somewhere other than the refrigerator or oven. Nor does it necessarily in anything that is a few days old, or spends the night on your counter. I still remember with a pang a superb fish soup lost one New Year's morning after a friend thought it was pure poison because it had been sitting out all night. I am fairly sure he wasn't right, and I am completely confident that it was spiritually wrong. To make the most of your work, consider, at least once, dipping your toes into the pleasures of room-temperature food.

All cooked vegetables, whether boiled or roasted, become wonderful salads. They need only a handful of toasted nuts, chopped fresh herbs, a few vinegar-soaked onions, and a sharp vinaigrette. It's really all most food ever needs. The combination may be the universe's only reliable youth serum.

A vibrant vegetable salad

~

2 cups cooked vegetables
¼ cup chopped almonds or walnuts
¼ onion of any color or a shallot, thinly sliced into half-moons
red wine vinegar
a pinch of salt
½ teaspoon mustard
olive oil
¼ cup roughly chopped parsley or mint
¼ cup roughly chopped turnip greens or radish tops or another
    peppery-tasting leaf
a squeeze of lemon

Let the vegetables come to room temperature. Remove them from the refrigerator when you get home from work so they can warm up slowly, or speed them up by putting a bowl of them near a lit burner or on a warm oven.

If you didn't toast nuts during the week's cooking, toast them now in a 400-degree oven, checking them after 5 minutes, then periodically until they are lightly colored. Shake them off their tray.

In a bowl big enough to hold all the vegetables, soak the onion in vinegar with a pinch of salt for 10 minutes. Add the mustard to the bowl and mix it in. Let it sit for another 2. Add the vegetables, toasted nuts, and a long drizzle of olive oil, then the herbs, greens, and squeeze of lemon. It should all taste refreshed.

Then, the variations are endless. For roasted cauliflower or broccoli, plump a small spoonful of golden raisins in warm wine vinegar. When they're soft and fat lift them out of the vinegar and mix them into a cup of toasted croutons, add a long pour of olive oil, and mix the heady croutons with the vegetables. Add a spoonful of roughly chopped capers, a small handful of pitted olives, freshly chopped mint, and a drizzle of olive oil.

Or for beets alone, soak thinly sliced red onion in vinegar for ten minutes, mix it with the cold roasted beets, scatter the mixture on a plate, and top it with halved boiled potatoes or boiled green beans, or raw tomato that you've salted and dressed separately with good olive oil; or arrange the beets over thin slices of salted avocado.

In Japan, cold sweet potato salads are made with the dark, pink-skinned sweet potatoes called *satsumaimo,* which we eat here deep fried as tempura, or drink distilled into the bracing liquor *shochu.* In Peru, cold sweet potatoes are sliced, skins on, and served chilled, with spicy, citrusy ceviche. Cold sweet potatoes used to be common here, too. "Take an old cold tater and wait" was a shush issued to whining children in the 1920s. It was, according to the sweet potato board, cold *sweet* taters to which the reprimand referred, which were traditionally sliced and served cold to sop up pork cracklings.

For a version of the Peruvian sweet potato salad, slice sweet potatoes into half-inch rounds. It's fine if pieces crumble and fall apart. Slice a shallot into thin rounds and soak it in lime juice or white vinegar and a little salt for ten minutes. Chop a big handful of cilantro and a whole fresh jalapeño. Stir it all together with a handful of roasted peanuts, letting the sweet potato break up into pieces, like potatoes are wont to do.

Chilled greens become a lovely salad. Remove them from the refrigerator, quickly chop them, and mix them with a sprinkle of lemon juice, or a sprinkle of sesame seeds or nothing at all, and a drizzle of olive oil.

II.

I ate one of the best sandwiches I can remember in a tiny, cramped sandwich shop in Florence, Italy. It was of oily, garlicky cooked spinach, layered on thick-crusted bread with mozzarella, salt, and black pepper.

I make a similar one at least once a week with cooked kale, collard greens, or chard instead of the spinach, which is expensive and cooks down too dramatically for me. I don't warm the greens, so the sandwich doesn't take any longer to make than one of sliced ham. Mozzarella is delicious. Ricotta is an especially good and messy substitute, and any cheese will do.

I also make sandwiches of cold roasted cauliflower and broccoli. This is just as simple. Chop the vegetables once or twice through. They can be alone or combined. Thickly slice and toast bread, rub it with garlic, drizzle it liberally with olive oil, and lay the vegetables on one slice. Thinly slice a little red onion and soak it in red wine vinegar, then sprinkle the slices over the vegetables. If you like, add a little handful of olives, or a few thin slices of prosciutto, a big handful of roughly chopped parsley. Cover with the second slice and eat. If you want a warm sandwich, heat a cast-iron pan and press your sandwich between it and another heavy pan, or toast it on an indoor grill.

To make a sandwich of roasted beets, sprinkle them with a little more red wine vinegar and mix in a big handful of chives, mint, or chervil. Soft boil one egg per sandwich. Slice the eggs into thin rounds across. Slice and toast bread and spread each piece thickly with butter; lay slices of egg over the buttered toast. Squeeze lemon juice lightly on the slices and salt them, add a few grinds of freshly cracked black pepper, then spoon the pickley beets over the top and cover with a second slice of toast.

Or make a more vegetal version of a hummus sandwich. Chop and smash roasted squash, root vegetables, and sweet potatoes to the consistency of a chunky spread. Mix in a little lemon juice, chopped parsley, mint, or basil, and a drizzle of olive oil. Toast hardy, grainy bread or pita. Layer the smashed vegetables and herbs inside.

III.

Some great food thinkers have the oddest things to say about soup: "A soup must be fresh," or "A soup must taste of its ingredients." Those are true of a lot of foods, but they are plainly false for soup.

The best soups are a day old. Soup mustn't be fresh, but mature. They needn't taste of their ingredients, but only give their ingredients somewhere to be left off and picked up again.

I learned to make soup from my mother, whose *potages* contained whatever was around, much of it already cooked: roasted root vegetables, boiled potatoes or turnips, an odd handful of herbs. She served them throughout my childhood, doused with good olive oil and topped with crisp croutons. They were a day old or older. Their ingredients were older yet, and they were delicious.

To make a good, honest, authentic potage, like my mother's, slice half an onion and a clove of garlic. Cook them, salting as soon as you add them to the pan, with a half teaspoon of fresh thyme in a little butter and olive oil, until tender. If they start to brown, add a few drops of water. Add any combination of roasted squash, root vegetables, and sweet potato and an equal quantity of stock or water. Let it all simmer for half an hour. Purée in a blender in batches, blending more solids than liquid. If it begins to seem too liquidy at any point, leave some of the broth behind. If it needs more liquid, judiciously add some of what you have left; you can always add more. You can make this days in advance. Warm the soup up slowly in a pot before eating.

If you want a soup of cauliflower or broccoli, begin it the same way, omit the thyme and add a quarter cup of olive oil before blending it and a dab of cold butter once you have. Eat either à la my mother, drizzled with olive oil and topped with crisp croutons.

Or put two cold, peeled roasted sweet potatoes into the bowl of a food processor. Add a few generous spoonfuls of melted butter, a splash of cream, and a quarter teaspoon of smoky paprika. Purée it until it's completely smooth. Warm it slowly in a pot over low heat, adding a combination of chicken broth and coconut milk until it just seems souplike. Serve squeezed with lime and scattered with chopped cilantro.

For beet soup, do everything just as you do for the squash and root vegetable soup, but serve it cold, drizzled with yogurt, sour cream, or crème fraîche.

There is an eye-roll-worthy restaurant chestnut that "today's soup is tomorrow's purée." It is also true. Tomorrow, cook a cubed, peeled potato separately in boiling water, drain it, smash it through a potato ricer or food mill, and mix it into your cold leftover soup. Warm it over low heat in a little pot with a tablespoon of butter. When it's warm, add a drizzle of cream, call it a purée, and serve.

IV.

Or make risotto according to the instructions on page 121. While the rice is cooking, chop three or four roasted beets into small cubes—small, not perfect. Drizzle them with a little red wine vinegar and olive oil and taste them for salt. Put the bowl close to the cooking rice to warm. When the risotto is nearly done, add a big handful of chopped thyme and parsley, if you have it, and a lot of grated Parmesan.

Put a big ladleful of risotto into wide shallow bowls, making a little hollow in the center of each bowl of risotto. Fill each hollow with a heaping spoonful of beets. Drizzle with olive oil, add a few cracks of black pepper, and top it all with more Parmesan.

I make this sort of risotto with other vegetables, too, the same way, after they've taken turns as purées.

Or chop cooked vegetables up, add a little good fat, and bake it all. If you were worried, this keeps the future from seeming too fibrous.

Greens gratin

~

2 cups chopped cooked greens
1 cup béchamel sauce

For béchamel sauce
1 tablespoon butter
1 tablespoon flour
1 cup whole milk
2 tablespoons grated Parmesan

Make the béchamel sauce by melting butter, adding flour, and mixing it over low heat until it just comes together. Heat milk to just above room temperature and add it slowly to the flour-butter mixture, whisking constantly. Continue to whisk until it's boiling, lower to the lowest possible heat, and cook for 20 to 25 minutes, until the raw flour taste is gone. Remove it from the heat and add the grated Parmesan.

Thoroughly butter a 6- x 4-inch gratin dish, roasting pan, or casserole. Mix the greens and the béchamel well. Taste the mixture. It should be rich and highly seasoned. Add it to the buttered dish and sprinkle with another ½ tablespoon Parmesan. Bake at 400 degrees, rotating it periodically if it's cooking faster at one part than another. Cook until it's bubbling, set, and slightly colored at the edges.

Cool to just above room temperature and serve it with a large spoon, not trying to make squares, which will not work, but rather scooping an oval mound for each serving.

Reheat single servings, or as much as you think you're going to eat, on subsequent days in a 350-degree oven until it's warm.

Béchamel sauce is also delicious to mix with pasta before baking it. If you like the idea, make twice as much béchamel and warm the second cup over low heat before you use it.

This is similar and similarly good.

Hot, toasty cauliflower or broccoli

~

½ onion, sliced thinly into half-moons
1 to 2 tablespoons olive oil or butter
optional: 2 chopped anchovy fillets
2 cups chopped roasted cauliflower or
　　broccoli
1 tablespoon chopped mint, parsley, basil,
　　or any combination
Toasted breadcrumbs

Sauté the onion in the olive oil or butter. If you are using anchovy, add it to the onion and cook it together. Cook until the onion is nearly tender. Lightly oil or butter a 6- x 4-inch gratin dish or roasting pan. Mix the vegetables into the onion and add the herbs. Spread the mixture in the dish and bake at 400 degrees for 20 minutes until it's bubbly. Top it with breadcrumbs to cover well and bake for another 5 to 10 minutes, until the breadcrumbs are lightly browned and it is warm throughout when tested with your finger.

V.

Turn the ends of your batches into one big curry. This is good with everything other than beets, which leave their garish stain on everything.

End-of-the-week vegetable curry

½ onion, cut into large dice
peanut oil or olive oil
salt
½ teaspoon, combined, ground turmeric, ground
*   cardamom, and ground cumin*
½ teaspoon flaked chile; if you have a whole, fresh chile,
*   mince it and use instead*
½ cup cooked chickpeas or black-eyed peas, canned or
*   cooked from dried*
½ to 1 can coconut milk
1 cup other liquid (chicken stock, strange liquid
*   requisitioned from cooking vegetables, or water)*
2 or 3 pieces lemon rind
optional: 1 teaspoon Thai or Vietnamese fish sauce
2 cups cooked vegetables
½ cup toasted peanuts
Fresh lemon juice
Fresh mint or basil leaves

Cook the onion in peanut or olive oil, adding salt as soon as you add the onion. Add the spices and the chile. Once the spices are fragrant, add the beans, then add all the liquid and lemon rind. Cook, stirring occasionally, at below a simmer until the beans are very tender, about ½ hour. Add the fish sauce if you are using it. Add the vegetables and peanuts and cook for 15 minutes on low heat. When everything seems integrated, taste the curry. Add salt if it needs it and a big squeeze of lemon juice. Serve on rice, topped with fresh herbs.

By the end of the week, you will have eaten vegetables a dozen ways a dozen times, having begun with good raw materials only once. You will also have had a number of satisfying conversations. You will have eaten a raw bite of kale stem and wondered whether next time it should be pickled. You'll have tasted a particularly soft, cold, vinegary beet, and realized you wanted to make beet soup again and serve it cold. You will have been silently practicing that ancient conversation in which cooks and their materials used to converse, feeling out unfamiliar conjugations, brushing up.

Then there is the breed of vegetable that strides at its own pace, regardless of yours. It has a brief season and is probably laborious, needing to be shelled or shucked or peeled, then leaving you a tiny pile of its edible self.

But it is invariably this vegetable that tastes so resonantly of its moment in the year that the surrounding months echo with it. There are festivals organized around this sort: in Spain there's one for the sweet, leggy onions called *calçots*. Everyone runs out and picks them, builds big fires, roasts bushels and bushels, makes *romesco* sauce, and gets drunk, eating as many as they can. In Italy if a vegetable's festival is not on the calendar, it's tacitly observed: there will be picnics when the first wild asparagus arrive. This sort of vegetable is impractical if you're trying to look ahead, but is very good at making you stop and look around.

One of the most common in our soil is English peas, which arrive, adamantly, in the spring. English peas need shelling, but they need it for only a few weeks, which makes the process bearable, and not a little grounding. My restless mind has found no better palliative: after a little time with the gratifying solidity of a bowl in my lap and the sound of legumes pattering into it, I always feel as though some cobwebs have cleared.

Children must help shell peas. In a world of things too big, getting peas from pods is a chance for pea-sized people to exercise authority. Always told to put things back where they found them, here, children have it right. Pea shelling goes only in one direction: dig, disperse, and never look back.

Shell English peas by digging a fingernail in by their stems and sliding your finger along their seams, seam side down, over a bowl. Keep a second bowl for everything that isn't a pea.

Children love all pea and bean shelling, but if you ever find fresh chickpeas, you will have found any child's new best friend. They're bright green, with a little lightly pressurized air inside their pods that makes them pop when punctured. I have never seen as joyous a spate of bean work as when I handed a four-year-old a bowl of fresh chickpeas. It was a short spate, but a committed one. Little hands are also good at snapping snap peas, whose threads, which come loose once their ends are snapped, make a curly pigtail when pulled.

Probably the best ways to cook English peas are either to boil them or put them in a shallow pan with barely enough water to come halfway up their sides, a nice-sized pat of butter, and a little salt and quickly heat them until they're tender and bright green.

English peas also have pods that taste of the essences of the vegetable itself, from which you can make the most perfectly sweet, pea-green stock to use immediately, or freeze so that you can have a pea-green echo down the line.

To make pea-pod broth, put all of the pea pods you have into a pot. This can include snap pea ends. Add the tops or skins of two onions, a clove of garlic, a bunch of parsley stems, and a few peppercorns. Cover it all with two inches of water, bring to a boil, then let cook at just below a simmer for an hour. Strain the broth.

If you want to use your broth immediately, make a pea soup that is "pea" emphasized and underlined. Cook a little bit of onion in butter until it's tender, salting it immediately, add whatever peas you've shelled, and cook them, just barely covered in pea stock, until just tender, then purée it until it's smooth. I like to drink this from a glass, and cold.

What is more enticing and confounding than an artichoke? I am among the class of human who is powerless against my love for them. The class's other members are far more august. I recommend Pablo Neruda's "Ode to the Artichoke" to anyone who loves the thistle already and to anyone who doesn't, because the poet's love is probably enough for two.

Even if you are not enticed by the poem or the vegetable, they are conceptually confounding and illuminating in that the artichoke you plan to eat—an artichoke's rich, metallic-tasting heart—emerges only after you've peeled off half its body.

Artichokes must be plucked down to their softest layer of leaves, then have their sharp little hats sawed off, then their fuzzy chokes cruelly scooped from their middles, then their stems peeled with a peeler. Artichokes are a strange, sweet investment. When I was growing up, my father's favorite saying was: "If you're gonna be a bear, be a grizzly." They are difficult and worth it, and when I decide to cook artichokes, I bearishly cook as many as I can.

Once you've cleaned them, the cooking part is easy. Halve small artichokes and quarter larger ones. Put them in a pot in a combination of water and olive oil, a sprinkle of white wine, a single bay leaf, a very big pinch of salt, and a few sprigs of fresh thyme. Simmer them until they're completely tender, testing by tasting pieces of several stems.

Though artichokes do not have shells to be made into artichoke stock, as English peas do, what is left at the bottom of the artichoke pot is the artichoke's bequeathal. It contains all of its certainty, its tinny insistence. There is more on what to do with such a treasure in the next chapter, called "How to Catch Your Tail." For now, pour it into a jar, knowing that for a little while at least, the uniqueness of the artichoke is yours.

Though plucking artichoke leaves doesn't mend all cracked spirits as firmly as pea shelling, it has its own curative power. There is a Dutch saying: "Bitter in the mouth cures the heart." If you happen to have a friend shaken by heartache, hand over a bag of raw artichokes. Once she has relieved them of their leaves, encourage one brave bite. Between the meditative peeling and the bitter taste, she should be completely healed. If there are no artichokes around, raw dandelion greens are a good substitute.

It would be a kerchief-wringing tragedy if Italians were to miss a vegetable in its transient ripeness. If an edible plant resolutely thwarts all attempts at practicality, a ceremony is devised to take advantage of it, no matter how short its season.

The best such ceremony I've encountered is for fava beans. Fava beans might be the most labor-intensive of all vegetables. There are only a few beans per Suessian pod. You need to buy more than a pound to get three-quarters of a cup. And once you've gotten them out of the thick pods themselves, there is still a rubbery skin around each bean.

Instead of trying to figure out a way to get the beans all shelled, peeled, and cooked in time for dinner, tenacious Italians have decided the beans should be shelled and peeled at the table, by whoever wants to eat them. Each bean is then eaten raw directly from its pod, dipped lightly in salt. They are accompanied by a wedge of the lightest yellow cheese, called *marzolino* after March, the month in which fava beans are harvested and the cheese is made.

It doesn't sound like much of a meal, but a fava bean, with its tastes of the beginning of the green part of the year, has an absorbing flavor, and you get fuller than you think. This is partly because it takes a while to do, and there is bread and prosciutto, and chilled white wine, and chillier March air; also because it is very filling to slowly eat a meal together at the table, making it as you go.

To shell fava beans, put one index finger on either side of the spot where it looks like a bean is and pop the bean out, through the pod, using your thumbs. Favas launch and bounce, so be prepared to chase them down.

Fava beans are also delicious eaten as a salad, after their rubbery second skin has been removed. This is easiest to do after quickly dunking shucked beans in boiling water. Remove each rubbery skin, using your nails. Mix them lightly with olive oil, a squeeze of lemon, and fresh mint. Or stew peeled favas with sliced garlic and parsley or savory then toss them with hot pasta, or smash them into a topping for grilled toast.

A good strategy for odd, unfamiliar vegetables, strange and lovely ones that interest you but you don't know quite what to do with—a clump of wild mushrooms, or marigold-yellow squash blossoms, or the little squashes themselves, blossoms still attached—is to buy a few, put flour in a bowl, mix just enough seltzer in to turn it into a paste, let it sit for an hour, then add a touch of salt and more seltzer until the batter looks like cream.

Then fry them, hot and quick, to be eaten immediately with nothing in mind but the crisp, salty vegetable itself. Heat a little grapeseed oil or peanut oil in a pot, cut your oddity into small branches or batons, and when the oil is hot enough that a speck of flour sizzles, dip the pieces in the batter, fry them, and let them drain for a minute on a paper towel. Then sprinkle them with a little more salt and eat them.

It sounds like a vague prescription for cooking any unfamiliar vegetable. Any vegetable? you wonder. Can any vegetable be made sense of just by being fried? My response is my father's other favorite saying, also ursine: Does a bear . . . ? And so on.

Four

How to Catch Your Tail

As is a tale, so is life.

—Seneca

The bones and shells and peels of things are where a lot of their goodness resides. It's no more or less lamb for being meat or bone; it's no more or less pea for being pea or pod. Grappa is made from the spent skins and stems and seeds of wine grapes; marmalade from the peels of oranges. The wine behind the grappa is great, but there are moments when only grappa will do; the fruit of the orange is delicious, but it cannot be satisfactorily spread.

The skins from onions, green tops from leeks, stems from herbs must all be swept directly into a pot instead of into the garbage. Along with the bones from a chicken, raw or cooked, they are what it takes to make chicken stock, which you need never *buy*, once you decide to keep its ingredients instead of throwing them away. If you have the bones from fish, it's fish stock. If there are bones from pork or lamb, you will have pork or lamb stock.

Parsley stems and scallion tops, too, must be saved. Both can be chopped more finely than their softer parts and used in tandem or instead. Mint stems should be soaked in red wine vinegar, creating minty vinegar with which to make minty vinaigrettes; cilantro stems are just as good as their leaves.

Citrus peels are some of the most often forsaken tails. Before juicing them, remove the zest from one or two oranges or lemons and combine a spoonful of their zest, a half clove of finely chopped garlic, a big handful of roughly chopped parsley or mint, and a little crunchy salt, and you have a gorgeous and quite sophisticated sauce for sprinkling over boiled chicken or poached eggs.

Or remove citrus peels with a vegetable peeler, finely slice them, and simmer them in sugar syrup made from one cup water and one cup sugar. Let it cook for fifteen minutes, with a small plate holding the peels down, until the liquid has thickened. Keep the citrus syrup in your refrigerator, and let it warm up before mixing it into tall glasses of cold seltzer and ice to make homemade sodas. Garnish them with fresh mint.

I have a frugal friend who bakes and deep-fries potato skins. These are delicious, free, and worth keeping in mind if you have a pot of oil ready. Carrot peels, turnip peels, and beet skins are only good for mulching, but vegetables will grow from soil into which their less composed selves are mixed, and owe their predecessors for the assistance.

Some ingredients only grow their tails in their cooking. There are few ways in life to bottle a process, an experience. The closest may be scrapbooks, but you must unlock something in you for them to work. But at the bottom of any pot of vegetables or beans or grains or meat are unrepeatable flavors themselves, all the alchemy of today's cooking distilled into a liquid you can neatly pour into a glass jar.

The lovely, oily liquid left once a vegetable is cooked is a perfect concentrate of everything that went into its cooking. It should be treated as a potion that has collected the imprint of the good butter and olive oil, cloves of garlic, lemon peels, sprigs of thyme, splashes of wine, cracks of pepper, and vegetable that created it.

Use the potion from your Italian frying pepper pot to drizzle over rice. Or add it to a pot of warming tomato sauce. Save the lovely green murk from the Swiss chard pan to warm the Swiss chard tomorrow, which will be happier for the chance to spend time with yesterday's more experienced cooking. The drippings from a pan of roasting meat are delicious on hot toast or mixed into cooked rice or cooking beans, or soups of either.

Or combine a potion with an end so boisterous it seems to shout "beginning." Tail ends of loaves of bread are as good as their heads, and perhaps more useful. Among their dozens of talents is turning into soup. Warm olive oil, add a sliced garlic clove and a finely sliced leek, cook them slowly for a few minutes, add four cups of cubed, crustless stale bread, two cups of any meat broth, two of any combination brothy potions—of the kind that may or may not have once rubbed shoulders with broccoli or a pan of buttery corn—and let it cook into a thick, unrecognizable, delicious soup. Eat it drizzled with a lot of olive oil and grated with fresh Parmesan.

Or do the most sensible thing that you can in most kitchens at most times, which is put the tail ends of everything in a pot, season it well with salt, add a bit of cubed potato and some butter, and simmer it until it is all tender.

Unless you're looking at a tail end of vegetable that has actually changed states —solid to liquid or, worse, to gas—its yellowed parts can be cut off, and it can be added to a pot containing sautéed onion, a chopped potato per three cups of vegetables, and meat or vegetable stock or water to cover. Find a turnip that missed the week's roasting, asparagus bottoms, cabbage cores. As long as a soup's ingredients are born in the same season, they will meld together perfectly in a pot and can then be blended until creamy. If there is a final cup of cooked beans or lentils that needs somewhere to go, once you've blended it this sort of hodgepodgey soup is the place.

We all have potionlike liquids around already. If you did not cook yesterday, glance around, and when no one is looking, swiftly tug on someone else's tail. The strong flavors left in the olive oil from a jar of dried tomatoes or marinated mushrooms will taste of tomatoes or mushrooms; the olive oil from a jar of anchovies of the little fish. Though you didn't marinate the vegetable or cure the anchovy, someone did, and either ingredient will have imparted flavor to its surroundings.

I would like to smartly advise you to label and date your potions well, so that you know their vintages and contents. But while I am very good at saving and storing things, I am terrible at labeling them. My refrigerator contains precariously full jars and tipping-over glasses of unidentifiable liquids. The best I can say is that it is worth *trying* to do. Then, if you fail, you can resign yourself to felici-tous discoveries when it is artichoke broth you sip in order to make a fair identification, and infelicitous ones when it's pickle brine you gulp just before mistakenly pouring it into a soup.

The amount of food you have left from a meal is always the per-fect amount for something. It may not be enough for a repeat of the first meal: a single bowl of beef stew is not stew for four. It is, though, just right for four hot beef sandwiches on warm little buns, with thinly sliced cabbage and pickles alongside.

A few tails are usually glad for each other's company. Combine the rest of the leftover stew with another day's boiled potatoes, smashed with a bit of olive oil, and the final bite of the sautéed greens. Spoon it into a ceramic dish, top it with crisp breadcrumbs, made from the tail ends of bread, and bake it until it's bubbling.

Almost all tail ends meet up neatly with the emblematic begin-ning: the egg. Last night's Thai green curry, or Indian *saag paneer* is the filling for today's frittata. Omelets, which provide the gracious foil of soft, simple egg, are especially good at making less dramatic meals from restaurant leftovers, which are usually so strongly sea-soned that eating them untransformed the next day can feel like meeting someone at the breakfast table in full makeup.

You're more likely to look seriously, and eagerly, at a small amount of something that's well fit into its container than some-thing deserted in the last, sad corner of a big bowl out of which everything else has been scraped. Store your tails in transparent glass containers the right size for them. It is important that they be transparent so that when you open up your refrigerator you don't see a stack of opaque plastic boxes, but purple eggplant, or turmeric-hued chickpeas. Keep the containers near the front of your refrigerator where you can see them.

Catching one's tail is a curious business. We watch dogs in their constant, fruitless chases all the time. Plato thought tail chasing not only practical but divine. He wrote that the mystical symbol for infinity, a snake swallowing its tail, was the perfect being: it made what it ate and ate what it made, needing nothing but its own existence for perpetual life.

I like to imagine Plato's resourceful snake quite happy feasting on his tail for eternity. We, however, don't have to gulp our tails down whole. We can season, rearrange, heat, chill, enliven, transform. We will find not infinitude but a detectable completeness in our finer version of his routine diet.

When we leave our tails trailing behind us we lose what is left of the thought we put into eating well today. Then we slither along, straight, linear things that we can be, wondering what we will make for dinner tomorrow. So we must spot our tails when we can, and gather them up, so that when we get hungry next, and our minds turn to the question of what to eat, the answer will be there waiting.

Five

How to Paint Without Brushes

One can paint without brush, ink, or paper.
For the gesture must be conceived in such a way that
when one makes it, it was already there.
— Shi Tao, *The Sayings of Friar Bitter Melon*

If we were taught to cook as we are taught to walk, encouraged first to feel for pebbles with our toes, then to wobble forward and fall, then had our hands firmly tugged on so we would try again, we would learn that being good at it relies on something deeply rooted, akin to walking, to get good at which we need only guidance, senses, and a little faith.

We aren't often taught to cook like that, so when we watch people cook naturally, in what looks like an agreement between cook and cooked, we think that they were born with an ability to simply *know* that an egg is done, that the fish needs flipping, and that the soup needs salt.

Instinct, whether on the ground or in the kitchen, is not a destination but a path. The word *instinct* comes from a combination of *in* meaning "toward," and *stinguere* meaning "to prick." It doesn't mean *knowing* anything, but pricking your way toward the answer.

If you are to start down this path, you must feel charged with using your senses, imagining them as hands that nudge you forward and hold you up when you get unsteady, and even when you fall.

You must taste and taste. Taste everything, and often. Taste even if you're scared. There are ideas for what to do if food tastes too salty or spicy or plain in "How to Snatch Victory from the Jaws of Defeat." Only by tasting can you learn to connect the decisions you make with their outcomes.

Listen as though you could cook something just by hearing it. A piece of fish is ready to be flipped when it sounds like it is, and no number of adjectives about that sizzle will be as useful as listening to the fish in your pan tell you when it is.

Smelling we can't help. Our noses keep us hungry, and they stay sharp even when our minds get dull. For your nose to be as useful as it can be, associate what you smell with what you taste and see and hear. An onion that's still too crunchy smells different from one that's tender. When you can distinguish one smell from another, you'll know how far along your onions are, whether you can see into their pot or not.

When you touch the food you cook, you develop intelligence in your fingertips. I cook mostly with my hands: they're calibrated, by now, to turn things at the right moments, to choose correct amounts of salt. They seem to know before I do when to stop squeezing a lemon, or how much parsley to grab.

No matter how well a cookbook is written, the cooking times it gives will be wrong. Ingredients don't take three or five or ten minutes to be done; it depends on the day and the stove. So you must simply pay attention, trust yourself, and decide.

As for what else you need in order to cook, there are too many equipment lists in the world already. A meal is cooked by the mind, heart, and hands of the cook, not by her pots and pans. So it is on the former that I recommend focusing your investments.

My pots and pans are big and old, and I have only a few. I prioritize size and sturdiness. I have a big pot for boiling. It fits a chicken and vegetables, or two pounds of pasta nicely. A chef I know cooks at home in an old tin camping pot because it's a good size and water boils quickly in it. Anything capacious enough for water and ingredients, no matter what it looks like, will do you fine. I have a big, heavy cast-iron pan; a deep and warped high-sided frying pan for sautéing greens; a scarlet oven-safe casserole, its inside very stained; a nonstick omelet pan, badly scratched, leaving it decidedly "stick."

I have a very little pot I found forlorn on someone's stoop—if I'm heating soup for one or boiling a single egg, I like to have the meal fill up the pot it's cooking in. I have a monstrous colander. It is nicked and dented, but I can drain pasta for a crowd without the bottom noodles suffocating, and I can boil four bunches of beet greens and drain them all at once.

My knife I cherish. It has a pretty, eight-inch-long blade. A fellow cook at Chez Panisse used to call it a "lady's knife." It was a gift from my brother, and I keep it clean and sharp. I also have a small paring knife, bought at the hardware store, and a heavy, sharp, serrated knife, for cutting hard-crusted bread. My kitchen table can be cut on, and is, but I also have a few big wooden cutting boards.

My glass roasting dishes I've had since college. I have a few cookie sheets, surely bought by a roommate and stolen unintentionally by me. I try to have a tart plate, but often find, midtart, that the one I'm using is someone else's, and then I hope that he or she has mine.

I have a deep, beehive-shaped mortar and pestle I bought in Thailand, and every day nuts or garlic or anchovies or herbs need to be pounded up, so it stays front and center. I have measuring cups and spoons. I have learned, though, reading old cookbooks, that it used to be a regular practice to give measurements in wine glasses and teacups. I can think of no reason not to develop your own system of weights and measures.

I have a rice cooker, which I trust completely; if you have one or buy one, make sure it's not a substitute for learning how to cook rice. Pay attention to how long it boils and how long it simmers. This goes for other kitchen gadgets. If you have a Crock-Pot or a slow cooker, watch its behavior. Then you will know what to do when it breaks. Even egg slicers and olive pitters have something to teach. Unless you are an aspiring laser beam, your microwave won't teach you anything. Use yours as a bookshelf, or to store gadgets you don't use.

I have a jar full of wooden spoons, almost all burned from my bad habit of leaving them in the pot I've been stirring. A writer named Patience Gray recounts the provenance of her favorite wooden spoon in a book called *Honey from a Weed*. It came flying out a kitchen window at the climax of a couple's squabble, and she picked it up and kept it.

I buy a wooden spoon whenever I see one I like because I may need to throw something, and a passerby may need one. They're perfect, too, for checking doneness of certain ingredients. There's nothing that does this with more certainty: when a piece of onion, garlic, carrot, or celery can be easily broken with a wooden spoon, then, and *exactly* then, it is done.

My favorite wooden spoon has a little round cup at its end, designed not for stirring but for tasting. Its sharp lip is like the rim of a bowl, which means that I don't use it to test for doneness. It is the only one in my kitchen that is not burned.

I have a funnel for pouring olive oil from a can into smaller bottles and a conical sieve for straining stock. It's helpful to have a blender, and my strategy of buying cheap ones and then not understanding why they break isn't efficient. Other pans and dishes of various sizes meander in and out of my life, pleasant, passing things I seem to need when they're there, and not once they're gone.

You can gather all of that, in whatever versions. You can also cook well, not in different pots and pans, but in the ones you have. As long as you taste curiously, and watch and feel and listen, and prick your way toward food you like, you will find that you become someone about whom people will say that cooking seems to come naturally, like walking. They will say it and it will be true.

That is my advice then, on experience and equipment. Consider not minding whether you *know* the answer, and not filling your kitchen with tools, but becoming, rather, the kind of cook who doesn't need them.

Six

How to Light a Room

Turn a shack over to a lover; for all its poverty, its lights
and shadows warm a little and its humbled surfaces prickle
with feeling.

— Robert Capon, *The Supper of the Lamb*

Little flourishes, like parsley, make food seem cared for. They are as practical as lighting candles to change the atmosphere of a room.

Fresh herbs have always been relied on to perk up whatever needs perking. Parsley, in particular, has long been called into duty when things were fading: in ancient Greece, anyone or anything on its way out was said to be "in need of parsley." The goddess in charge of the herb, Persephone, was both queen of the underworld and goddess of spring. Whether to speed passing or revive, parsley has always tapped at the junctures where the here has begun to slide into the hereafter.

I recommend buying a bunch of parsley whenever you can. Then, once you have it, act as children do when handed hammers and suddenly everything needs pounding.

Whether because it is plain, or because it is aged, or because it is there and you want to enhance it, everything needs parsley. Newborn as spring, a poached egg needs parsley. Hot white rice, freshly boiled potatoes, pasta with butter and cheese all need parsley by the handful. So does leftover rice, the last of yesterday's boiled potatoes, a frittata of Monday's pasta with butter and cheese.

They need parsley to make them all brighter and more present, and because you will feel more present when you eat them. Scientists continue to study what satisfies us in eating. It's not a simple chemistry of starches and proteins. We feel sated when our senses have been animated and our brains' activity has had time to register our guts'. Our mouths love plenty, but so do our eyes. An abundance of fresh parsley may *only* be of parsley, but it's an *abundance*.

Pick parsley leaves off their stems not for anything in particular, but so that they're ready to use. You're more likely to reach for them if they are.

Pick the leaves by pinching each where leaf connects to stem. This goes quickly if you focus your attention on the leaves, not the stems. If you are ever too scattered to focus, which I sometimes am, use a sharp knife and cut lightly where leaf and stem meet. Save all parsley stems. You need them to make any soup or pot of beans worth its weight in water. There's a lot of shilling for soup and stock and beans in this book, and every recipe wants parsley stems.

Then roughly chop a big handful of parsley. It's nice to have not just the *impression* of a leaf, but the *experience* of it when you eat one. I find that I only want to chop herbs finely if they're going to be scattered over the clearest broth, whose only other ingredient is four grains of rice, where ascetic and aesthetic balance must be maintained. Otherwise, I go at them with a knife, briefly and cleanly, and leave the pieces big.

Once parsley, or its fellow soft herbs—basil, chives, tarragon, dill, and cilantro—have been quickly chopped, throw a generous handful directly over your rice or potatoes or pasta, and watch the meal begin to prickle with feeling.

Mediterranean food especially likes basil and mint. South American and Asian food like both of those plus cilantro. Gallic food loves licoricey tarragon and sweet chives. Everything likes parsley as much as everything needs it, which is the reason it is the herb I keep most regularly on hand.

A flourish of fresh herbs does a similar thing when you add it to food while it's cooking. A little tarragon or basil is wonderful in softly scrambling eggs or little turnips and radishes and peas, cooking in butter. I like to add cilantro, chopped roughly, stems included, to cooking leeks, cabbage, or stewing tomatoes. It's nice to add an herb to a dish twice, once while it's cooking and then again raw, on top, once it's cooked.

Hardier herbs, like rosemary and thyme, can take high heat. They are good for adding to food that you're roasting. Include a few sprigs of either in pans of roasting vegetables. Or put them under the skin of a roasting chicken, or inside a whole roasting fish. They also perfume rice nicely, added to a pot at the start of its cooking.

Parsley leaves stay good, picked off their stems and stored in a closed container, for weeks. I used to follow common advice to store herbs in a jar of water in the refrigerator and cover their leaves with a damp towel. I invariably knocked the jar over at some point, and the herbs seemed to wilt just as quickly as if they'd stayed in plastic bags.

All the rest of the herbs stay good for longest kept whole and dry, laid side by side in single layers in paper towels. Stack the layers in a roasting pan and wrap it tightly in plastic. When you remove herbs to use them, rewrap the remainder just as well. An airtight container with a snap-on lid would be simpler, and I often think I should get one.

There are other even more practical ways to keep herbs from going bad. Simple herb oils are a magical condiment. *Salsa verde,* for which there is a recipe on page 17, is one. There are dozens even simpler, made only by chopping and pounding a raw herb, a touch of garlic, and setting the happy green mixture awash in good olive oil.

Fat helps unlatch flavors. The subtlest tastes of the most sheepish bowl of rice or bowl of lentil soup will slide giddily along fatty molecules. Our taste buds must be as animated as our eyes. An herby oil makes you satisfied, or at least pleased, with less food, which you enjoy more.

All of the world's peasant cuisines rely on this trick to make food better, regardless of how common it is or how little of it they have. Indian spices are heated in clarified butter, *ghee,* before they're used. Rustic French puréed soups of turnips, asparagus, or spinach get a little butter added as they finish cooking. The Mediterranean shellacs its food with olive oil before lifting its forks.

I make parsley oil whenever I have parsley. I do it while I'm waiting for water to boil or an oven to heat. It's inexpensive and everything it's drizzled on is cheered up by it. To make dark green, lovely parsley oil, chop the leaves off a bunch of parsley, smash a clove of garlic to a paste with a little salt, and douse both in olive oil.

Combine herb and oil here with volition. It is not damp herb you want, but a lusty, deep, spoonable sauce that assures sliced tomatoes get eaten deliberately, with eager hands spooning garlicky green sauce onto each.

Add another chopped fresh herb to your parsley oil and have an oil that tastes just as herby, and different. Add half as much as you have parsley. Marjoram or sage make especially delicious oils for drizzling over beans or meat, or try mint, which is good anywhere. Add the zest of a lemon to make it brighter.

Add freshly grated Parmesan and pounded up toasted walnuts, and you will have pesto. Pesto can be made from any herb or leafy green. If you have an herby oil already, add the cheese and nuts and mix it all in a bowl.

The most common pesto is made from basil. Because basil browns and changes flavor quickly once it's cut, it's not good for turning into herby oil, but very good for quickly chopping and pounding raw into pesto.

There are some edible already-made basil pestos, but they are pesto birth to death. It's more practical to buy fresh basil so that you have *it,* nuts so you have *them,* and a wedge of Parmesan cheese and bottle of olive oil, which will all be more useful to you, after you've eaten a bowl of pasta with pesto and spread the rest on a sandwich, than an empty plastic container.

Make basil pesto by toasting a handful of pine nuts, walnuts, or pecans, pounding a half clove of garlic to a paste with salt, combining them and a cup of freshly grated Parmesan cheese in a food processor, and filling the rest with at least three cups fresh basil. Blend it quickly in pulses, adding olive oil until it looks like pesto.

Or substitute a combination of arugula and parsley for basil. In the winter, quickly dunk cooking greens in well-salted boiling water, drain them well, and use them instead.

You can also store your herbs chopped up in butter. A little herb butter is a graceful thing. It can be made with any herbs soft enough to easily bite through. It can also be made with whatever quantity of herb you have. If you've only a few leaves of herb, your butter will be lightly perfumed. If you have a lot, it will be thickly green.

Bring a stick of unsalted butter to room temperature. Roughly chop herbs and smash them into the butter with a wooden spoon. Spoon the herb butter onto a piece of plastic wrap, then form it into a tube, twisting each end.

A little shallot, chopped finely and added to the butter along with parsley, makes the traditional French accompaniment to steak, *maître d'hôtel* butter. I find a bit of grated ginger works magic on mint butter.

Herb butters are, like pesto, for sale, and very expensive, in gourmet grocery stores. If you make your own, you save thrice: eight dollars on herb butter, the remainder of a bunch of herbs that might have gone bad, and a meal from monotony. Herb butters stay good in the refrigerator for a month, or in the freezer for four.

Or chop any herbs finely and add a handful to plain yogurt to make a light, tangy sauce for drizzling over lamb chops, soup, or rice. Or mix herbs into mayonnaise to gussy it up.

There is no rule for which herbs to mix with olive oil, which with butter, which with yogurt, which with mayonnaise, just as there is none for deciding which herb to scatter over anything.

So go by geography. Cuisines that cook in olive oil use herbs that grow well in the same climate as olive groves, like parsley, marjoram, thyme, rosemary, and sage. They are best for herby oils. Cuisines where food is cooked in butter have their own herbs, like chervil and tarragon. Where yogurt is treated as a sauce, mint, cilantro, and dill are prolific. I can't think of anything that doesn't taste good in mayonnaise.

Frying the leaves of parsley, rosemary, or sage is a good if messy way of making an especially elegant garnish from something ordinary. Fried herbs' colors and shapes crystallize. Fried parsley becomes a little soldier. Fried sage is an exaggeration of the leaf's almost animal curve. Fried rosemary looks like rosemary would in the realm of ideas.

To fry herbs, make sure they're dry and separate all but rosemary leaves from stems. Rosemary can still be in small clumps. Heat four inches of peanut oil or grapeseed oil in a pot into which you can just fit a slotted spoon. The smaller the pot the better. When the oil begins to shimmer, drop in a needle of rosemary. The oil is the right temperature when the rosemary needle causes a lot of commotion. Once it does, add the herbs, in batches of a handful each, keeping them separated by type.

Have a plate with a paper towel on it handy. When the oil stops bubbling voraciously and starts just barely simmering, the herbs are done. They should all still be bright, bright green. Scoop them out and let them drain, in a single layer, on the paper towels. Sprinkle them lightly with salt. A light shower of any or a combination of fried herbs is lovely on little lamb chops, and they're quite wonderful mixed lightly with toasted breadcrumbs and scattered over boiled or roasted meat or fish.

When it has cooled, strain the oil and save it to use for frying herbs again.

If you're down to your last few leaves of a bunch of herbs, chop a handful of olives or capers, or both, mix them with the herbs you have, add good olive oil to *that,* then drizzle or dollop.

If you're out of herbs completely, find another candle. Scatter toasted breadcrumbs or toasted nuts on anything at all, proudly and liberally. Or slice onion as thinly as you can, soak the slices in vinegar, then drain and scatter them instead. If there is no onion, zest some lemon peel; if there is no lemon peel, find a jar of sauerkraut, drain a little, mix it with good olive oil, and call it cabbage relish.

If, on the other hand, you ever find that you're well stocked in ambiance, but that the room itself has disappeared, make a meal of atmosphere. In Southeast Asia, bowls bursting with basil, mint, and cilantro are put directly on tables alongside bowls of rice or broth or plain noodles. The herbs are left on their stems so that you can make salads, as goats do, while you chew. If there's nothing to make except the plainest, sparest meal, put whatever green and lively things you have in a bowl and brighten your meal as you go.

You could also follow the direction of an early nineteenth-century paean to herbs written by M. Grieve. She recommends a whole herb meal: an herb omelet, filled with thyme, tarragon, and chives; a salad of chives, tarragon, and mint, dressed with mustard, sugar, and oil; sandwiches of nasturtiums. Begin yours, instead, with this soup of herbs, then have a salad of a handful of arugula leaves, whole leaves of parsley, basil, mint, and tarragon. Then little toasts with mint butter or herby oil or an omelet filled with toasted breadcrumbs, which is as delicious as it is strange.

Minestra di herbe passate
~

> 5 tablespoons butter
> ½ carrot, chopped
> ½ onion, chopped
> 8 cups herbs: cilantro, parsley, whole chives, spinach, sorrel,
>   lettuce leaves
> 2 small potatoes, peeled and cut into chunks
> 1 tablespoon salt, plus to taste
> 4 cups water or more to cover
> lemon juice

optional: croutons, chives, herby oil, sour cream,
    yogurt to garnish

Melt the butter in a big soup pot. Add the carrot and onion and cook until tender. Add the potatoes, water, and salt. Bring to a boil, reduce the heat, and cook at a simmer until the potatoes are completely tender and beginning to fall apart. Add the herbs. Taste the soup and salt until the broth tastes good. Blend in batches until as smooth as possible. If the soup seems fibrous, pour it through a fine-mesh sieve. This can be served hot or cold.

Squeeze with lemon juice just before serving and top with little croutons and any other herbs or garnishes.

There is a lot of good advice available on growing herbs on your windowsill. My best is that if you're uncertain about the greenness of your thumb, buy herbs as small, sprouted plants at farmers' markets from people who've gotten germination down.

If it is your first time, choose likely successes. Most herbs retain their personalities from soil to soup pot.

Scientifically, herbs are classified into the carrot family and the mint family. The first has feathery leaves: parsley, cilantro, fennel, dill, chervil. The second contains basil, thyme, mint, rosemary, oregano, savory, sage, and tarragon. Its leaves are unbroken, each determined to get to the point.

If an herb will stand up to being fried in oil, or if it can be mixed with garlic and olive oil, it will generally grow easily and well. These are mostly the mints. If an herb prefers to be quickly, carefully chopped and mixed with butter, it is finicky at being grown. These are mostly the carrots.

The exceptions are tarragon, which is in the mint family but needs to be treated carefully and prefers butter to oil, which I've never had any success growing; and parsley, which is unlike the carrots in that it can be treated like a hammer or chopped with one, and like them in that I still can't get it to grow well.

My guess is that my trouble with the latter goes back to its tie to Persephone, who might like to keep her hold on parsley tighter than I wish she would. Happy to let it sprout in soil, happy to let it give food new life or ease it to a quiet end, but unwilling, at least in my herb box, to abide an in-between phase.

Seven

How to Have Balance

Almost every wise saying has an opposite one, no less wise,
to balance it.

—George Santayana

I n *How to Cook a Wolf,* M. F. K. Fisher gives the best dietary advice I have read. She says: "Balance the day, not each meal in the day." She explains that we can still eat healthfully without trying to get fruit juice, hot or cold cereal, scrambled eggs with bacon, and buttered toast packed into the first meal of the day, and soup, beef, mashed potatoes, lima beans, and Waldorf salad packed into the second, which her contemporaries were.

Here is her further guidance:

"Breakfast then can be toast. It can be piles of toast, generously buttered, and a bowl of honey or jam. You can be lavish because the meal is so inexpensive. You can have fun, because there is no trotting around with fried eggs and mussy dishes."

She is right. Breakfast *can* be toast; so can lunch be, or dinner. "Breaking bread" means eating. "Our daily bread" means food. It is also called the staff of life, which I like: bread there, all life leaning against it. Our lives don't lean against it anymore: we've decided that bread is bad for us. Our staff has broken, and that is part of why our diets seem so hard to get in balance.

Bread can be the *thing* you're eating, not a prelude to the meal, or an afterthought. It is not bad for you. Whether as piles of toast, generously buttered, or thick slices rubbed with garlic and drizzled with olive oil, eating bread with intention is a good dietary strategy.

I can think of no better way to get good, healthy vegetables, lush, ripe, and in season, to the middle of your plate than to let them balance on freshly toasted bread. Instead of worrying about lots of ingredients with which to trot around, buy a loaf of bread with a hard crust. Pick it based on how enticing it looks, and on how good it smells. Pick something that is round and fat or, if it is oval, that still has good girth at its ends, so you can get a lot of big, healthy pieces out of it. Make it a loaf that will require slow, deliberate chewing.

Then let the rest of your meal be vegetables. Cut thick slices of bread, drizzle them with oil, and toast them in a hot oven or on a grill. Let them get nicely charred, then rub each slice lightly with the cut side of a clove of raw garlic.

In autumn, roast a whole butternut squash (for instructions, see pages 39–40). Smash it in a bowl with good olive oil, a little freshly grated Parmesan, and a lot of freshly cracked black pepper. Spread the squash thickly on the toast, drizzle it with more olive oil and a squeeze of lemon juice, and sprinkle it with roughly chopped toasted almonds.

In winter, sauté Swiss chard or kale in a lot of garlic and olive oil. Top pieces of toast with ricotta or goat cheese, then piles of garlicky greens. Squeeze each with lemon juice.

In spring, cook English peas or asparagus in a little butter and water. Top each toast with a brothy spoonful of vegetables and drizzle it with crème fraîche or sour cream, then a few cracks of black pepper and chopped mint, tarragon, or chives.

In summer, thickly slice tomatoes. It's best if they're different colors. Lay an array on each toast, salt them well, drizzle each with good olive oil, and top with torn basil. Or roast zucchini or eggplant in an oven or on a hot grill, dress it with vinegar when hot, and top the toasts with it.

For people who say that bacon is a vegetable: cook sliced garlic over very low heat in butter and a little water until it is completely tender and stewed. Top toasts thickly with stewed garlic, then very thinly sliced bacon or pancetta. Cook each toast under a broiler until the meat is crisp and its fat has seeped into the bread.

Use bread to balance your budget as much as your diet. Local vegetables are especially worth their cost if you're eating *them,* prepared simply and well, mounded on a big piece of toast. As is good bread. As is the good olive oil you will drizzle, as lavishly as you want.

Your bread doesn't have to be in the middle of the plate. But if it is not your meal, let it help you relish what is. Choose a piece of good bread *instead* of a second pork chop or second helping of lasagna. Use it to sop up your chop's lovely juices or wipe up the last of the lasagna's sauce. This will make your meal easier on your stomach as well as your pocket.

If you're going to choose a food not to make at home, choosing bread represents a judicious division of labor. Bakers are devout and singular people, with firm beliefs in the secret lives of the yeast starters they tend. Their ovens are hot, and they can smell when bread is nearly done, then done. I am not devout and singular enough. In general, my loaves come out insensibly hard and flat.

I keep trying, though. I've had some success with this recipe, and there is often great balance to be found in making one's staff oneself. It isn't mine, but recipes are never anyone's.

Jim Lahey's no-knead bread

~

3 cups all-purpose or bread flour and more for dusting
¼ teaspoon instant yeast
1¼ teaspoons salt
1⅝ cups water
cornmeal

In a large bowl, combine the flour, yeast, and salt. Add the water and stir until blended; the dough will be shaggy and sticky. Cover the bowl with plastic wrap. Let the dough rest for 18 hours at warm room temperature, around 70 degrees. (How pleasant!)

When the dough's surface has begun to bubble, lightly flour a big cutting board and place the dough on it; sprinkle it with a little more flour and fold it in on itself once or twice. Cover loosely with plastic wrap and leave it there for 15 minutes.

Using just enough flour to keep the dough from sticking to the work surface or to your fingers, gently and quickly shape the dough into a ball. Generously coat a smooth towel with flour and cornmeal. Put the dough, seam side down, on the towel and dust with more flour. Cover with another smooth towel and let rise for about 2 hours. It should more than double in size and not spring back when poked with a finger.

Heat the oven to 450 degrees. Put a 6- to 8-quart heavy cast-iron, enamel, Pyrex, or ceramic pot with a lid (I use my heavy Le Creuset Dutch oven) in the oven as it heats. After 30 minutes, carefully remove the pot from the oven. Slide your hand under the loaf on the towel and turn the dough over into the pot, seam side up. Don't worry about its appearance. Shake the pan once or twice to distribute the dough; the rest will straighten out as it bakes. Cover and bake 30 minutes, then remove the lid and bake another 15 to 30 minutes until the loaf is browned. Cool on a rack.

My mother met a woman in Meursault she described as the best tart maker in the world. The woman had a paper bag of breadcrumbs ground perfectly fine, fluted tart tins, and ceramic pie pans. She lightly tapped her cold butter and flour together on a cold marble slab, rolled it, by my mother's description "Once! In each direction," and then her crusts were done, dusted with crumbs, filled with the summer vegetables of Burgundy, and so.

I have a certain tart dough that I make. It doesn't rely on cold butter, which starts to sweat too quickly on my warm, uneven wooden table, and it doesn't toughen up when I roll it "Twenty times! Willy-nilly." It's accommodating because it's made with olive oil. That also makes it sturdy, obviating a need for breadcrumbs at its bottom.

Thankfully, tarts did not come into being because pastry needed to be filled, but because ingredients needed somewhere to go. Even if the wizardry of flour and water frightens you, as it does me, it is undeniable that once you have a crust, any filling becomes a meal. This makes tarts too useful to be permanently scared of, and this rather unflappable dough makes it seem silly to have ever been.

This makes enough for two tarts; the half you don't use keeps in the refrigerator for a week or frozen for six months. The reason to make twice as much is that the measurements are even; it's also nice to have dough made.

Olive oil tart dough

~

2½ cups all-purpose flour
⅓ cup best possible olive oil
½ cup ice water
1 teaspoon fine sea salt

Mix all the ingredients together in a bowl. If the dough doesn't stay together, add a touch more ice water and mix to integrate.

Divide the dough in half. Roll each half into a ball, then flatten it into a disk. Save the half you're not using. Let the half you are using sit in the refrigerator for an hour. While it is chilling, heat the oven to 400 degrees.

Remove the dough and roll it into a ¼-inch-thick round on a floured surface.

Lightly grease the bottom of a 9-inch pie plate and dust it with flour. Lay the crust in the pan. Trim the excess with a sharp knife. Prick the bottom a few times with the knife's tip.

Fill the crust with aluminum foil and fill the foil with dried beans or pie weights. Cover the exposed rim of the crust with a crust guard, or make your own with a long piece of tin foil.

Bake for 20 minutes. Remove the foil and pie weights but leave the crust guard, then bake for another 15 minutes. Remove from the oven.

For a very good, basic tart filling that makes a perfect bed for any vegetable, whisk one and a half cups of ricotta, a quarter cup of good olive oil, two tablespoons cream, a half teaspoon kosher salt, two egg yolks, and a pinch of chopped fresh thyme or rosemary. This makes a very rich, salty custard that if there are no vegetables is a gratifying filling on its own.

Cook whatever vegetables you have or like. In the spring, cook a bunch of scallions or asparagus or the tiny wild leeks called ramps until just tender in well-salted water. In autumn or winter, roast and smash a squash, or sauté greens. In summer, toss a pint of cherry tomatoes with a tablespoon olive oil and a tablespoon chopped rosemary and roast them for thirty to forty-five minutes until they're collapsed. They look more peaceful cooked and with a crust containing them than they ever do when they're rolling about.

Cool any cooked vegetable and cut all but the cherry tomatoes into two-inch pieces. Fill the tart with ricotta custard and bake at 400 degrees, with the edges of the crust uncovered, for fifteen minutes, until it is just barely firm to the touch. Scatter any vegetables you've cooked in a firm single layer over the ricotta and bake for another ten minutes. Let the tart cool and eat it at room temperature. This tastes good for days.

Once something is framed in crust, it seems worthy of framing. Almost anything can be loosened with a splash of cream and put inside a crust. Lightly mix sautéed onions with cream, and strew them over the ricotta custard, or dot the custard with tomato sauce, leaving out the cream. Or leave out the ricotta and fill the crust with leftover curried eggplant or beef stew. I always thought anything but a bean made a good tart, but according to my mother, her guru in Meursault made a good one of lentils.

Cookbooks from cuisines that hold bread in high esteem all contain legion recipes that depend on stale bread. They're never listed under "stale bread," which can make them hard to spot. That is because stale bread is simply an ingredient, the way onion or garlic is.

Some of the best stale bread recipes are for bread soups. I'm sure bread soup sounds strange. The logic of bread soup is the logic of croutons, inverted. If good, hard bread improves hot liquid, hot liquid improves good, hard bread.

Bread soup recipes are comically nitpicky about how stale and rugged their main ingredient must be. Authentic recipes for the French *croûte au pot,* which means "crust in a pot," rigidly call not for stale bread but for only stale bread *crusts* to be cooked with the fat from a pot of boiling meat until they stick to their pot's bottom, then served with the broth from the boiling pot ladled over the top. A recipe for onion bread soup from *Simple French Cooking* by Richard Olney demands stale bread that is "coarse, vulgar, compact." We have all tossed loaves for meeting that description at some point.

Stale bread cannot be bought. It must be waited for, which gives all dishes containing it the weight of philosophical ballast, as well as dietary and budgetary ones.

Probably the most delicious bread soup is *ribollita,* the famous bread soup of Tuscany. As a Tuscan friend witheringly explained to me once, *ribollita* does not contain *any* procurable ingredients: "You don't buy ingredients for *ribollita.* You have them."

Here is a recipe for a less than authentic *ribollita.* The truest ones require that you "have" the exact contents of the average Tuscan larder.

Ribollita

~

> *olive oil*
> *1 medium onion, diced*
> *2 cloves garlic, sliced*
> *2 stalks celery, diced*
> *salt*
> *½ cup fresh parsley and rosemary, roughly chopped*

½ teaspoon chile flakes
3 peeled whole tomatoes
1 bunch leafy cooking greens like kale, Swiss chard,
    or collard greens, stemmed and chopped
¼ cup water
2 cups cooked cranberry beans, cannellini beans,
    or chickpeas
2 cups broth from homemade beans, or any combination
    chicken stock, liquid from cans of tomatoes, and water
1 piece Parmesan rind
2 cups good, stale bread without fruit or nuts or seeds,
    crusts removed, torn into rough ½-inch pieces

Heat ¼ inch olive oil in a large pot. Cook the onion, garlic, and celery in the oil, salting them as soon as you add them. Once they have begun to soften, add the herbs and chile flakes. Add the tomatoes, breaking them up with a spoon as they soften, and cook over medium heat for a few minutes.

Add the chopped greens and the water. Cover the pot and cook over low heat until the greens are wilted. Add the beans and broth and Parmesan rind. Bring it to a simmer, then add the bread and ½ cup olive oil. Cover the pot, turn the heat as low as you can, and cook for half an hour, checking occasionally to make sure it isn't burning, and adding a little bean broth or water if it seems too dry. The bread must cook, and absorb everything it can, and then melt into the soup.

Stir in another ½ cup olive oil, taste, and remove the cheese rind. Serve warm, topped with freshly grated Parmesan and freshly ground black pepper.

You can also be simpler. I subsist contentedly through the winter on a basic bread soup that's true to the spirit of bread, which is that if you have it, all you need to turn it into a meal is whatever else you have.

I would repeat this in every chapter if I could. To make basic bread soup, heat a half cup olive oil in a soup pot. Cook a cup of any combination garlic, onion, leek, and celery, finely sliced, until tender, salting the vegetables immediately to keep them from browning. Add a half cup roughly chopped fresh parsley and rosemary or the leaves from a bunch of celery, four cups cubed stale bread, crusts removed, and, after stirring well, four cups any combination vegetable cooking liquids, meat broths, and bean broths you have, and the rind of a piece of Parmesan. Let it cook covered for twenty to thirty minutes, adding water if it starts to stick, until the bread has broken down completely.

All bread soups are somewhere between soup and solid. The best way to tell if yours is done is by knowing it will thwart attempts to classify it as one or the other and, instead of trying, take it off the heat when it tastes good. Remove the cheese rind. Drizzle heavily with olive oil, grate with Parmesan cheese, and top with freshly cracked black pepper.

Bread soup recipes recommend serving them "very hot." Whoever wrote the original ones knew that no matter how slim the pickings for your pot, with the temperature of the liquid inside, at least, you could be spendthrift. It feels nice to be unstinting with some part of a dish. I let bread soup cool before eating it because I like it better lukewarm.

Leftover bread soup should be formed into little cakes and panfried in olive oil. These might be better than the soup that precedes them, and probably better than the bread before it. At the restaurant where my brother is chef, the kitchen makes *ribollita* throughout the winter but never serves it as soup at all. The soup is cooked, then left to get cold and absorb its flavors for a few days. It is then made into gorgeously nubby little golden pancakes. By the time it reaches your plate, every part of the dish has been deliberately aged further, lovingly neglected by skilled hands.

Just as easy and delicious as bread soup is bread salad. To make it, toast torn pieces of stale bread in a hot oven with a lot of olive oil, combine them with a handful of vinegar-soaked onions, as many juicy, raw tomatoes, or garlicky, oily roasted vegetables as you have, a handful of herbs, more olive oil, wait for twenty minutes, and eat.

There are a number of ways to store bread. My Tuscan friend buys fresh bread every morning after her coffee. When she gets home, she files the rest of yesterday's loaf in a cupboard cluttered with identical packages. When the cupboard gets full she retrieves the bags, makes a big pot of soup, and then begins again.

My mother only nominally concedes control of her kitchen to the disorder that stales bread. As soon as bread begins to dry, she moves it along. She will not go to sleep until each heel or uneaten slice has been cut into neat cubes, tossed in oil, toasted until crisp, cooled, tidily packed into plastic bags, then labeled, dated, and frozen. It has always seemed neurotic, but I grew up on broths and soups of this or that, and ate them happily, because they were good but also because of the inevitable crunch of toasted stale bread on top.

I like croutons torn, which leaves crags and edges for things to settle in. To make croutons, cut the crust off drying bread, then tear the rest into pieces of similar size, coat them with olive oil, spread them on a baking sheet, and bake them in a 400-degree oven for ten to fifteen minutes.

Gather them to one side of the pan and redistribute when you notice they begin to brown. When they're crispy, they're done. Salt them lightly, let them cool, put them in glass jars, or in plastic bags if you're freezing them. Store them in the refrigerator for two months, in the freezer for six.

Or make breadcrumbs. Grind crustless bread roughly in a food processor. Mix them with olive oil until well coated. Bake them in a single layer in a pan in a 400-degree oven. Check them after five minutes, using a spatula or spoon to gather and redistribute them. Cook them until golden brown and crisp. Remove and shake onto a plate immediately to stop their cooking. Once cool, keep breadcrumbs in a ziplock bag at room temperature for a few days, or refrigerate or freeze for up to three months.

I usually wait to do any of that. I leave bread in a paper bag for two days. Then I store it in a plastic bag. Then, depending on how industrious I feel, I quickly tear it into croutons, or make bread-crumbs, or leave it whole and freeze it in whatever form, which means that my freezer has a big hunk of bread in it, but it gets used in good time.

⚬≫⚬

In *The Cooking of Provincial France,* which M. F. K. Fisher also wrote, there is a description of her Sunday ritual of going, after long walks, to a noisy beer hall in Strasbourg to order a Muenster plate: "a large piece of strong runny cheese, a bowl of finely minced raw onion, a smaller bowl of caraway seeds, plenty of good, crusty bread."

That sounds to me like a fine meal. It also sounds like a balanced one, and I'm glad to hear how well she took her own advice.

Meals in which cheese is allowed to take the place of another protein are no worse for your arteries and as good for your soul as any others. I don't like to think of food as carbohydrates and fat because it gives an incomplete picture of how we digest. Belly laughter must burn calories, and good conversation helps speed what needs speeding.

But here nutritional science verifies what my gut knows: fat does not make you fat absolutely. It does absolutely make you full.

Eating a piece of cheese instead of meat is a good allocation of digestive resources. If it's not slathered *on top* of a steak but in its place, there's no reason a large piece of strong runny cheese, or whatever cheese your beer hall serves, can't be a meal, eaten with good bread.

The diet of the animal whose milk is used must be balanced, too. Cows were designed to eat grass, not corn—which they're fed in the factory farms that disgrace our erstwhile prairies. When cows eat their natural diet, especially an array of grasses, bright green in spring, light and dry in the summer, their milk has high levels of conjugated linoleic acid, believed to fight cancer. It doesn't clog us up the way milk or cheese (or meat) from cows raised on corn does.

It's also a good allocation of environmental resources. The managed grazing of pastured animals is as good for land as factory farming is bad for it. And it carries a karmic bonus. An animal you milk parts only with her milk. Tomorrow, she will go on munching grass. Her inclination will inspire her to make more milk, and your cheese maker to make more cheese, and so it will go.

Cheese making is more remote a skill than baking. It requires access to certain grasses at certain times of year, and a long, old knowledge of cultures and molds, and dark caves in which to age slowly evolving milk.

You can practice making bread. I see improvement in my little clodlike loaves all the time. But when it comes to cheese making, you haven't a chance. You can spend a lifetime and still not make a Tomme de Savoie to rival those of alpine *fromagères,* who keep track of where the greenest grass is and take their animals to graze on it. It's a good justification for guiltlessly buying cheese already made. It is a good justification, too, for buying pricey, finely crafted cured ham. It would take another lifetime before any of us could make prosciutto like those made by families in Friuli who have been at it since before Italy's unification. And the last hardened slice of prosciutto can be added to your *ribollita* to infuse it with centuries of aggregated skill.

There are a few ways to learn about cheese. The first is to read about it. There are a lot of good cheese books. They contain lists of what and where and how it was made and what to do with it.

A faster, more nourishing route is to talk to someone behind a cheese counter. You will get to taste, and you will do a great good deed. Cheesemongers are categorically zealous. Their counters are their pulpits, and they live to share their gospel. You will notice, if you approach one with a question, his eyes widen with joy and lips quiver with excitement at a chance to spread the Word.

You will also get good stories. Cheese makers are incorrigible romantics. It is part of what inspires zealotry in their acolytes. Tommes from Bordeaux, raw sheep's milk cheeses from Sardinia, creamy Robiolas from the Piedmont region of Italy, and hundreds more that are made from the milk of cows and sheep that have never been fed by human hands, are referred to as *sotto cielo,* Italian for "under the sky." There are American romantics in the bunch, too. A cheese maker in California uses only musical terms—*adagio, rondo, nocturne*—to refer to her cheeses.

If there's no cheese counter at your store, look for small logs of chèvre, or goat cheese. They're young, and fresh, and straightforward tasting, and they're sold at most grocery stores.

Chèvre is good as it is, but to get it to carry more of a meal's weight, marinate rounds in olive oil and herbs. You will be doing some romancing of cheese yourself, and it will last longer.

Marinated goat cheese

~

> four 4-ounce logs plain goat cheese—organic is better
> olive oil
> 1 bunch thyme
> 2 cloves garlic, peeled
> 1 tablespoon fennel seeds, toasted
> 1 teaspoon salt

Cut the cheese into rounds. Getting them cold before you do so makes this easier; keep whatever cheese gets stuck in the plastic wrappers and, in the end, shape it into rounds the size of the ones you've cut. Pour a little olive oil into a bowl and dip each round in it to keep it from sticking to all the others. Put the herb sprigs, garlic, and fennel seeds into a glass jar, then add the cheese carefully. Sprinkle salt in as you go to distribute it. Cover it well with oil.

Store the jar in the refrigerator for at least 4 days before eating. It will keep for up to 3 months.

In small Italian groceries, delicate-flavored fresh ricotta is made every day. Freshly made ricotta is exquisite. You can also get honest-tasting ricotta in any grocery store. It's not made of milk from happy grass-munching cows, but it's affordable and good.

I like it on toast. A lot of it, thick and cold, and probably a lot of toast, too. And herbs, and olive oil, and vegetables if there are any.

Ricotta is also good for cooking. It turns easily into a crustless tart, which gives you a chance to add a few good eggs to the equation.

Savory baked ricotta

~

32 ounces soft ricotta
¼ cup very good olive oil
2 egg yolks
¼ cup roughly chopped fresh thyme, rosemary,
    marjoram, parsley, mint, oregano leaves
salt and freshly cracked black pepper to taste

Heat the oven to 425 degrees. Mix all the ingredients well in a mixing bowl. Add salt judiciously until it tastes a tiny bit less seasoned than you think it should be. A lot of water will evaporate while this bakes.

Spread the mixture into a 9-inch pie dish. Bake it in the middle of the oven for 30 to 35 minutes. The top will develop a toasted, brown skin. It will inflate slightly and then deflate when you take it out. This is good at any temperature. Store it in the refrigerator.

All other cheese simply likes condiments. The condiments can be the Strasbourg Muenster plate's finely chopped onion or pickles of some kind, or a chutney, or a relish, or marmalade, or mustard.

Put bread and cheese, and whatever condiments you've chosen, on the table. Serve them, a salad, and not much else.

⸎

They represent a different kind of balance, but wine and beer are the third member of this holy trinity of fermented things. Though it's not our custom, a meal of bread and cheese doesn't seem quite a meal without at least a glass of one of them accompanying it. Since eating bread and cheese with conviction isn't our custom either, we might consider swallowing the trinity *in toto* and adding a bottle of beer or wine to steady any table trying to balance with only the other two on it.

Eight

How to Season a Salad

How one learns to dread the season for salads in England.
—Elizabeth David, *Summer Cooking*

A salad does not need to be a bowl of lettuce. It just needs to provide tonic to duller flavors, to sharpen a meal's edges, help define where one taste stops and another begins.

Italian salads are often just a single raw or cooked vegetable, sliced thinly and dressed with a drizzle of vinegar and olive oil. In France, they are happy little mops of celery root, doused in vinegar and mixed with crème fraîche and capers. In Greece or Israel, salads might be cucumbers and mint, or roasted eggplant, or spiced boiled carrots. There is a delicious Palestinian salad made only of preserved lemons, roughly puréed, and eaten cold with warm pita bread. Elizabeth David suggests, after her lament about her native England's bad salads, "a dish of long red radishes, cleaned, but with a little of the green leaves left on."

Cold roasted beets, sliced or cubed, drizzled with vinegar, and mixed with toasted nuts and olive oil are a wonderful salad. So is roasted broccoli, tossed with vinegared onions and a light smattering of dried chile. So are green beans, boiled until just cooked, cold and sliced thinly, tossed with peanuts and crisp scallions and rice wine vinegar and sesame oil. So is boiled cauliflower or potatoes, already nicely salted, drizzled with vinegar and oil, with a big handful of chopped olives and capers mixed in. Anything, cooked or raw, cut up a little, mixed firmly with acid, salt, and a little fat, laid carefully on a plate, or spooned nicely into a bowl, is a "salad."

A salad simply is too wonderful a moment in the meal to waste on assumptions. Because a salad *can* be made of anything, make one of an ingredient about which you get excited, or of whatever looks most lively, or of whatever you have around already. Do that instead of automatically buying lettuce, or wishing you were happier eating the sallow lettuce you have.

Parsley makes a very good salad. I have seen the humble leaves do a salad's duties on several occasions. At the wonderful little restaurant Prune, it is served next to two gloriously rich marrowbones and buttered toast. No lettuce on earth is a better-suited foil to that fatty combination.

When friends and I opened a restaurant in Georgia in a summer too hot for lettuce to grow, I decided that if parsley could do what needed doing for bone marrow, it could do it for a hamburger. So I listed "parsley salad" on the menu.

Our general manager made little signs to put on tables that explained that lettuce was a seasonal crop, printed with a solemn "Why we don't have lettuce," but other than a few noisy ones, customers ate their parsley salad unquestioningly. There were even requests for more parsley salad, once the days cooled down and our farm's young lettuces needed to be picked and served instead.

Parsley salad

~

> 1 bunch flat-leaf or curly-leaf parsley, stems removed and
>   leaves roughly chopped
> 1 shallot, thinly sliced
> 1 teaspoon drained capers
> 4 cornichons, thinly sliced
> juice of 1 lemon
> 3 tablespoons olive oil
> salt and freshly ground black pepper

Mix the parsley, shallots, capers, and cornichons. Mix the lemon juice and olive oil together and add to the salad. Sprinkle lightly with salt to taste. Top with freshly ground black pepper.

Other humble ingredients make similarly fine analeptics. Use a vegetable peeler to peel long slices off carrots. Fill a bowl with the carrot ribbons, add a light sprinkle of toasted cumin or coriander, a little vinegar and salt, then dress it with a lot of good olive oil.

Or slice celery thinly on a long diagonal and, omitting the spices, do the same.

Rich, piquant rémoulade salads, usually made from celery root, are in season when the ground ices over and the only vegetables available are fibrous roots. If you ever wonder whether all vegetables really can become salads, stop and look at a celery root, with its grizzled, warty skin. In France, it's waited for all year long, itself a reason to look forward to the arrival of shorter days.

Root vegetable rémoulade

~

3 celery roots or parsnips, or 1 rutabaga
white wine vinegar
salt
1 cup crème fraîche or homemade mayonnaise
freshly ground black pepper
2 tablespoons drained capers, roughly chopped
lemon juice
olive oil

Peel the vegetables. If it is celery root, cut the skin off with a knife. Cut them into thin slices, then into matchstick-sized pieces. Put the pieces in a bowl, douse them well with white wine vinegar, and season with a little salt. Let them sit for half an hour, mixing occasionally, then put the vegetables into a colander to drain. Press down on them well, several times, then transfer to a mixing bowl. Mix in the crème fraîche or mayonnaise, adding more to taste as needed, a lot of black pepper, and the chopped capers. Just before serving, add a squeeze of lemon juice and a drizzle of olive oil.

Rémoulade, designed to tame cold-season vegetables, could tame cardboard just as easily. If you end up with old, tough green beans, slice them very thinly, and treat them to the same smoothing over. Use rémoulade to make a salad of anything but tender spring and summer vegetables, which it would wilt, leaving the delicious sauce a cold, untested puddle.

Another good cold-weather salad is cabbage, thinly sliced out of its tight-leafed hermitage, well salted, dressed with rice wine vinegar, drained, then mixed with a big handful of roasted peanuts or toasted sesame seeds and sesame or olive oil, for a lovely, elegant, and nutty slaw.

In summer, the ingredient you see piled high and regally on Italian tables is raw zucchini, soaked through with lemon and good oil. In spring, when they are still small and tender, little tan artichokes, dressed as simply and firmly. Slice zucchini in half lengthwise, so that you can put a flat surface on a cutting board, then slice toward the board, safely and thinly. If you're making a salad of artichokes, clean them to their tender lightest green leaves, then slice them as thinly as you can. Try to make the slices of either vegetable leaflike in aspiration, if not appearance.

Put the slices in a mixing bowl, add a big squeeze of lemon or a drizzle of white wine vinegar and a small handful of salt, let it sit, then dress with olive oil, mixing it through with your hands, and lay the salad out on a platter, making sure everything is well coated and glossy. A handful of herbs will do nothing but good, as will a scattering of toasted walnuts or almonds, or a grating of hard Parmesan.

Fat raw asparagus, radishes, and spring onions, all thinly sliced, just barely stilled by lemon and oil, also make wonderful salads. As do radishes alone, either served whole and cleaned, like Elizabeth David's, or thinly sliced. As do snap peas, and English peas, little green beans, and young fennel.

Fruit makes especially refreshing savory salads. Almost any fruit tastes good sliced, laid out on a plate, and sprinkled with salt and olive oil. Most taste good with herbs, or onions, or olives, or chiles, or nuts added, too. At the starts of their seasons, when they're still bitter and tart, apples and pears jump at the chance for a salad's eye view of the world. Slice either thinly. In a small mixing bowl, squeeze a good amount of lemon juice over whichever, add a pinch of salt, let it sit for a few minutes, then add a handful of whatever fresh, soft herb you have, drizzle with olive oil, and lay the salad on a plate.

At Chez Panisse, we made a salad that included as wide an array of citrus as I've ever seen: wedges of the basketball-sized fruit called pomelo, which when peeled contains a fruit the size of a softball, blood oranges, Cara Cara oranges, navel oranges, pink and canary yellow grapefruits.

You don't need all that. Cut the peels off a few of any citrus fruits with a sharp knife. Doing this allows you to remove some of their bitter pith. Slice them across into thick rounds and lay them gently overlapping on a plate. Scatter each slice with flaky salt, a little thinly sliced, vinegar-soaked red onion, a healthy handful of pitted and roughly chopped olives, a dusting of chile flakes, and a long pour of good olive oil.

Salads of grains and beans are light, but filling, and taste clear. They are especially good for taking to work, because they are best dressed ahead of time and allowed to marinate. They are also good with one or two soft-boiled eggs halved and placed on top.

This salad is a good defense to pitch against the armies of salad stores that surround workplaces like attacking ants, all effective at supplying office workers with bad, expensive salads.

Rice or lentil salad

~

2 cups cooked rice or lentils
2 tablespoons chopped fresh oregano
½ cup pine nuts, walnuts, or almonds,
    toasted and roughly chopped
2 tablespoons drained capers
a big pinch of chopped fresh chives
basic vinaigrette, to taste

Make basic vinaigrette (page 100).

In a bowl, mix the rice or lentils with the oregano, nuts, capers, and chives, then drizzle in the dressing, tasting as you go.

You can make this just as well with leftover rice, lentils, or beans as with freshly cooked ones.

For lunch or dinner, make what is called *salade composée,* or composed salad. The ingredients of composed salads aren't mixed, but laid side by side. The French *salade niçoise* is a famous one, made of tuna, little new potatoes, green beans, and wedges of ripe tomato.

More adaptable is *salade canaille,* which translates as "salad of the scoundrel." It must be made of a rabble: the rice salad you made yesterday in one pile, lightly dressed beets in another, vinegary potatoes, a handful of fresh herbs, maybe some marinated peppers. It should be a hoi polloi until it is on your fork.

Lettuce has a season. It has delicate leaves, susceptible to heat, drought, flooding, and bugs, so its season is a short one. When lettuce is in season, buy whatever looks like a healthy head of it. Its name doesn't matter as long as it looks lively and fresh.

Buy lettuce at farmers' markets if you can. If there isn't a farmers' market near you, looking for local lettuce still makes sense because if you can't find any, it means it's the season for another kind of salad.

Lettuce you buy in whole heads is just as convenient as lettuce that comes prewashed and precut if you wash and dry it all at once. It will be there, ready, as easy to reach for, but healthier and better tasting, than the kind that comes in astronaut bags.

Prepare whole heads of lettuce by paring the leaves off their cores with a small knife. Lettuce leaves will stay good longer if they're cleanly cut. Do this by holding the lettuce and cutting around each core carefully, which saves you a cutting board. Drop the leaves directly into a sink filled with water. Save outer, browned or yellowing lettuce leaves for soup.

Move the lettuce around in the water with your hands. If you've bought good, local lettuce there may be dirt, mud, bugs, worms, all signs of its good provenance, all worth removing.

Spin lettuce dry in small batches in a salad spinner. Hand the job off to a little person as early as you can. I always liked this chore, and I think it made me love lettuce as protectively as I do. If you've conscripted help with spinning, instruct your helper to lift the leaves out of the colander when they're dry, instead of pouring the whole thing out, which will return the water that's been spun off to the leaves. If you don't have a salad spinner, air dry the lettuce by laying cloth towels on your counters and placing leaves on them to dry.

Store the leaves in single layers between cloth or paper towels in a well-wrapped roasting pan or plastic container, just as you store herbs. Make sure lettuce is completely dry when you put it away. If it is dry and stored like this, even the most delicate leaves will stay impeccable for two weeks.

I believe lettuce salads can only be good if they're dressed with your hands. Your hands can dress each leaf in a way tongs can't. Leaves are either delicate and must be lifted about lightly, or hardy and need dressing massaged into them. You must taste leaves as you dress them to figure out when you've added the right amount of dressing, and it's easiest to do if you've got your hands in the bowl already. And though I have an unseemly habit of doing all cooking with my hands, including turning little brown roasting chickens in their hot pans, most people don't have that many opportunities to touch food while they are preparing it. Raw leaves provide a good burn- and bacteria-free opportunity to do so.

A lettuce salad's dressing should not be its nemesis. It should only be what the lettuce needs. Choose the dressing for a lettuce salad based on the lettuce, instead of beginning with a recipe or a bottle of dressing. Delicate butter lettuces and other thin leaves need little.

Their dressing should be almost gestural, just a light squeeze of lemon and olive oil. Other lettuces, like oak leaf or young romaine, like basic vinaigrette.

Here's a basic vinaigrette that can be varied with the addition of garlic, pounded to a paste with salt, and can have vinegars substituted in and out.

Basic vinaigrette

~

1 shallot
¼ teaspoon salt
1 teaspoon Dijon mustard
juice of ½ lemon
1 tablespoon red wine vinegar
1 clove garlic
⅓ to ½ cup olive oil

Mince the shallot as finely as you can. Put it in a bowl with the salt, mustard, lemon, and vinegar. Smash the garlic once with your hand or the handle of a knife, then add it to the bowl. You'll remove it before dressing the lettuce. Let it sit for 5 minutes. Mix in the olive oil. It doesn't need to become uniform in consistency. Taste by spooning a little on a leaf. Remove the garlic clove, and dress the lettuce by drizzling with vinaigrette and mixing with your hands.

Whenever you make vinaigrette, keep it around and use it until it's gone. Make adjustments to it that are right for the kind of lettuce you have.

Here is a gutsier one. I'm not a "salad is health food" person, but if ever there were a food designed to straighten out squiggly lines, it would have to be a salad of bitter greens from the chicory family—escarole, frisée, radicchio—or bitterer ones yet, like dandelion greens, dressed with a vinaigrette with enough bite to match.

Dogged vinaigrette

～

1 clove garlic
4 anchovies, chopped
salt
¼ teaspoon mustard
1 teaspoon lemon juice
1 tablespoon red wine vinegar
1 teaspoon white wine vinegar
⅓ to ½ cup olive oil

Pound the garlic and anchovy and a tiny pinch of salt in a mortar with a pestle or on a cutting board. Add it to a bowl with the mustard, lemon juice, and vinegars. Let it sit for 5 minutes. Whisk in the olive oil. Dress tough leaves with this and some vim and vigor. Make sure to massage it through the leaves.

A big wedge of iceberg lettuce needs a creamy dressing.

Creamy vinaigrette

～

1 clove garlic, pounded to a paste with salt
1 teaspoon red wine vinegar
1 cup of crème fraîche or mayonnaise
1 teaspoon heavy cream or buttermilk
salt
a squeeze of lemon
1 tablespoon olive oil

In a mixing bowl, mix the garlic with the vinegar. Lightly mix in the crème fraîche or mayonnaise and cream or buttermilk, careful not to whip. Add salt and lemon juice to taste, then drizzle in the olive oil. Serve mixed with iceberg lettuce leaves or spooned over a wedge of it.

Lettuce salads should be simple, with only one or at most two other ingredients. Thinly sliced cucumbers *or* thinly sliced radishes, and if you twist my arm, okay to both.

If you add other ingredients to lettuce salad, keep in mind that you are never dressing the dish "salad," but rather dressing each ingredient. If you were making a stew, you'd season the stew, not its carrots in one corner of the pot, then the meat, then the potatoes. A salad is the opposite: you season its carrots, its meat, its potatoes.

An irony of default lettuce salads is that lettuce is, of all salad ingredients, the ingredient that needs the least dressing and mixing, and the one that often gets overdressed while ingredients that need dressing end up neglected. Salads of more than one ingredient should be dressed in stages, with the hardier ingredients dressed in the salad bowl first, then the more delicate. The first ingredient, well dressed, in turn dresses the second. Lettuce is always the most fragile ingredient in a salad. It should always be added last, when everything else is already dressed and ready to go.

It's not just the lettuce-as-salad protocol that needs flipping on its head, but the whole idea that lettuce is only good eaten cold. I like this recipe from Elizabeth David's book *Summer Cooking,* because it continues to flip and flip. It is for *laitue au jus,* or lettuce with gravy.

"Cold crisp lettuce with the rich gravy from a roast poured over it, hot. Exquisite with the hot meat or bird, especially if it has been cooked in butter and flavoured with garlic and wine. Dandelions or Batavian endive can also be used for this salad."

This is a good reminder of two things. First, the omission of a comma between *cold* and *crisp,* which is David's not mine, reminds that "cold crisp lettuce" is the kind of lettuce you're after. It is not a series of qualities appended to the vegetable, but what the vegetable itself must embody. Second, as in the recipe for rice and lettuce soup on pages 120–21, it is important to remember that lettuce can be served hot, and may even, especially if there's a plump zucchini or two around to be eaten raw, be better that way.

We must choose our salads well and put seasons of dreadful salads far behind us. When we do we'll find ourselves, all assumptions pushed aside, already and always our salad salad days.

Nine

How to Live Well

<hr />

Si stava meglio quando si stava peggio.
We were better off when things were worse.
—fifteenth-century Tuscan saying

Beans have always been associated if not with poverty, with the sweating classes. Fava beans, whose slightly bitter flavor is so refreshing it's common to see them being peeled and eaten raw, were called, in ancient Rome, *faba,* a play on words with *faber,* the Latin word for "worker." The Roman physician Galen said of beans: "Legumes are those grains of Demeter that are not used to make bread." He then chose them over less wholesome wheat loaves as the staple of Roman gladiators' diets.

Most of us regard beans with suspicion, as we do stale bread and cooking in water. Prejudices are always best dispatched, but not always unfounded. When food is boiled badly, it's fair to turn away from it, and if stale bread isn't cooked with, or toasted, but served dry and harsh, it's awful.

Beyond the indelible stain the poor little things will never shake, the distaste we feel for beans is not unfounded either. Our beans are rarely as good as they can be. They're usually so bad, in fact, that basing an opinion of their merit on prior experience is very much like deciding you don't like Bach after having heard the Goldberg Variations played on kazoo.

I suggest you set your doubt aside, fill a pot with cold water and two cups of dried beans, put it on your counter, and leave it there overnight. You will be on your way toward making beans that taste like those that have fed laborers and fighters for centuries.

You will also have plowed effortlessly through the hurdle of "soaking beans," a hurdle whose existence and gnarliness is a pure invention of food writers' proclivities for making cooking seem difficult.

The way to keep bean soaking from getting in the way of your cooking beans is to detach the process from today's hunger and expectations and pour dried beans into a pot and cover them with cold water whenever you think of it. Their needing to stay where they are until being cooked tomorrow won't be a problem, and you'll have soaked your beans.

A lot of bean recipes advise soaking in the refrigerator: beans are vegetables, and warmed too gently in water may think they're being asked to sprout. I soak mine wherever there's room in the kitchen, and they keep their vegetal ambitions well in check for a day.

Once the sun has set and risen, drain the beans through a colander and cover them by two inches with fresh, cold water. What gets flushed out of the beans on their overnight wallow is what inspires musicality in eaters. Feed their soaking water to your plants, who will digest it more quietly, if you like.

If you didn't put two cups of beans in a pot of cold water last night, get on the bandwagon today by putting them in a pot, covering them with five inches of water, bringing it to a boil, turning off the heat, and leaving them sitting in hot water, covered, for an hour. Then drain them and cover them with new water. This has the same effect as overnight soaking and is a good alternative.

The cooks who make the best beans are the ones who hold simplicity in high esteem. Romans and Tuscans value spare eating and living. Both of their legislative histories are peppered with sumptuary laws limiting the length and content of meals, passed whenever their citizens' affection for simple living got flabby.

Tuscans, though, make the best beans. They are known in Italy as *mangiafagioli,* or "bean eaters." Tuscans believe that frugality is next to godliness and give the humblest ingredients their finest treatment. Tuscan cooks are extravagant with good olive oil, pressed from dark trees, and with vegetable scraps and Parmesan rinds, which, along with salt and more of that fine oil, make transcendent pots of beans.

Those odds and ends are as crucial to pots of beans as fresh water. Your pot will benefit from a piece of carrot, whatever is left of a stalk of celery, half an onion or its skin, a clove of garlic, fibrous leek tops. If you must decide what to save for your chicken pot and what for stock and what for beans, save your fennel scraps with pots of beans in mind. I make notes to myself after meals, and there are enough torn pieces of paper attesting that "The best bean broth has fennel in it!" for it to have become axiomatic.

Your pot also wants parsley stems, whole sprigs of thyme, and a bay leaf. It can all be tied into a neat bundle in cheesecloth or with kitchen twine, or it can be left bobbing around, as everything in my bean pot always is.

Beans need salt. There is a myth that adding salt to beans keeps them crunchy and unlovable. Not cooking beans for long enough keeps them crunchy, and undersalting them is a leading culprit in their being unlovable. They also need an immoderate, Tuscan amount of olive oil. This is different from adding oil to a boiling pot of water for pasta. Pasta doesn't cook in its water long enough to benefit from the oil, and you use only a small amount of pasta's cooking water to help sauce and noodle get acquainted.

The liquid in a bean pot becomes broth as beans cook in it just as the water in which you boil a piece of meat does. No ounce of the water that goes into a bean pot should be discarded. Tuscan food is based as much on the broth made by the beans on which Tuscans lavish their affection as on the beans themselves. Harold McGee, who writes about the chemistry of food simply, writes that beans make their own sauce. He is right. Their sauce must be well made and it must be kept.

Cooking beans is like boiling a chicken or boiling an egg: only their water boils, and only for a brief second. The rest of their cooking is slow and steady. Light the burner under your beans, and as soon as the pot has come to a boil, turn the heat down to just below a simmer. Gray scum will rise to the top of the pot and gather around the edges. Skim it off and discard it.

The best instruction I've read for how long to cook beans comes from a collection of recipes called *The Best in American Cooking,* by Clementine Paddleford. The book instructs to simmer "until beans have gorged themselves with fat and water and swelled like the fat boy in his prime." The description is so perfectly illustrative I don't think anyone should write another word on the subject. I don't know who the fat boy is, but I feel I understand his prime perfectly, and it is what I want for my bean.

As they cook, beans should look like they're bathing. Their tops should stay under the surface of the liquid, or they will get cracked and leathery, and they shouldn't ever be in so much water that they're swimming. Taste their broth as they cook to make sure it is well seasoned. It should taste not like the pleasant seawater of the pasta pot, but like a sauce or soup.

The second good piece of advice from the same book is in one of its recipes for black beans: "Soak beans overnight; drain. Put in pot, cover with water. Add onion, celery, carrot, parsley, salt, and pepper. Simmer until bean skins burst when blown upon, about three hours." This is the only recipe I've ever read that takes the doneness of beans as seriously as it should be taken: a cooked bean is so tender that the mere flutter of your breath should disturb its skin right off.

Beans are done when they are velvety to their absolute middles. You should feel, as soon as you taste one, as though you want to eat another. The whole pot is only ready when five beans meet that description. If one doesn't, let the beans keep cooking. (My "five bean" method is good, but ever since reading Mrs. Paddleford's book, I feel like a brute when I practice it, and am quite intent, moving forward, on whistling the skin off a bean.)

Cool and store your beans in their broth. The exchange of goodness between bean and broth will continue as long as the two are left together, and the broth helps the beans stay tender through chilling, freezing, and warming up again.

Those are instructions for cooking all beans. The only exception to these instructions is lentils. On the timescale of beans, lentils are instant. They do not need to be soaked and take only a half hour to cook. It is smart to keep cans of cooked beans around, but there is no reason to buy precooked lentils. Cooking them from dried does not take any more planning than putting a pot of water on the stove, lighting a burner, and opening a plastic bag.

Other than how good they are when they're cooked well, and how many good meals you can get out of them, beans are economical because they're a cheap habit. I keep an assortment of different beans stored separately in little glass jars. I have jars of little green French flageolets, marsh-brown cranberry beans, inky black beans, turtle beans, speckled Jacob's cattle beans, and plain burnt umber kidneys.

Pots of beans have an admirable, long-term perspective on eating. It's the same to them whether you eat them tonight or in three days. Beans get better over a few days' sitting, gorged and swelled, like happy fat boy. Any longer and you should freeze them, but they'll thaw ungrudgingly when you want them back.

A bean pot has a lot of meals in it, and you've already done much of the cooking you need to for many. A bowl of *pasta e fagioli* is a pot of boiling water away. Bring a few cups of beans and broth to a simmer in a deep pan or pot along with the rind from a piece of Parmesan. Smash the beans with a spoon as they warm. Cook a short pasta like ditalini or orecchiette until it is still quite firm. When the pasta is nearly done, remove the cheese rind from the beans and scoop the pasta into the bean pot to finish cooking. Serve drizzled with olive oil, and top with freshly cracked black pepper and freshly grated Parmesan.

Simple and delicious beans and rice also only requires that you boil a pot of water and add rice. Warm your beans in their broth until they're very hot, make rice, and ladle the beans on top. Or, if it's spring, cook halved little white turnips with their long greens still attached, or English or snap peas in butter and bean broth or water, and cut little wedges of artichokes and cook them in olive oil and butter. When everything is tender, combine it in one big pan, add beans, a lot of broth, and a big handful of whatever soft herbs you have—chervil, chives, mint, fennel fronds, celery leaves—and ladle the bright, springy stew over rice. If you don't want to make rice, add a little extra butter and herbs to the vegetables and beans and serve it over toast.

A deeply comforting supper for one or two is beans and egg. Warm cooked beans in a little pan. Add sautéed kale, or roasted squash, or a little bit of roasted tomato, or add nothing at all. Crack an egg or two onto the beans, cover the pan, and cook. If you have stale bread, put a toasted piece, rubbed with garlic, in each bowl. Spoon the beans and egg over the toast, salt each egg, grind it with fresh black pepper, drizzle the beans and egg copiously with olive oil, grate them thickly with Parmesan, and dine like a Roman plebeian, or a Tuscan pauper, prince, or pope.

Cassoulet is a bean dish from southern France, where austerity is not considered next to godliness. If you can tell such things from what people eat, for Toulousians, pork, goose, and duck, all slow-cooked in fat, occupy that station.

Traditional cassoulet contains all three, plus copious quantities of fat, pork skin, and a great quantity of beans. If they were lingering, any vestigial associations between bean meals and deprivation should be erased by the very existence of cassoulet. To make an authentic one, follow any of a million good recipes. They're involved but worth the trouble.

Or make a simpler, utterly satisfying version by cooking a mixture of finely chopped onion, carrot, and celery, called mirepoix, in olive oil, browning a small, garlicky fresh sausage per person, spooning beans and mirepoix into a baking dish big enough to fit them happily, and nestling the sausages among the beans. Add bean broth to come up just halfway and put it in a 300-degree oven.

It takes about an hour for the sausages to cook through at low heat, which gives them time to get tender and for the beans to sip up some of their juices. Take the dish out when it's bubbly and the sausages are cooked, scatter the top heavily with toasted bread-crumbs, then put it under the broiler for a few minutes, until the top is crisp and brown.

There are similar dishes, made of mostly beans with some meat, in every bean-eating cuisine in the world. They range from franks and beans to black-eyed peas and ham, from chili to the majestic Brazilian *feijoada*. The principle of all is the same and the principle is good.

If there's already meat on the table, or you can go without, skip the sausages and ladle beans an inch or two deep in a small ceramic roasting pan and turn them into a rustic, herby French bean gratin. Cook mirepoix as above and mix it into the beans. Bake the gratin in the oven until it begins to bubble. Mix a big handful of any combination of chopped parsley, rosemary, and sage into toasted breadcrumbs, top the gratin thickly, and let it cook until the top is quite brown.

The world of bean soups is populous. Its population is for the most part exemplary. If you'd like to make the most straightforward one, put more broth than beans in a pot and heat it up. For the second most straightforward one, purée the mixture with a little olive oil and a squeeze of lemon.

Minestrone is much more than a bean soup; it is the complete expression of the bean's generosity, its raison d'être. Minestrone underlines all sensible cooking practices. Like the other great Tuscan soup, *ribollita* (pages 85–86), minestrone is a beacon. If you have the ingredients to make either one of those soups, two of which are beans and their broth, it means you're cooking steadily, buying good ingredients and saving the parts of them you don't cook immediately to cook later.

Minestrone is a precisely seasonal soup: it should reflect the season inside and outside your kitchen at all times. The beans you have cooked will always be at its center, but the rest will change throughout the year. In the winter, it will be chock-full of beans and pasta and thick enough to stand a spoon in. In spring, you will leave out the dark greens and include English peas and new onions; in summer, include the first slim green beans and basil, and little zucchini and ripe tomatoes, cut into cubes.

Minestrone is the perfect food. I advise eating it for as many meals as you can bear or that number plus one.

Minestrone

~

1 cup diced onion, carrot, celery, leek, fennel
3 cloves garlic, sliced
½ cup olive oil
a small pinch of chile flakes
the end of a piece of cured meat or hard salami, diced
1 cup any combination parsley, thyme, marjoram, basil leaves
2 to 3 cups roughly chopped any combination kale, collard
    greens, Swiss chard, spinach, mustard greens, dandelion
    greens, broccoli raab, escarole, cabbage (cooked or raw),
    any stems and leaves, ribs, and cores, cooked or raw
½ cup whole tomatoes, well chopped, or drained canned
    tomatoes
optional: ½ to 1 cup chopped root vegetables (if they are there
    and need to be cooked, or cooked and need to be eaten)
6 cups cooked beans
a Parmesan rind
8 cups any combination bean broth, stock, and liquid from
    cans of tomatoes
1 cup small pasta such as orecchiette, little tubes,
    or small penne
pesto, olive tapenade, fresh ricotta, or parsley for garnish

Cook the onion, carrot, celery, leek, fennel, and garlic in the olive oil until tender in a big pot. Add the chile flakes and any cured meat. Stir to combine. Add the herbs, greens, tomatoes, root vegetables, beans, and cheese rind, crushing the tomatoes against the side of the pot. Add liquid to cover. Simmer for 45 to 60 minutes, until everything has agreed to become minestrone. Just before you eat the soup, cook the pasta in a pot of salted, boiling water, only enough for the soup you're planning to eat that week, and add it to the week's soup. If you freeze minestrone, cook new pasta whenever you eat the minestrone you've frozen.

Garnish with pesto or olive tapenade, or a big dollop of fresh ricotta, or simply parsley.

I once lived with a Tuscan in a house in San Francisco. I would cook a pot of beans weekly, and our bean meals followed a regular pattern. The cooked beans would sit in their broth for a half hour, contenting themselves with their last swallows of olive oil and herbs. When my Tuscan decided their time was up, he would stand ceremoniously, clear his throat, slice bread, open wine, and put olive oil on the table.

Then we would eat just beans and bread, and we would drink wine. I would do it all happily, he intently, glowing with genetically imprinted joy at his great fortune to be sitting there, eating beans, beans, beans.

There are a good number of bean-loving Americans who agree that cooked beans need no further fussing, and eat beans, on their own, as whole meals, as Tuscans do. In New Mexico, big pots of beans are cooked studded with pork and served for dinner. They're called *borrachos* and eaten plain and hot with an accompanying stack of warm corn tortillas and beer. In Texas, the same beans, cooked the same way, are called *frijoles* and are eaten plain and hot with plenty of corn tortillas and beer. In the South, you can still get bowls of black-eyed peas or crowder peas accompanied by chopped scallions and watermelon pickles and pepper vinegar to eat with sliced white bread and beer.

Tuscans may treat dried beans with reverence, but it is a fresh bean they worship. When you know the taste of a fresh bean, you taste in dried ones the invisible mark all true loves bear: a memory of what it was we first fell in love with. Fall in love with a fresh bean, and you will stay in love with a dried one.

Fresh beans are in season in the summer, and come in as many shapes and colors as you can imagine. To shell fresh beans, practice a technique a friend calls "the twist and tickle": twist a bean's ends, one in each direction, and then, once its seam opens, tickle its beans into a bowl. This won't work for fava beans. Their pods' insides are sticky, and if you tickle them, they tickle back.

I usually use up my bean broth in minestrone or a bowl of pasta, or warm it up and make some odd, delicious thing of stale bread and whatever else is around, and probably cook an egg on it in the end. But I've been served plain bean broth twice, and been inspired to serve it myself several times.

The first time it was served to me was at a convent in Oaxaca, Mexico. The broth was the first course of a meal so pure and simple, the air seemed to thin as we ate. The soup was smooth and golden and tasted of grass. After it there were five tiny, glossy meatballs, on a pool of serene, dark amber tomato sauce. It was a simple meal, and it was calming.

The second time was in a weathered dining room in Turin, Italy. The broth was ladled out of a ceramic jug in which beans had cooked in the fireplace. The beans themselves were served separately with torn kerchiefs of fresh pasta, but the beanless soup was hot and each spoonful told the story of the beans' slow bubbling amid herbs and garlic.

If you decide to serve bean broth, I have only the advice of a guest to whom I served it once. He thanked me for the meal after saying good evening, and suggested that the next time I might serve it hot. If you serve bean broth as soup, do remember what I forgot and was too proud to rectify during dinner. If you are ladeling it from anywhere other than an earthenware jug in a fireplace, the broth will have cooled as it sat and need to be ladeled into its own pot and heated up again before being served.

The writer Waverley Root did a thorough survey of Italian food, top to bottom, in his book *The Food of Italy*. He was deeply enamored of the noble Tuscan and insisted that the Tuscan obsession with frugality was nothing but "finesse."

I cannot associate the word *finesse* with bean cookery. It doesn't take finesse, but dried beans, good olive oil, a big pot, and time to do it well, and it takes only common sense to appreciate.

But there is great dignity in allowing oneself to keep clear about what is good, and it is what I think of when I hear the term "good taste." Whether things were ever simpler than they are now, or better if they were, we can't know. We do know that people have always found ways to eat and live well, whether on boiling water or bread or beans, and that some of our best eating hasn't been our most foreign or expensive or elaborate, but quite plain and quite familiar. And knowing that is probably the best way to cook, and certainly the best way to live.

Ten

How to Make Peace

───────────────────────────────────

Her ways are ways of pleasantness,
and all her paths are peace.
—Proverbs 3:17

A lot of rice turns any amount of anything else into a meal. A small helping of meat perched upon a bowl of rice makes a meal of meat; a single egg with a bare scattering of scallions, or five cubes of eggplant, four peanuts, and three leaves of basil seem like square meals if their spareness is offset by a generous bowl of rice.

A recipe by the Italian cookbook writer Marcella Hazan calls for chopping olives and parsley, mixing them with boiled rice, and serving the dish as one would pasta. It sounds lean but good. I like another Italian recipe, from the cookbook *The Silver Spoon,* that says to cook a pound of spinach in salted water, sauté it in a lot of butter, boil rice in the spinach cooking water, and serve bowls of the rice topped with the buttered spinach and a lot of grated Parmesan.

These dishes work not just because rice is filling, but because rice has a knack for making any small thing you top it with seem like what you're tasting the whole time. A friend named this effect the "bean principle" after I served him a bowl of bean broth into which a few precious beans had escaped. The absence of beans, he said, made him appreciate the ones that were there more acutely.

It should be called the "rice principle" since it's the dietary strategy of most of the world's nearly seven billion inhabitants, who live on rice and whatever is placed, to be acutely savored, on top of it.

Rice is a good reminder that all of our appetites are similar. The rice principle does not just feed Asia and Italy, but Spain and all the Middle East, and dozens of other cultures where small amounts of ingredients are cooked and served amid large quantities of rice.

It will do for you what you believe food should, no matter who you are. Gourmets are satisfied: the seductions of rice are whispered of; it can be topped with buttered spinach and Parmesan or shaved with white truffles, and to the palates of children who still think eating a beastly reality of life rice remains agreeably anodyne.

Unlike eggs, which we make *too* mechanically, we don't make rice mechanically enough. It's worth making a pot of rice without planning for anything but to be hungry. There are a lot of rice recipes that begin: "Start six hours ahead," or "Rinse each grain thoroughly, three times." There is also ubiquitous Minute Rice, and rice that comes already cooked, needing only to be reheated. Aim, peacemakers, for the third way.

In Italy, white rice is simply cooked in salted water, like pasta. This is how it's done in England, too, and is a perfectly good way to cook rice. Bring a pot of water to a boil, salt it more lightly than for pasta, then add the rice and cook it at a fast, rolling boil. Check it as often as you want. Strain it when it's done. Spread it on a baking sheet on the counter to keep it fluffy.

You can also use a rice cooker. I use mine religiously. If you have a rice cooker, you can drop your bags the minute you enter your kitchen, add rice, a pinch of salt, and press start, all before you take off your coat. It will be cooked before you've even settled into being at home.

Do the same without a rice cooker by putting rice and salt in a pot with the prescribed amount of water, bringing it to a boil, then lowering it to a simmer, covering it, and cooking it for twenty minutes. This is worth knowing how to do, so that if your rice cooker breaks, you can still eat rice. Measuring cups are unnecessary in the two latter scenarios: the ratio of rice to water is all that matters. If the instructions on a bag of rice say a cup of rice to two cups of water, it can be a teacup of rice to two teacups of water.

We fear this method because we fear mushy rice. I've had to cook my way *through* mushy rice to get to fluffy rice. If you decide to cook through, too, there are good recipes for what to make with mushy rice on pages 235–36.

Then approach dinner, as most of our fellow eaters do, with the rice principle in mind. Fill deep bowls with rice and put an array of ingredients in little bowls on the table. This turns a miscellany into an exciting meal that you can call "rice bowls." They will be closest to Indian *thali* meals, where a beautiful succession of strongly fla-vored tomato sauce, coconut chutney, and thin, fragrant lentil soup are served with as much rice as you can eat.

The only requisite ingredient for your own version is a bowl of any shape or color of hot rice.

Serve one thing that's warm: each bowl can get a newly fried egg on it, or hot stir-fried spinach or scallions, or vegetable leftovers, like sautéed kale or roasted squash. If it's a leftover vegetable, chop it, warm it in a pan with a bit of broth or water, then mix it with a drizzle of vinegar and a handful of toasted sesame seeds, or peanuts, and top the rice with it or serve it in a bowl alongside.

Serve a little bowl of something cool and raw: thinly sliced rad-ishes, chopped cucumbers drizzled with vinegar, thick slices of avo-cado, chunks of tomato, fresh herbs.

Serve one vibrant, intense-flavored thing: spicy pickled chiles, a homemade salsa of scallions, herbs, and vinegar, Korean *kimchee,* Indian pickled mango.

I like a little can of sardines, too. If you don't, try leftover beef, chicken, or pork, cut into cubes and panfried.

Or softly scramble eggs and add a handful of roughly chopped ripe tomato, salt, and a handful of fresh cilantro at the very end, and serve it on hot rice. I existed on solely this and sautéed eggplant for a month in China. The first I ate because it is humble but exquisite. The second is because *eggplant* is one of the few words I can pronounce perfectly in tonal Mandarin.

For a truly pacifying rice dish, make rice and lettuce soup. I first made this soup after looking at a head of lettuce and wondering why I'd never seen lettuce risotto on a menu. I didn't get the answer, because I then began wondering why no one ever boiled risotto rice. I'm sure lettuce risotto is on a menu, and it's just a menu I haven't seen. And people surely do boil risotto rice, and ought to, because it turns out wonderfully.

I passed this recipe along to a friend who reported that it was "butter's highest and best use, because the lettuce becomes an expression of butter . . . sweet, crunchy, innocent butter."

Rice and lettuce soup

⁓

1½ onions, medium diced
2 tablespoons butter
salt
⅓ cup parsley leaves, roughly chopped
½ cup Arborio rice
8½ cups chicken stock or combination chicken stock and water
1 very big head lettuce, such as romaine or other crisp leaf; about
    16 cups very, very loosely packed

Cook the onions in butter in a medium-sized pot, salting them once you have added them to the pot. When they're softened, add the parsley. Add the rice and liquid. Let it cook about half an hour until the rice is completely cooked through, and then for another 20 minutes until it's jagged around the edges. Turn off the heat. Taste for salt. Cut the lettuce in thin ribbons. When you're ready to eat, warm the soup up, add the lettuce to the soup, and mix it through.

Serve each bowl with rice mounded in the middle and more liquid poured over. Drizzle with good olive oil and crack fresh white pepper over it, or black if you don't have white.

The best example of the rice principle is also the one we think is the fanciest. *Risotto* needs clarifying. The plainest risotto calls for rice, onion, white wine, butter, broth, and Parmesan cheese. If you have those ingredients, which you probably do, you have a perfect version of that famous dish.

The many elegant risottos you've seen on menus or tasted are slight variations on it, the ingredients that define them used as minimally as possible. Lobster risotto may be made with broth of simmered lobster shells, but there will only be a little lobster atop your broad bowl of rich rice. Risotto Bolognese will seem plump and meaty but won't contain much meat. A few wild mushrooms, their scraps simmered into earthy mushroom stock, sliced thinly and sautéed in a hot pan with butter and dropped onto each bowl makes the finest mushroom risotto.

Except for risotto Milanese, always served topped with a piece of beef shank called osso buco, risotto with meat is not an accompaniment to the meat but the main dish, and a very good way to serve a lot of people on a little meat and a lot of rice.

I make risotto by chopping half an onion medium fine and cooking it in butter. I add a cup of rice, stir it a few times, add a quarter cup of white wine, let the alcohol burn off for a minute, then add hot chicken, beef, or fish stock by the ladleful, keeping the rice at a low bubble the whole time. If a dry spot in the risotto pan doesn't get immediately refilled with starchy liquid when I push the rice away, I add more stock. I keep it going for about twenty-five minutes, then turn it off, add a big squeeze of lemon, a lot of grated Parmesan, and freshly cracked black pepper. You can certainly use more specific recipes, but none should be much more complicated than that.

The most illuminating addition I've read is by Elizabeth David, who seems always to have had the right terminology for everything. Her risotto instructions say that the rice should be "impregnated" by butter before the wine is added. The rice goes from being transparent to being opaque, and seems filled up.

Maybe the truest evidence of the almost sacramental simplicity of Italian risotto cooking is a dish called *risotto in cantina* for which risotto is made with onion, wine, butter, and broth, and then served in a bowl of sharp white wine, which is, we are firmly instructed, not to be mixed with the risotto, but dipped into before each bite. That is from Elizabeth David, too, who remarks that she doesn't know why it sounds so enticing. Neither do I, but it does, doesn't it?

The Neapolitan street food *arancini* are a spectacular use of leftover risotto, which after sitting for a night becomes claylike and can be shaped around little pieces of cheese, rolled into balls, dipped in breadcrumbs, then deep fried. You can also simply shape cold risotto into little cakes and panfry them in olive oil until golden brown.

Always make more rice than you need for a meal. Asian cultures make fried rice, for which rice must be a day old. What makes fried rice good is every grain getting a chance to fry individually in hot oil. I've tried to make fancier fried rice by cooking a pot of rice especially for frying. It was mushy and inferior. (Thank heavens for the occasional, calculable superiority of old things.)

My favorite is Thai fried rice.

Thai fried rice

~

1 tablespoon peanut oil
2 shallots, sliced into thin rounds
1 Thai bird's-eye chile, sliced into thin rounds
2 cloves garlic, smashed once or twice
1 cup yesterday's cooked rice
salt
½ cup chopped cucumber, radish, or green tomato
2 cups chopped cilantro or a combination of basil,
   cilantro, and mint
a big squeeze of lime, plus lime wedges for serving
½ teaspoon sugar
2 teaspoons Thai fish sauce
optional: 1 fried egg per person

Heat the oil in as wide a pan or wok as possible. You need enough hot surface area for every grain to fry. Once the oil has begun to smoke, add the shallots, chile, and garlic, then immediately add the rice. Spread it out over the whole surface of the pan. Salt it lightly.

When it seems like every grain has had time alone with the hot pan, scoop the rice into the middle of the pan, add the rest of the ingredients, and toss it all well. Serve with a lime wedge per bowl. This is most delicious with a fried egg put atop each bowl.

Fried rice is the rare meal for which it's sensible to make only as much as you'll eat in one sitting. The main ingredient is already cooked, and the rest takes four minutes. A single batch of cold, left-over rice can keep you in fresh fried rice for a week. This is a very good meal to eat alone.

Whatever hasn't been fried must be turned into rice pudding. We do not make enough rice pudding, probably because we do not make enough rice.

Rice pudding

~

2 cups yesterday's cooked rice
2 cups coconut milk
1 cup heavy cream (you could use all coconut
    milk also, but I like the combination)
¼ cup plus very scant ⅛ cup raw sugar,
    or ¼ cup white sugar
½ cup raisins (I like the littlest ones
    but any are fine)
1 teaspoon vanilla
½ teaspoon cinnamon
a few grates of nutmeg

Combine all the ingredients in a small pot. Let it heat to just under a boil. As soon as you see the first bubbles, lower it to a quiet simmer. Cook it with the intention of the rice absorbing everything. After about 50 minutes, it should be very pudding-y, with a tiny bit of swim left to it. Hot, medium, or cold, this is good. In my constant economy and curiosity, I have made this from rice cooked with peppercorns in it, and rice cooked with cardamom in it, and rice cooked with turmeric in it. All good, good, good.

In 1952, Charleston's *Post and Courier* suggested that grits were the real peacekeepers. Given enough grits, it declared, "the inhabitants of planet Earth would have nothing to fight about. A man full of [grits] is a man of peace."

Although Southerners have never been our most pacific citizens, it's true that we all fight less when we eat well, which an abundance of grits guarantees.

The paper was also right because grits and polenta, their identical twin from across the ocean, are vehicles for butter, cream, and cheese, and most tempers can be at least a little cooled by large quantities of those.

I cook grits and polenta interchangeably. This might affect my credibility, but they are both ground corn, and they both taste good with the other's traditional accoutrements: a bowl of grits is delicious with Bolognese sauce, as is polenta with shrimp or pulled pork.

It is also an authentic approach. Traditionally, grits and polenta, like risotto, are not intended as a rich accompaniment to the main event. They are the main event. Polenta Bolognese, like risotto Bolognese, is mostly starch and a little meat. The same is true for shrimp and grits. Whether I cook grits or polenta, it's not the side dish, it's *the dish*.

Cook either grits or polenta by putting a pot filled with five cups of water on the stove to boil. Use as big a pot as you would for pasta. Once the water is boiling, salt it less heavily than for pasta, and pour in a cup of grits or polenta, whisking as you do. Once it's integrated, lower the heat to below a bubble and leave it on the lowest possible flame, whisking it once every ten minutes or so, for forty-five minutes to an hour, until it stops tasting soapy, which it will until it is done. Add a half stick of butter and stir well.

Keep polenta or grits in a pot over very low heat while you're eating. This will keep them soft and, once everyone has eaten his or her share, make them easy to pour into a baking pan, so that you can have grilled polenta tomorrow.

Though all either needs is butter, cheese, or cream, both polenta and grits are good destinations for leftovers. One summer I witnessed some of the finest polenta meals I've ever seen, assembled by my brother, who was cooking at the time in the little town of Vicenza, Italy. He meticulously arranged bowls of the prior night's cooked kale, a little bowl of olives, a pile of olive-oil-poached salt cod, and a few thin slices of fatty salami alongside a bowl of buttery rewarmed polenta. He dined on it at 5 a.m. on Sunday mornings, then finished with an espresso and got to work.

Warm some garlicky sautéed cooking greens in a pan. Find leftover roasted squash and season it with a little red wine vinegar, dig out some olives and a wedge of Parmesan cheese. Put grits or polenta in a bowl, assemble your leftovers on top, drizzle with balsamic vinegar or olive oil, or both, and grate it all heavily with Parmesan cheese.

Or serve grits or polenta with beans ladled over. Or cut salami into slices on a long bias and brown each slice in a pan. Add red wine vinegar to cover and a spoonful of tomato paste. Let the slices of salami simmer until they've begun to soften, then spoon three or four pieces per person over each bowl of grits or polenta. Top each with chopped fresh parsley and grated Parmesan cheese.

Store leftover grits or polenta poured into a baking or roasting pan. You can leave the pan, cut or uncut, covered or uncovered, in the refrigerator for days. Once its contents have hardened, cut them into wedges or squares, drizzle them with oil, and grill or fry them. Serve a big square of panfried polenta topped with garlicky greens, a poached egg, and a heavy grating of Parmesan cheese.

If you decide you want to eat grits or polenta soft on a second day, break them into pieces, put them back into a pot, and heat them, adding a little water and whisking vigorously until they become creamy. You can go in both directions a few times.

If you crave something even more tranquil make *polentina*. This is as unlikely a soup as one made of risotto rice and lettuce. It has no bon mot attached. It is just deeply comforting to know how to make such a thing.

Polentina

~

6 cloves garlic, sliced
2 tablespoons olive oil
salt
8 cups chicken stock
1 small bundle parsley stems, thyme, savory, and sage,
    tied together with twine
½ cup polenta

Cook the garlic in olive oil in a big pot, salting it as soon as you add it. Add the chicken stock and herbs and bring to a boil. Lower to a simmer. Add the polenta slowly, whisking it in. Cook for an hour until its soapy taste is gone. Remove the herbs. Serve topped with a poached egg.

Rice and ground corn are both pacifists and peace. They fill bellies and cracks in our meals, and they fill the cultural divisions in our appetites, which really, in the end, are the same.

Eat a meal of rice or grits or polenta. Or eat a meal of farro, the Italian grain that can be cooked and eaten the same way. Or the Peruvian quinoa, with its strange cowlick at top. Or the underestimated barley, which should be freed from murky beef and mushroom. Eat any as often as you remember to. If you have great meals of them, and they don't cost much and haven't taken much time to make, then, I think, you will be at peace.

Eleven

How to Feel Powerful

The stove, the bins, the cupboards, I had learned forever,
make an inviolable throne room. From them I ruled;
temporarily I controlled. I felt powerful, and I loved
that feeling.

— M. F. K. Fisher, *A Gastronomical Me*

No matter what else is in my cupboards, I try to keep at least one jar or can each of anchovies, olives, capers, and astringent pickles, like gherkins, or cornichons. They are not all universally loved, but few powerful things are. The key to making them as useful as they can be is knowing how to exercise their power well. They each contain enough potency in their tiny preserved selves to do most of what needs doing.

Anchovies divide us into lovers and fighters. No one is neutral. The little fish elicit wistful gazes from their adorers—if you love them you wonder when you will get your next one—and shudders from objectors, far more numerous, who can't fathom the injustice of ever having to see one of the nasty things again.

If you have ever tasted a good anchovy, you will know that nastiness is not in the fish's nature. Freshly caught and gutted, their tiny tails left on, then quickly packed into salt, they are meaty, beautiful little things.

When you open a jar or tin of them, their thick salt smell is the first thing that escapes. Once they've been soaked for ten minutes in warm water, they emerge, tails and fins still attached, whole, looking very much like they did when they were first pulled from water. These anchovies, when stripped of their bones and tails, taste clean and fresh and have a depth that can only come from deep in the dark sea.

Most of the anchovies served in restaurants are bad, filleted before they were preserved, and then preserved carelessly. They taste fishy and often a little acrid. If they weren't bad to start with, they're usually stored badly, dry, instead of nicely shined with olive oil.

The best anchovies will have been preserved in salt. One way to unite the camps is to buy them. Then, ten minutes before you're planning to cook with them, dig the number of anchovies you want out of their salt and soak them in a bowl of water until they've begun to soften and their salt rubs off easily.

Under a slowly dripping tap, run your thumb along each side of the little fishes' backbones until you can lift the fillets off. Pull off the back fin and tail and lay the fillets on a paper towel to drain. While they are draining, replenish the salt in the remainder of the jar or can with kosher salt, making sure the remaining whole anchovies are well covered, and store it in the refrigerator. Store any anchovies you've filleted and not used completely submerged in olive oil. Not enough of us do this, which accounts for the matte pallor of the fillets that show up flumped on top of our Caesar salads.

Or buy the best olive-oil-packed fillets you can. I avoid the ones folded over capers, only because I don't understand why it was done.

You can buy anchovy *paste* in tubes. It means you avoid the small mess of anchovy skeletons and oil sloshing, but paste means you can't decide you would like a whole anchovy on an egg or sandwich or salad. Plus, the oil anchovies are stored in is an ingredient. I add it to anything I'm using the fish themselves in, or for the beginning of a pasta sauce that will have fish in it, or to a pan of roasting vegetables.

A good way to get anchovies' dense, rosy little selves to show what they can do is to make *bagna cauda*. (This means "warm bath.") *Bagna cauda* is a buttery dip that is a lovely way to start a meal and incredibly economical. The contents of a single jar of anchovies make enough for a big group of people.

You need to reconceive both the dip and the dipped to make sense of this. Fill a plate with sliced boiled potatoes, thin wedges of raw cabbage, wedges of soft-boiled egg, lightly boiled celery, and leaves of endive, then spoon the rich sauce over each one as you eat it.

Bagna cauda

~

½ cup good anchovy fillets	4 cloves garlic, pounded to a paste
⅔ cup olive oil	with salt in a mortar with a
2 tablespoons butter	pestle or on a cutting board
	salt

Chop the anchovies roughly, then pound to a paste as you would garlic. Heat a little of the olive oil and all of the butter in a small pot over low heat. When the butter melts, add the garlic and stir over the lowest heat possible, making sure it doesn't brown. Add the anchovies and cook the two together for 5 minutes, stirring occasionally. Keep the heat very low; turn it off periodically if the pot starts sizzling. Once the bagna cauda *has begun to darken, add the remaining olive oil and a small pinch of salt. Let it cook at below a simmer for 15 to 20 minutes.*

Serve this warm. There are special pots sold especially for it. I serve it in the pot in which it cooked, moving it back to the stove for a minute when it cools down, warming it up again, then returning it to the table.

Turn your leftover *bagna cauda* into a Caesar-like dressing by whisking in the juice of a lemon, one raw egg yolk, a half teaspoon mustard, and a tablespoon water. Toss it with romaine or escarole and croutons, and shave Parmesan cheese over the top.

———

Shrimp eating is environmentally treacherous these days, but if you find wild-caught or sustainably farmed shrimp, buy them whole and head-on. Mix ten finely chopped anchovies into a stick of room temperature butter. Blister the shrimp, still in their shells, heads still attached, on a very hot grill. Slather them with anchovy butter and serve alongside bread.

Nothing spruces up plain boiled eggs better than a sliver of a shiny anchovy fillet laid over a half of one. It's hard to think of anything else that does as much for as little fuss as anchovies do for the *bigoli in salsa*—pasta with onions and anchovies—on pages 148–49.

I challenge anyone to find me a situation a good olive can't fix. A lot of people don't mind olives, and many like them, and few find them repellent. This is lucky, because they're versatile, can be a dish's anchor or its sail, and it takes only a precious few to do either.

When someone does object to olives, as with anchovies, it is not to olive qua olive they object. Olives are inedible raw, off the tree. They have to be cured. Some are treated well, cured in plain salt or salt water or lye. Others are pained little things, drowned in harsh brine and robbed of everything that made them worth preserving in the first place.

There are plenty of good olives around. They can be buttery, or tart, if that is how you like them, but they should never taste crabby or mean.

A lot of stores have big tubs of olives you can taste. If you find yourself at a store with tubs, sample their contents and choose the simplest tasting, or choose a few kinds, and decide as you cook with them which you like. Avoid olives that come already seasoned with herbs and garlic. The olives may be good, but the herbs or garlic may not, and they will ruin things.

If you're buying jars of olives, the tiny eggplant-hued niçoise olives are delicate tasting and all-purpose. Black, wrinkled, salt-cured Greek olives are also delicious. I also like the mossy little

French *lucques* or *picholine* olives. Greek kalamata olives may be the only jarred olives you can find and they are usually fine.

If none of those are available, buy any olive in a jar, not a can. If you can only find green cocktail olives, buy them. Unless you're deeply committed to their bright red pimentos' pickliness, remove the garish things before you begin cooking with the olives.

Olives taste more like themselves if they're bought with their pits still in. To pit olives, put a handful of them onto a clean flat surface and press down on them firmly with the bottom of a ceramic ramekin or sturdy mug. Move the ramekin or mug back and forth a few times while pressing on it. The olives will smash and let loose their grip on their pits.

If that sounds like a hassle that will stop you from cooking with olives, follow the lead of olive-loving cultures. It is a common practice in Italy, France, and Greece to put little olives, pits intact, on pizzas and tarts. The responsibility of pitting olives is passed on to their eaters, who are expected to have the foresight to keep from biting into one.

If you don't pit olives for a dish that *isn't* a pizza or tart, a vegetable stew, for example, or the chicken dish below, and you have any leftovers that you plan to repurpose into a frittata or gratin, pit the olives before you do. Otherwise, they will hide, unseen, beneath egg or breadcrumb, and attack unsuspecting teeth like guerrillas.

Olives aren't often enough asked to fit into their surroundings. They usually seem tossed in the general *direction* of a dish, or dumped straight onto salads, which get dark and damp, or added into sauces at the last minute, so that there is resistance on the olive side and resistance on the sauce side, and no time to resolve it.

Olives have to be thoughtfully deployed, or their strength is a disadvantage. Instead of looking for a recipe, cook whatever plain ingredient you have using a cooking technique that is tactical deployment of olive.

This works well with chicken. Buy a good chicken. Salt it as you would for boiling and cut it into pieces, leaving them on the bone.

In a deep, oven-safe pot with a lid, brown each piece, skin side down, well. While the chicken is browning, thinly slice any vegetable you have: if it's autumn or winter, it can be cabbage or waxy potatoes. If it's spring, little carrots and spring onions. If it's summer, roughly cubed zucchini and tomato.

Once the chicken pieces have browned, remove them from the pot, add two cups of the vegetables you sliced, a handful of whole, drained olives, pitted or unpitted, and a few long slices of lemon peel.

Salt the vegetables lightly and cook them until they've just begun to soften. Nestle the pieces of chicken among them skin side up, making sure the olives and lemon peel are well distributed. Let it all cook, covered, in a 375-degree oven until the chicken is tender and the vegetables are cooked, uncovering it for the last few minutes so that it all ends up darkly roasted. Serve the chicken and vegetables with lemony olives scattered over each piece.

(Dried fruit, which is also preserved and its flavor concentrated, works like olives, and is used in place or in tandem throughout northern Africa and the Middle East. Its deployment should be similar. Add a handful of chopped dried figs, dates, raisins, or apricots to your chicken pot, with or instead of olives. A tiny sprinkling of dried cinnamon and ginger is good in that case.)

Deploy olives tactically to make pasta sauce. Cook a little sliced garlic in a pot with a lot of oil and a small shake of chile flakes. Add a big handful of drained olives, pitted or unpitted, whole or chopped. Let them cook for thirty seconds, then add a can of peeled tomatoes and its liquid, and simmer for an hour until it's rich and sweet. To turn this into the spicy, slightly oceanic puttanesca sauce, add four roughly chopped anchovies when you add the olives and a pinch of well-drained capers for the last fifteen minutes of the sauce's cooking.

Olive pastes are some of the handiest sauces to keep around. I can't think of anything that isn't improved by a spoonful of one. Make a basic olive paste by finely chopping olives, pounding a little garlic with salt, and mixing in a good amount of olive oil.

There are a million variations, most of them good, each with its own name. In Greece, olive paste might have a few drops of vinegar added. In Italy, there may be chopped fresh rosemary—if you're eating beans or bean soup, I recommend this variation. When olives and garlic and earthy rosemary plop down onto hot beans, something quite extraordinary happens.

I grew up eating very garlicky tapenade, the Provençal version, which includes finely chopped capers and anchovies. One day my mother would add lemon zest, and another mix in a few warm chickpeas, another day a lot of parsley. She would lightly spread the tapenade on little pieces of toasted dry baguette and called them "olive toasts."

To make olive toasts, thinly slice any bread you have, toast it, rub one side with raw garlic, drizzle the toasts lightly with olive oil, then top each with a big spoonful of tapenade, made by adding some capers and anchovies to your plain olive paste. For a variation on that, top each with a torn piece of mozzarella and toast until the cheese melts. For another, put a sliver of vinegar-marinated roasted pepper on each one.

There is nothing more perfect in spring or summer than a plate of lamb chops or grilled chicken or steak or fish, thickly topped with fragrant spoonfuls of tapenade, with chilled, simply boiled vegetables alongside. Except, perhaps, for ripe zucchini or tomatoes, cut in half, roasted until their insides can be scooped out, then their flesh mixed with tapenade and a handful of breadcrumbs, and filled back into them, all of it roasted further until the vegetables are brown and bubbling. Or perhaps leftover sliced potatoes, little cooked turnips, or green beans mixed with big spoonfuls of tapenade, thinned with a drizzle of olive oil, served with a tiny bit of chill still on them.

The very end of a batch of olive paste should become vinaigrette. Whisk in a tiny bit of mustard, a few drops of red wine vinegar, fresh lemon juice, and olive oil, and mix with romaine.

Capers are as odd and wild as birds. They are the original nipped buds, picked from their scraggly bushes early in the morning, on their way to becoming tiny, petaled flowers, just before they're won over by the sun and convinced to bloom. I believe I can taste the power of their foiled entry to the hot day each time I eat one.

Like anchovies, capers taste more like themselves—peppery and a little pebbly—if they're stored in salt, not brine. If you find a jar of plump, salty, good ones, buy them. If you don't, brined capers are fine.

Soak salt-packed capers in warm water until they don't taste salty. You may have to drain them once or twice, refill the bowl with water, and let them soak again. If you buy capers in brine, keep the brine after you have used up the capers. It is useful for pickling chiles and onions, and a few drops are good in a martini or a Bloody Mary.

Use capers to make a delicious sauce for chicken or fish. Heat a little butter in a pan, and when it begins to brown, add a small spoonful of well-drained roughly chopped capers, a big squeeze of lemon, and a handful of chopped parsley. Turn off the heat. This is as good on eggs or toast as on meat.

Capers can also be added directly to cold leftover boiled potatoes, or roasted cauliflower, or anything else that needs a little vibrancy. Scatter a few into bread salad, or over a sandwich of olive-oil-packed tuna and slices of hard-boiled egg.

Capers like all kinds of fat, and somehow get it to firm up: capers in butter, capers in olive oil, tiny crisp fried capers, capers delicately strewn over soft, rich cheese are all good. If something ever seems too rich or oily or creamy, a caper will negotiate a painless détente.

You can make your own caperlike ingredient from the edible flowers called nasturtiums. If you ever see them with their little seed pods, which look like chickpeas, still attached, pick as many as you can. When you get home, make a quick pickle brine, like the one on pages 208–9, or heat up leftover caper brine you've kept, adding a little vinegar and a dash of sugar to freshen it up. Put the seed pods in a jar, pour the hot brine over, and let them sit for at least three days before eating them. They taste peppery and caper-like and will store, refrigerated, for months.

A pickle is the same but different. Gherkins, called cornichons in French, smart a little when you eat them. There's no cooking or soaking. They are firm, no-nonsense things, and bristle if they're asked to change.

Cornichons are usually located just next to the anchovies, olives, and capers in any grocery store. Your choices will probably be limited to one or two good, comparable French brands.

If you need cheering up, eat them straight. If your food does, I suggest making a relish. Relishes are uninhibitedly joyful sauces. The relishes that come on hot dogs aren't joyful, but saccharine, which is why it's worth making your own.

For a simple one that calls only for the other powerful ingredients in your cupboard, combine equal quantities of drained chopped capers, pitted chopped olives, a chopped anchovy fillet or two (or five, depending on your taste), and twice as many finely chopped cornichons as capers and olives. Mix with just enough olive oil to loosen. Try this on cold potatoes, or cold roast chicken, or in an omelet of boiled beef.

One of the best pairings in condiment history is of pickle and egg. The aggression of the pickle and self-possession of the egg are a perfect match. A condiment recipe from the first known cookbook, Apicius's *De re coquinaria,* calls for mixing the yolks of two eggs with celery salt, the squeezed juice of the celery-like plant lovage, and ground peppercorns. It is for serving with *scilla,* big shrimp found in the delta of the Liri river. The celery and lovage are not pickled, but potent, and mixed with the peppercorns, must act very pickley. Whether you use jarred cornichons or juice of lovage, the combination of sharp green flavor and egg is a delicious one.

There is nothing better for cold asparagus, or cold potatoes, or any cold boiled meat than a relish made of both pickle and egg. It is also so like an egg salad that a sandwich could be made of just it and a scattering of fresh herbs.

Sauce gribiche

~

> 1 hard-boiled egg, yolk and white separated after it's cooked
> salt
> 1 teaspoon Dijon mustard
> ⅓ cup olive oil
> 1 teaspoon white wine vinegar
> 1 teaspoon finely chopped cornichons
> 1 teaspoon drained whole capers
> ¼ cup (lightly packed) chopped mixed herbs:
>   parsley, chervil, and/or tarragon
> freshly cracked black pepper

Smash the egg yolk and a small pinch of salt with the mustard. Mix in the olive oil with a spoon. When it is fairly well combined, add the vinegar and mix. Add the rest of the ingredients, including the cooked egg whites.

Tartar sauce suffers a fate both alike and opposite to that of the anchovy. Skeptics should be seduced to try good anchovies. Enthusiasts should be cautioned away from the sweet glop that passes for tartar sauce.

A good tartar sauce should be piquant and powerful. It is much better made at home—where you can guarantee its potency—than purchased.

Here's one.

Tartar sauce

~

1 cup homemade mayonnaise
⅓ cup chopped cornichons
3 tablespoons chopped capers
3 tablespoons roughly chopped parsley leaves
1 tablespoon lemon juice
1 tablespoon white wine vinegar
optional: 1 tablespoon olive oil
a single drop hot sauce
salt

Mix everything lightly into the mayonnaise, only whisking in the optional olive oil if the sauce threatens to get thin. Taste for salt.

I also have this more elaborate recipe by the Louisianan writer Lafcadio Hearn.

1st:—Catch a young Tartar: for the old ones are very tough and devoid of juice. To catch a Tartar is generally a very unpleasant and at all times a difficult undertaking. A young Tartar will probably cost you at least $10,000—and perhaps your life—before you get through with him: but if you must have Tartar sauce you must be ready to take all risks. Having procured your Tartar you must kill him privately, taking care that the act shall escape the observation of the police authorities, who would probably in such a case be strongly prejudiced in favor of the Tartar. Having killed, skinned and cleaned the Tartar, cut off the tenderest part of the hams and thighs; boil three hours, and then hash up with Mexican pepper, aloes and spices. Add a quart of mulled wine and slowly boil to the consistency of honey. You will probably find the Tartar sauce very palatable; and if hermetically sealed in bottles with the addition of a little Santa Cruz rum, will serve for a long time. The rest of the Tartar will not keep, and must be disposed of judiciously.

I have not tried his, but still prefer mine, which seems to require less planning and exertion of its cook.

Twelve

How to Build a Ship

If you want to build a ship, don't drum up people
to collect wood, and don't assign them tasks and work,
but rather teach them to long for the endless
immensity of the sea.
—Antoine de Saint-Exupéry

There are times when I can't bear to think about cooking. Food is what I love, and how I communicate love, and how I calm myself. But sometimes, without my knowing why, it is drained of all that. Then cooking becomes just another one of hunger's jagged edges. So I have ways to take hold of this *thing* and wrest it from the claws of resentment, and settle it back among things that are mine.

The first is remembering that ill-tempered as I am, I resent everything sometimes. I get infuriated by the weather and missed trains and missing buttons. I think that cooking *must* be allowed to swell to contemptible proportions when it seems contemptible, just like other disproportionately terrible annoyances, and then allowed to shrink when it is time.

Then the question is: How do you fall in love with it again, or if it has never made you truly happy, fall in love with it for the first time?

My answer is to anchor food to somewhere deep inside you, or deep in your past, or deep in the wonders of what you love.

We have different loves. Mine are food and words. Others' are how buildings slant away from dark sidewalks, or how good it feels to solve an equation. I say: Let yourself love what you love, and see if it doesn't lead you back to what you ate when you loved it.

It helps me to think of meals I've cooked or eaten before, if not for the food, for the light in the room or in the sky when I ate. What the light looked like, or what music was playing. It doesn't take more than my opening a window, head lifted to the air, for the sound of glass against a marble table, or the rustle of the wind to remind me that I've sat at marble tables outside, drunk out of glasses, listened to their light clatter on the table, noticing a rustling wind.

I may not remember what I ate, or whether it was the lunch where I realized I do not like black pepper to have been ground before I use it, or the one where I spilled water in my lap, but I will remember how the day felt on my face, and my creative soft self will have been awakened. So I listen hard. I listen with the purpose of remembering. And this digging into sounds and into days I have heard and felt roots future meals in the unchangeable truths of past ones.

Let smells in. Let the smell of hot tarmac in the summer remind you of a meal you ate the first time you landed in a hot place, when the ground smelled like it was melting. Let the smell of salt remind you of a paper basket of fried clams you ate once, squeezing them with lemon as you walked on a boardwalk. Let it reach your deeper interest. When you smell the sea, and remember the basket of hot fried clams, and the sound of skee-balls knocking against each other, let it help you love what food can do, which is to tie this moment to that one. Then something about the wind off the sea will have settled in your mind, and carried the fried clams and squeeze of a lemon with it.

The smells of a fireplace or wood fire are some of the best. Decide you will replicate the meals those smells remind you of, no matter if they're hot dogs and Boston baked beans, or corn, or cinnamon toast eaten off paper plates. If it's hot dogs or cinnamon toast that reminds your heart that it can be moved by food, make hot dogs or cinnamon toast.

Or instead of eating hot dogs or toast, think of sausages, and how fun it is to spread anything with mustard, or with the smell of cinnamon in your nose, open up a cookbook to look for a recipe for apple cake.

When I smell charcoal, I remember a meal at a folding table at the side of a river in Laos. A woman manned an oil drum cut in half, a hot blackened grill over its top, and coals spread in its belly. She grilled chicken legs, bones removed, until they were charred, their meat turned the color of dark honey. They were sent to the table with sticky rice, packed into little wicker baskets by her tough hands, along with ceramic crocks of red chile paste.

I cannot smell charcoal or wet river rock without smelling, too, grilling chicken, and steaming rice, and remembering how for days my hands were stained with chile. It does not matter what river or what food. Tug your memories back into the kitchen with you and you'll find yourself less separate from the idea of making food.

I like to read descriptions of food in books. If I'm feeling resentful of cooking, I never pick up anything useful. I will only read a cookbook if it is one in which the poetry of food comes alive on the page.

I have a dog-eared copy on a bookshelf near the kitchen of *The Taste of Country Cooking* by Edna Lewis. Ms. Lewis was a chef from Virginia who wrote about Southern cooking so beautifully that when you read what she writes, you can taste the seasons and the fields vegetables were picked from, and the temperature outside when jam got made, and what the wind felt like when quails were hunted. Writing about the Virginia summers of her childhood:

> *Most farmers had their own icehouses, but we got ours from the icehouse at Lahore. We used it for making ice cream, lemonade, cooling the milk, and sometimes drinking water. It was a great treat to bring the ice home in a burlap bag, chipping off small pieces to eat on a hot day.*

It is hot, then, and I want to make lemonade, and feel cold ice on my fingers.

Or I read passages from children's books, which often contain the most limpid descriptions of food. The writer E. Nesbit's stories seem to always end when, after quarreling, getting lost, getting stung, children find themselves—warm and tired in hay barns—eating cold chicken, bacon, boiled eggs, ripe tomatoes sprinkled with salt, and siphons of seltzer. Her stories leave me wanting to run and scrape and quarrel and eat cold chicken and ripe tomatoes, and those are all pleasant things to want to do. So, I am again excited about the way a meal can bring a day to fizzy, perfect completion.

One spring I reread *The Wind in the Willows,* remembering having been bewitched as a child by what its animal citizens ate. I found this description of Water Rat's picnic:

> *"There's cold chicken inside it," said Rat briefly, "cold-tongue-cold-ham-cold-beef-pickled-gherkins-salad-french-bread-cress-sandwidges-spotted-meat-ginger-beer-lemonade-soda-water—"*
>
> *"Oh stop, stop!" cried the Mole in ecstasies: "This is too much!"*
>
> *"Do you really think so?" inquired the Rat seriously. "It's only what I always take on these little excursions . . ."*
>
> *Rat rowed silently down the river, while Mole took in all the new sights, smells and sounds, and trailed his paw lazily in the water.*

For a week, I had a solid sense that my days were a cool river. I made cold beef and pickled onion sandwiches for lunch, and ate watercress salad, and drank not lemonade, but beer.

I am probably most helped by reading books written by people who were moved by what they ate, and could not tell a story without telling what was eaten. Ernest Hemingway, who never made explicit what could be implied, could not help describing food. He wrote about foods that were wild and cold: oysters, brook trout, wine.

And when I read this one, which I do when I'm really embittered about cooking and eating and being hungry in the first place, I think "Oh, yes." And something settles. In *A Moveable Feast,* he wrote:

> *As I ate the oysters with their strong taste of the sea and their faint metallic taste that the cold white wine washed away, leaving only the sea taste and the succulent texture, and as I drank their cold liquid from each shell and washed it down with the crisp taste of the wine, I lost the empty feeling and began to be happy and to make plans.*

Thirteen

How to Find Fortune

There are riches there, lad, fortune enough for all the
country round but not a soul sees it!
—Anton Chekhov, "Happiness"

S ome vegetables are persistently underestimated. If you ever
find yourself longing to cook a good vegetable but there is none
in sight, get a deep pot and dig eight to ten plain, big, dusty onions
from your pantry, or the cold, dark onion bin at your nearest store.
Then caramelize them. Cut off their tops, then cut them in half
through their roots, then lengthwise into slices about a quarter-inch
thick. Warm three tablespoons of butter and three tablespoons of
olive oil in a big pot. When the butter is melted, add the mountain
of onions, a small pinch of sugar, a big pinch of salt, and a branch of
fresh thyme, and stir it all well. Cook the onions over medium-low
heat, stirring them occasionally. Add occasional sprinkles of water
if the onions begin to stick. If they start to sizzle, lower the heat
and cover the pot, then uncover it when the cooking has slowed.
This will take forty-five minutes to an hour, and the whole mass
will look soggy and unconvincing until right before the onions are
done, at which point they melt completely into a golden jam and all
of their sugars come out to toast.

Now you have a perfect vegetable base for a series of dishes. If it's
cold out, make soup. Our expectations of onion soup are as dingy as

our expectations of onions themselves. There is no better varnishing of either than the fine and heady humbleness of this one.

Onion soup

~

> 2 cups caramelized onions
> 1 tablespoon olive oil, plus more for the bread
> 1 tablespoon butter
> ¼ cup water
> 1 teaspoon flour
> 1 tablespoon sherry, wine, or Cognac
> 4 cups beef or chicken stock
> stale bread
> 1 clove garlic, halved
> freshly cracked black pepper
> optional: chopped fresh parsley

Cook the caramelized onions according to the instructions above. Warm them in the oil, butter, and water. Add the flour and stir it through the onions. Add the sherry, wine, or Cognac, and let it cook off for 20 seconds. Add the stock. Simmer for 15 minutes.

Grill or toast thick slices of stale bread. Rub each with garlic, then drizzle with olive oil. Ladle the soup, very hot, over each one. Top with chopped fresh parsley if you have it and freshly cracked black pepper.

There is a delicious Venetian pasta dish called *bigoli in salsa* made of only cooked onions with a few good anchovies sizzled and smashed among them, tossed with the thick spaghetti called *bigoli*.

To make *bigoli in salsa*, heat a little olive oil in a big, deep pan. Warm a cup of caramelized onions in it, and once they've begun to sputter, add six anchovy fillets, crushing them and mixing them with the onions.

Cook a pound of any long noodle in well-salted water. Penne is un-Venetian, but also very good here. When it is still quite firm, drain the pasta, retaining a glass of its cooking water, then add the pasta and a quarter cup of the cooking water to the pan of sauce. Mix it all well over low heat, adding more water if it gets dry.

When the noodles are completely coated in sauce and the pasta is fully cooked, remove the pan from the heat. Add a big handful of roughly chopped parsley and top with toasted breadcrumbs. A few salty pitted olives are inauthentic but a good addition.

In Nice and all around the Ligurian Sea, the same onions are spread on very flat pizzas, then sprinkled with fresh thyme, criss-crossed with anchovies, and dotted with tiny niçoise olives. The onions and anchovies get gloriously sweet and golden when the pies are baked.

To make a version, use a simple tart dough recipe, like the one on page 83, and fill it lightly with sweet onions and salty little fish, or just toast a few slices of bread, top them with the onions and fish, sprinkle on thyme and olives, then bake them in a hot oven.

Or make omelets and fill their centers with a spoonful of sour cream, caramelized onions, and a little toasted caraway.

My nearest small grocery has a dreary-looking hummock of shallots that squats next to the bananas and newspapers. Shallots are some of the best onions to roast. They simply need to be peeled, given a good dose of wine vinegar, and put in a hot oven. All onions are good roasted, though. If your grocery keeps a different kind of onion in that strange spot, it is what you should roast.

Vinegar roasted shallots

~

2 pounds shallots or other small onions	*1 tablespoon white wine or*
salt	*sherry*
2 tablespoons olive oil	*¼ cup water*
2 tablespoons red wine vinegar	*optional: a few sprigs thyme*

Heat the oven to 400 degrees. Trim the root ends from the shallots, trying to leave their layers connected at their roots. Halve or quarter them if they're bigger than a golf ball. Leave small ones whole. Peel them. Lay them tightly in a single layer in a deep roasting pan. Salt them heavily, then drizzle with oil, vinegar, white wine, and water. Scatter the thyme in the pan, cover tightly with aluminum foil, and put it in the oven. Check after 30 minutes by undoing the foil carefully and piercing the shallots with a knife. Make sure there aren't any holes in the aluminum foil, which will slow their cooking. Check them periodically. If you notice the roasting pan get dry, add a little water. When the onions are completely tender, remove the aluminum foil and return the pan to the oven, uncovered, long enough for any remaining liquid to evaporate and for the onions to get brown. These are as good at room temperature or cold as they are hot.

We also forget to cook scallions. I like to cook scallions in a very hot, well-oiled cast-iron pan, then, once their bulbs are sweet and tender and their green tops pleasantly charred, curl them under poached eggs. Sometimes I chop them once or twice and strew them over a piece of simply cooked fish, or slice them thinly and toss them into hot spaghetti along with a big squeeze of lemon, a little dried chile, and toasted breadcrumbs.

To cook scallions like this, wash and trim the roots off a few bunches. Heat a cast-iron pan until it's very hot. In a bowl, toss the scallions with olive oil and salt. Lay the whole scallions very close together in a single layer in the hot pan. Let each get well charred on one side, turn them all over and cover the pan with a lid, or fit a plate inside your pan to trap hot air inside, and let them finish cooking through, about three minutes.

Leeks are in the onion family, and are particularly important to keep in mind when you feel vegetable-poor. They last for ages, make wonderful side dishes and salads, and are indefatigably springy.

Cook leeks by first trimming off their dark tops and then their shaggy roots. Slice them lengthwise and soak them in cold water to get rid of the dirt between their layers. Bring a big pot of salted water to a boil, add the leek halves, and cook them until they're tender enough to be easily pierced with a knife. Remove them to a colander to drain.

If you want a salad, chill the boiled leeks. Put one or two pretty halves, cut side up, on each plate and drizzle each with mustard vinaigrette and a scattering of parsley. Add a soft-boiled egg, cut into wedges, and you have lunch. Any leftover leeks, roughly chopped, will do more to improve mashed potatoes than anything but melted butter can.

If you want a hot roasted side dish, lay the drained leeks, side by side, cut side up, in a small roasting pan. Drizzle them with oil, salt them well, and roast them like cauliflower or root vegetables, in a 400-degree oven with a few sprigs of hardy herbs scattered in the pan.

Celery is another untapped treasure of the vegetable world. In an anecdote about celery in *The Cooking of the British Isles* a Frenchman visits a British household and is served afternoon tea, including cakes, cucumber, watercress, and tomato sandwiches, bread and butter, and celery. "Celery?" the visiting Frenchman exclaims. "How strange." The host breaks a piece off, dips it in salt, and munches it with a piece of the bread and butter. "Celery," he says, "is very popular in England. If you were to stand on a hill during any Sunday afternoon in winter and listen carefully, you would hear a low, rustling, crunching sound. It is the entire English nation eating celery."

Our nation, too, enjoys hearing its low, rustling crunch, and it's especially pleasing to hear the echo across the Atlantic. We should eat it for that, and also because though it may have been invented to treat us to the cross-pond cacophony, it's more likely that celery was invented to be gently simmered with lemon until it stops crunching.

I recommend buying the leafiest, most complete bunch of celery you can. Every part of a bunch of celery can be used. Tough outer branches are perfect for stock, and there's no better ingredient for a capery *salsa verde* for eggs and no better herb for a pasta frittata than celery leaves.

Celery with lemon

~

1 large or 2 small bunches celery
2 tablespoons unsalted butter
water
salt
⅔ to 1 lemon, sliced into the thinnest possible rounds
½ cup toasted breadcrumbs
freshly chopped parsley or mint leaves

Cut the leaves from celery and set them aside.

Use the entire stalks of celery for this dish, except for the very bottom of each bunch, where the stalks come together. If any of the stalks look especially dark green, save them for stock. Cut the rest of the stalks into 3-inch-long pieces. Locally grown celery is stronger flavored and tougher. It needs to be peeled.

Put the celery, butter, and water to come halfway up into a pan that fits all the cut celery in one or two layers with 2 inches above it. Season it with a little salt, then layer the lemon rounds over the top.

Heat the pan over high heat until the water starts to boil. Turn the heat to low and cover the pan. Cook for 20 to 30 minutes. If you hear the pan start to dry out before the celery's cooked, add water by the drizzle until there's enough liquid in the pan to let it keep cooking without burning.

Check for doneness by removing a piece and tasting it. The celery should be easy to pierce with a knife and taste quite lemony. Uncover the pan and raise the heat to medium to let some liquid cook off and whatever is left thicken. This should only take a few minutes. Stir it occasionally to keep it from sticking. Let the pieces have irregular texture.

Top each serving with a small handful of toasted breadcrumbs and then herbs.

Or keep celery's crunch, but enjoy it sitting down. Thinly slice it, sprinkle it with vinegar and salt, dress it with olive oil, and eat it as a salad.

We disdain plain potatoes. But where potatoes are prized, dishes made from them are appropriately located at the intersection between the rooted and the divine. In *The Cooking of Germany*, the writer Nika Standen Hazelton tells a story of arriving in a town too late for dinner and asking where she could find anything to eat. Her inn's owner answered that there "was no food to be had at the moment, unless I wished to share the family's own 'heaven and earth,'" the name of a local specialty of potatoes simmered with apples.

I prefer to be lighter handed and lighter hearted. In late spring and summer look for small potatoes that are really "new," scrub and salt them well, and put them in a roasting pan with a bay leaf, a little water, and a drizzle of olive oil, and cover them tightly with aluminum foil. Roast them for forty-five minutes to an hour until they're completely tender. When they can be pierced easily with a knife, halve them and sprinkle them with a little white wine vinegar. Add roughly chopped chives or mint and a good, long pour of olive oil. These are as bright and shiny as the little apple of the earth is ever going to get.

If it's only big, ordinary Idaho potatoes you can find, cut them into cubes and boil them in salty water, beginning them in cold water, then bringing the temperature up with them in it. Mix them the same way, with vinegar and herbs and olive oil, and they still manage to taste fresh and true.

Cabbages do not grow underground but they are terribly neglected. A perfect way to flatter cabbage is to boil it. Cut a whole cabbage into fat wedges, leaving them attached at their core. Drop the wedges into well-salted boiling water, and cook them until the solid pieces of core are easily cut with a knife. Quickly drain and lay the wedges on a plate, add a long drizzle of olive oil and a splash of vinegar. This is heavenly.

Or roast cabbage, cut into thinner wedges, in a deep, covered roasting pan with a sprinkle of white wine vinegar, another of water, and a lot of olive oil, until it's tender within, golden without. Or slice it very thinly and cook it with olive oil and salt in a big pan.

I have heard of one lucky man for whom undervalued vegetables turned to solid gold. Here is the story as I was told it:

A farmer who grew acres and acres of onions became weary of trying to sell his onions at home, so he filled a carriage with bags of them and struck out to seek his fortune. After much journeying he reached a country where onions were unknown, and when he demonstrated their wonders to the royal court, the king rewarded the farmer by filling all of his onion bags with gold.

The farmer returned home and told his story. So his neighbor, a garlic farmer, took the same journey, to the same land.

The court was again bewitched, this time by garlic, and the night after a great feast, where garlic soup got the pulses quickened, and garlic chicken drove people to ecstasy, the garlic farmer was rewarded; his garlic sacks filled to brimming with treasure. The man drove straight back to his native land, aching to see his riches. When he finally arrived, he opened his bulging bags to find them full of the kingdom's most prized possession: onions.

Fourteen

How to Be Tender

‚óè───‚óè

Tenderness is the repose of Passion.
—Joseph Joubert

O f all of the people who have had opinions about whether eating meat is an evolutionary inevitability or an ontological
crime, none is so right as Hugh Fearnley-Whittingstall, who wrote
a very big, comprehensive book called *The River Cottage Meat Book*.

He starts it by answering the question all of us who write recipes
for meat should: "It seems obvious to me that the morality of meat
eating lies in the factual details of our relationships with the animals
we kill for food. It is what we do to them that counts."

It is.

I've looked at animals raised amid the roiled and rich chaos of
sun and dirt and barnyard. I've watched exchanges on farms where
things are slow and sensible: between pig and pig, pig and soil, soil
and sky. I've watched children care for animals and learn a little
bit about transience and wildness from it. I've also peeked over the
high walls of the factory farms behind which most meat is raised
and seen how beastly we can be to the animals we eat.

What we do to animals counts.

Other than arguments about the hypocrisy of treating animals
kindly before dispatching them (to which the fairest response seems

155

that no matter what happens next, good feed and good sunlight are appreciated when one is eating and sunning), the only objection I ever hear to buying sanely raised meat is cost.

Good meat only seems so expensive because we eat meat like children taking bites out of the middles of sandwiches and throwing the rest away.

There's not yet a cow with an eternal supply of steaks, a pig that's all loin, or a chicken that is all boneless white meat. Most meat on cows and pigs and chickens is bound in hardworking muscles, and we tend to avoid it because it needs to be coerced into tenderness.

Luckily, those hardworking cuts are more delicious than the idle ones. Barbecue comes from cuts from the shoulder and rib cage and animals' strong, tough chests. So do sausages and bacon. Ham is made from pigs' legs, osso buco from cows' shins.

They are also the simplest to cook. Reserves of fat are woven throughout them instead of huddled in a cap on their surface. This keeps them from drying out, even if you forget them or worriedly let them cook too long. Because they're the most numerous, they're also the cheapest. I take this all as a tiny divine nod in favor of thoughtful omnivorism.

If you agree, I recommend you put away all cookbooks except Hugh Fearnley-Whittingstall's and *The Supper of the Lamb* by Robert Farrar Capon. The first contains recipes that are as smart as its moral deliberations. The second, the single most sensible meat recipe I've ever read.

The recipe is called "Lamb for Eight Persons Four Times." It lasts half the book. (It's long but includes breaks like "God makes wine," and "Let us pause and drink to that," and "Another toast." You would be a slurry cook by the end of it.) It also produces thirty-two servings of food from a single leg of lamb.

I've never made it to thirty-two servings, but I won't buy meat unless it lets me make more than one. This helps from a budgetary perspective, and my soul is more settled when I make a little meat go far. It also makes buying meat at farmers' markets, or the humanely raised meat available at grocery stores, practical.

You don't need to serve an army or follow Robert Capon's directions for butchering meat and turning each piece into a different stew. You only need to do what it makes sense to do anyway: choose cuts from which you can most easily get the greatest number of meals, and cook them in the way that makes it possible.

Tougher cuts are best. They end up meltingly tender. They're easy to turn into several meals, and they don't suffer from reheating. You will be turning slow-cooked meat into one dish after another, not just warming it up, but it's good to know it won't toughen as you tinker.

The simplest way to cook hardworking cuts is slowly, in a pot. This is also the most resourceful way to cook meat. After it has simmered away with broth and a few vegetables, meat that has slow-cooked in a pot creates a second ingredient. This is as inevitable as bean broth from a bean pot. In addition to their meat, tougher cuts generously leave you soup or sauce.

There are a lot of terms for cooking meat in pots. "Stewing" refers to cutting meat up and cooking it covered in liquid. "Boiling" means cooking in water. "Braising" means cooking meat partially covered in liquid, usually other than water.

There also seem to be hundreds of slow-cooked meat dishes, each with a discrete set of steps and ingredients. There is chicken cacciatore, coq au vin, Irish lamb stew, pot roast, osso buco, and *boeuf bourguignon.*

Then the names of the cuts themselves: spareribs and short ribs, blade roasts, shoulder roasts, neck roasts, shanks, briskets, chuck eyes, eyes of round, London broil, and on and on.

None of it matters.

A parable explains this well. A rabbi is asked to teach a student the Bible while the student stands on one leg. The rabbi agrees and says: "Do unto others as they should do unto you. The rest is commentary."

Cuts of meat cook either quickly or slowly. The rest is commentary.

Steaks and chops and boneless chicken breasts can be quickly cooked on a grill or in a pan. Almost everything else needs salt, liquid, heat, and time. Though recipes for chicken cacciatore call for chicken legs, osso buco for shanks, *boeuf bourguignon* for beef and wine from Burgundy, the process for cooking each is the same. The sizes of the pieces of meat, the cuts, the amount and kind of liquid in the pot are only the elegant commentary that separates them.

Choose one of the good recipes for stewing or boiling or braising meat in Fearnley-Whittingstall's book, or wend and guzzle your way through Robert Capon's lamb stews, or go to your nearest source for good meat and buy three pounds of tough cuts.

As you shop, look at chuck eye and know it will behave like short ribs; expect shoulder and shin to perform the same. If it's economical, gather an assortment of odd cuts from the same species: I have been served from a deep, delicious pot of braised lamb that included lamb ribs, a rich lamb shank, and pieces of shoulder roast.

If the responsibly raised meat you find is sold frozen, buy it. Opinions differ, but I think that frozen meat is fine. Tough cuts freeze especially well.

Once you're practiced at this thinking, you can consider the least expensive way to buy meat. It is to organize a group of friends to buy all of the meat on an animal. It doesn't cost a farmer any more to feed an animal's steaks than to feed its ground beef, so if you buy it all you can pay the same for it all: instead of twenty dollars for steaks and seven dollars a pound for ground beef, you pay seven dollars for everything.

This will leave you with four hundred pounds of beef, or more than a hundred pounds of pork, and it's a big undertaking for everyone involved. The meat shows up butchered and frozen. You have to divvy up quick-cooking cuts and slow-cooking cuts, but once you have you will all have a consistent supply of locally raised meat in your freezers, and you can probe the elegant commentary of slow-cooking meat in as leisurely a manner as you like.

Unless you are positive your refrigerator and pantry are completely bare, return home with only the meat in hand. A pot of slow-cooking meat is an accommodating place. It is into it that any good-tasting odds and ends should go: little peelings from mushrooms, ends of bottles of wine or beer, skins from blanched tomatoes, tops of sweet peppers, ends of bunches of herbs.

Once you get home, salt your meat five times more heavily than you're comfortable doing. It's hard to get enough salt into dense, slow-cooking cuts. Salt needs to sit on all available surfaces for as long as possible and have a chance to journey in on its own.

If you plan to cook the meat today, leave it sitting at room temperature for three hours. If you are cooking it tomorrow, refrigerate it overnight and then bring it back up to room temperature before cooking it. It's worth cooking the meat you've bought even if you aren't planning on eating it for a few days. Slow-cooked meat improves with time. The best possible dinner of it tonight would contain meat cooked at least a day ago.

Here is a good recipe for slow-cooking meat. I call it "braised" because "braise" is a flexible term, and cooking it you should feel both flexible and in charge, which is most certainly what you are

Braised meat

~

3 pounds meat from a tougher part
    of a happily raised animal
2 tablespoons olive oil
salt
up to 1 cup clean vegetable scraps:
    onion, celery, carrot, fennel.
    If you've not got scraps, use pieces
    from whole vegetables
a bundle of parsley stems, sprigs of
    thyme, and a bay leaf

optional: ½ teaspoon spices
    such as fennel seed, cumin,
    and/or coriander
8 cups stock, heated if you've
    got time
2 cups white or red wine or
    beer, or a combination of
    any and the liquid from a
    can of tomatoes

Between a day and three hours before you want to cook the meat, salt it heavily.

If the meat has been refrigerated, bring it to room temperature two hours before you start cooking it.

Heat the oven to 300 degrees. Heat the oil in a pot big enough to hold the meat plus all the liquid. Add the meat and brown it on at least two sides over medium heat. Let it get quite brown, not mushy tan. Remove it from the pot to a plate.

Add the vegetable scraps and herbs to the pot, stirring them against the browned bits. If you're using spices, add them, too. Once the vegetables have begun to soften, add the meat, stock, and wine-beer combination, and bring almost to a boil. Lower to a simmer, cover tightly, and let cook for 3 to 4 hours in the oven until the meat is tender enough to fall apart when it's pressed with the side of a wooden spoon. Check the pot more frequently if you're cooking different cuts of meat. Smaller pieces of meat will get fully cooked before larger or denser ones. When any is completely tender, remove it.

Strain the vegetabley liquid through a strainer. Discard the vegetables and taste the liquid. If it's too salty, add a little stock or water or some tomato paste. If you're eating the meat immediately, once it's cool enough to handle, cut it into slices or pull it into large pieces. Skim whatever fat you can off the braising liquid. Serve the meat with a little of its liquid on warm polenta, boiled vegetables, or beans.

If you have time, refrigerate the meat in its liquid overnight or for a few days. Fat will harden on its surface. Remove it and save it to cook vegetables in. Slice or tear the meat, reheat it in a little liquid, and serve as above.

This is endlessly variable. Try adding a handful of dark, oil-cured olives and a few slivers of lemon or orange peel. Add trimmings from peppers or tomatoes. Or add a touch of cinnamon and a cup of roughly chopped dried apricots or figs, and serve the meat with couscous. Or add dried porcini mushrooms, and serve it on pasta, or add dried chiles and cilantro and serve it on rice.

Slow-cooking cuts of meat are neglected when it's hot out. That makes them especially affordable in spring and summer. Slow-cooking them in light liquids like orange juice and beer or white wine, then eating them chilled, or boiling and slicing them and making sandwiches or tacos are good strategies for staying in afford-able meat when the weather seems stacked against you.

Probably my favorite thing to do with leftover slow-cooked meat tastes best when it's warm out. I boil the tiniest, freshest new pota-toes I can find and chop an assortment of dill, delicate chives, cher-vil, tarragon, summer savory, celery leaves, and parsley, then slice spring onions and soak them in white wine vinegar, adding a small spoonful of strong Dijon mustard once they taste sweet, then a long pour of olive oil.

While the potatoes are still warm, I halve them and mix them with the mustardy onions and herbs, crushing them a little. Then I roughly cube whatever meat I have, still cold, spread it onto a plate, spoon the dressed potatoes over it, and top it all with more roughly chopped fresh herbs. This is also good with a few cold, roasted, vinegared beets. A delicious addition is cubes of the braising liquid that, cold, will be the consistency of Jell-O.

Or I make tacos. It doesn't take very much other than warming leftover braised beef or pork or lamb or chicken in a small pot and shredding it. Serve the shredded meat alongside warm, soft tortillas, sliced jalapeños, cilantro, shredded cabbage, sliced radishes, sliced scallion, and wedges of lime. Or toast tortillas over a burner and layer them with cooked beans and braised meat and braising liquid in a deep pie dish and bake it. Serve with the same accompaniments and sour cream.

This is also good. It is based on the Provençal meat dish *miro-tons,* which is made with leftover slow-cooked beef, flour, onion, tomato, a lot of butter, and breadcrumbs. This version is brighter and more vegetal.

Summer vegetables and slow-cooked meat

~

olive oil
2 cups zucchini cut into ¾- to 1-inch pieces
½ small onion, finely chopped
1 stalk celery, finely chopped
2 cloves garlic, finely chopped
salt
1 tablespoon tomato paste
1 tablespoon chopped roasted peppers
½ cup white wine
1½ cups beef stock or braising liquid
2 cups boiled or braised meat, cut into irregular
    ¾- to 1-inch pieces
1 cup potatoes, cut into cubes and boiled
½ cup chopped fresh parsley
1 tablespoon chopped mixed fresh thyme and rosemary
¼ to ½ cup toasted breadcrumbs

Heat the oven to 425 degrees. In a large sauté pan, heat the olive oil, add the zucchini, and cook without browning. When it's started to soften, add the onion, celery, and garlic, salting well. Let it cook until softened. Add the tomato paste and roasted peppers and cook over medium heat until the vegetables have begun to melt together, 8 to 10 minutes. Add the wine and 1 cup beef stock and cook it at a low bubble. When most of the liquid has cooked off, add the meat, potatoes, and the rest of the beef stock. Mix in the herbs.

Butter a deep, heavy pie dish. Spread the mixture in the dish and cook, uncovered, in the middle of the oven for 30 to 40 minutes until it's all bubbling, there's barely any liquid left in the pan, and the peaks of the meat and vegetables have begun to brown. Scatter the bubbling mixture heavily with breadcrumbs and return it to the oven. Let it cook another 10 to 15 minutes until the breadcrumbs are quite crisp.

If everyone has eaten firsts and seconds and you've served all the meat you cooked, you will still have braising liquid. If it contains bits of meat, warm it in a pot, add a great handful of parsley or basil, then toss it with hot pasta as you would any pasta sauce.

If it doesn't contain meat, it will still make a gratifying soup. Cook a little garlic and onion until they're tender, cut potatoes and root vegetables into cubes and add them, a little spoonful of tomato paste, the braising liquid, and water. Cook until the vegetables are tender, add a drizzle of vinegar and a big handful of parsley and serve hot. A cup of cooked beans is a good addition, if you need this to stick to your bones even more tightly.

Or don't braise tough cuts of meat, but instead do what cooks from where Switzerland and Austria and Italy meet in the mountains do. Slice them thinly and pound them into big, flat cutlets to be dredged in flour and breadcrumbs and quickly fried. This is an exception to the principle that tough cuts need to be slow-cooked, because you speed everything up with elbow grease by pounding tenderness into them: as fine an oxymoron as ever there was.

Thinly cut slices off a shoulder or leg roast. Pound them evenly until the slices are just still opaque, about a quarter inch thick. I do this with a dull-toothed meat hammer if I can find one. If not, I use the base of an empty wine bottle.

Season the cutlets with salt. Shake them quickly in flour, dunk them in beaten egg, then dredge them in fresh breadcrumbs. Lay them on wax paper. Heat two inches of olive oil in a sauté or cast-iron pan. Fry the cutlets in batches. These will stay crisp in a 200-degree oven for half an hour. Serve with tartar sauce (page 139), or just wedges of lemon.

Nearly half of every cow and a third of every pig and a quarter of every lamb must be ground. This is not because the meat is bad, but because a butcher's knife can't win every battle with bone. Ground meat is as good as the rest of the meat on the animal it came from, and probably the most affordable.

If you're buying humanely raised meat, ground meat may cost as much as steaks and chops from animals raised more dubiously. So you must stretch it over more meals, just as you do any other cuts.

One of the best ways to do that is to make Bolognese sauce. Sauce distributes goodness. It also gives you an opportunity to add butter, or luxurious dried mushrooms, or cream, or anything else you want to add to make your investment pay off.

This sauce has all of those, which makes it opulent without being expensive. It is the best thing I can think of to make with ground meat. It is delicious on pasta or polenta.

This is a version of a recipe adapted by Amanda Hesser from one by Heidi da Emploi.

White Bolognese

~

¼ cup finely chopped onion
⅛ cup finely chopped carrot
1 stalk celery, finely chopped
olive oil
salt
1 pound Italian pork sausage, removed from its casings,
   or ground pork plus 1 teaspoon chile flakes and
   3 leaves fresh sage, finely sliced
1 pound ground beef
1½ cups white wine
2 cups beef or chicken stock
1½ ounces dried porcini mushrooms
   rehydrated in 3 cups warm water
⅓ cup heavy cream
1 pound rigatoni or another short noodle or 1 cup polenta
¾ cup freshly grated Parmesan cheese

Cook the onion, carrot, and celery in olive oil until tender, salting them as soon as you add them to the pan. Add the sausage and beef, break it up, and brown it well. Add the wine and simmer until the pan is almost dry. Add the stock and simmer, uncovered, until the stock is nearly gone, stirring every now and again. Chop the rehydrated porcini into small pieces and strain the liquid through a coffee filter. Add the

porcini and strained mushroom broth to the sauce to cover the meat half-
way. Simmer until the sauce is loose but not soupy, 10 to 15 minutes.
Taste and adjust salt. It should be highly seasoned. Fold the cream in.
Remove from the heat.

   Bring a pot of water to a boil and cook pasta or polenta. Heat sauce
before mixing with the pasta or ladling over bowls of warm polenta.
Grate each bowl with Parmesan.

Or follow a recipe for meat loaf, but think of it as a terrine. I discovered this idea in an atrociously named book called *Pâtés and Other
Marvelous Meat Loaves*. The point of the book seemed to be that if
you cut it small enough, you could put any good ingredient into the
deep ceramic crock called a terrine, poach it in the oven in a bath of
water, as you would cook pâté or a traditional terrine, slice it into
thick pieces, and eat it with piquant mustard.

   Any meat loaf you make will be more tender if you cook it in a
pan of water instead of directly in the oven. Add more fresh herbs
than your recipe calls for, or add some sautéed mushrooms. Serve it
elegantly with a dab of mustard and a salad.

I taught classes in butchery one spring, instructing students in how
to take apart chickens and remove bones from legs of lamb. At the
end of each class, because nearly everyone rejected my suggestion
that bones go home with her, I took them home myself.

   They were the handiwork of new butchers, so were particularly
well endowed, but I didn't have to buy meat once that spring. I
dropped the bones in water with onion, fennel tops, and herbs,
removed bits of meat as soon as they were tender, and served fresh
chicken or spring lamb soup.

   If you can't afford meat, ask a farmer or butchers' counter for
meaty bones. Most have them and will either give them to you for
free or sell them cheaply. With a kitchen inventory more bone than
flesh you will eat finely.

If you need a meal from your bones immediately, put as many as you have into a pot just big enough to hold them. If you can wait, collect bones in your freezer until you have enough to fill your biggest pot tightly. Meat stock freezes well, so there's no reason not to make a big batch at once.

Put about two cups of a combination of aromatic vegetable scraps in a big pot. I usually use tips or ends of carrots, an onion half, onion peels, tough tops of fennel, outer stalks of celery, and parsley stems. Add a small handful of black peppercorns, bones, and water to just cover by two inches. I don't add salt. If anything else you're cooking ends up salty, it's good to know that your stock can save it.

Let the water come to a boil, then lower it to a bare simmer. Skim off the gray foam that gathers on its surface with a slotted spoon. You will need to do this periodically as it cooks, as often as the stock seems to want it. After three hours, taste a bite of vegetable, and taste a spoonful of stock by scooping a little into a spoon and sprinkling in a few grains of salt. The vegetable should be tasteless, having given all of itself to the stock, and the stock taste like light broth. Let it cook until the pot's contents match those descriptions.

Remove bones with tongs or a spoon, then pour the stock through a fine-mesh strainer into a container and refrigerate it. Any meat that's still clinging to the bones won't taste like much, but in a pinch can be picked off, mixed with mayonnaise, onions, and chopped pickles, and spread on toast.

Let the stock sit in the refrigerator overnight to give its fat time to rise to the top. The following day, scoop the fat off with a spoon. Save it in a jar. Use it as you would butter or olive oil.

Once you have stock, you will have already half cooked a number of meals. Sauté a little onion and risotto rice in butter and use your stock to make risotto. Cook a handful of dried noodles in it for noodle soup. Warm and add some cooked beans and greens to simmering stock, and poach an egg in it. Or toast stale bread, rub it with garlic, put it in a bowl, and top it with hot broth. You may not get thirty-two servings of food from your pot of bones and scraps but you will get into the high single digits.

If you can afford to buy meat, buy it on the bone. It will be less expensive with the bone than without it. This is senseless and a great boon if you're a stock maker. Whenever you can get a second ingredient still attached to your first, stop whoever is trying to remove it and ask him to hand it over.

Herodotus called fire a hungry creature that had to be fed, and when it had eaten its fill, died along with whatever it had eaten. This has always made me think of roasting meat.

Jean Anthelme Brillat-Savarin recounts a story in *The Physiology of Taste* in which he and his companions get to an inn whose kitchen has no provisions for their dinner. He spies a roast cooking on a spit in the dining room and inquires as to the identity of its owner. The inn's cook reports that it belongs to another party, sitting fatly a few tables over. Brillat-Savarin watches the roast turn, his eyes catch on its glistening juices, dripping onto the coals underneath it. He summons the cook again and asks about the fats and juices of the roast. The cook immediately sees the genius of the loophole.

The roast continues to cook sumptuously, browning slowly in the fire, its herbed and fatty juices becoming, once they escape the meat and skin, property of the inn in whose fireplace it cooks, and newly acquired by the hungry party smart enough to know their value. M. Savarin ends his story sharing eggs softly scrambled in the glorious, fatty meat juices with his companions and gloating about having gotten the best of the meat.

When we remove pots from the equation, a thoughtlessness sets into our cooking. We throw meat directly onto fire, and let the ferocious creature devour half our dinner. This is expensive and wasteful. The old gastronomist knew what we all must. There are ways to be resourceful in all kinds of meat cooking, and the better meal goes to him or her who finds the loophole.

Roasting is a good way to cook meat that doesn't have enough finely woven fat amid its fibers to cook for a long time. Roasting involves high heat and shorter cooking. Chickens are good roasted. I baste mine with butter the whole time they roast and they're delectable.

But when it comes to bigger animals, I am less interested in predictable racks and ribs than I am in roasts made from the less commonly eaten muscles in front of or behind them. My favorite cut of meat to roast is pork belly. The best recipe I've read for roasting pork belly is from *The River Cottage Meat Book.* It instructs that you get a big piece, three to five pounds, skin on. You then score it with a sharp knife, make a dark green paste of chopped thyme and sage and garlic, rub it vigorously into the slits in the skin, over the skin, and into the meat itself, then roast the slab of belly, skin side up, on a pan with sides high enough to catch its copious and quick-running fat. The herbs and garlic seep into the meat; the belly tenderizes as it cooks.

This is a fantastic thing. It is worth cooking, and far more worth sitting down to—big fork and knife in hand, iconic napkin round neck, damp forehead, and anticipatory drool—than almost any other piece of meat, fowl, fish, friend, or foe that comes to mind.

If you want a slab of pork belly before it is smoked and sliced into bacon, you will need to ask a farmer directly. Most will have a piece, or a pig ready to give it to you.

Another good, unpopular roast is a cut of pork leg, also called ham. Hams do not grow on their respective porcine bodies seasoned and smoked. Because of how rarely we buy them fresh, they're usually for sale at a good price. If you can find one on its bone, buy it and cook it that way. If yours comes boneless, inquire about the bone, which is a healthy big one, and makes good stock.

Because they are dense with muscle and not with fat, pork legs need to be put in a briny bath overnight. Osmosis draws water out of the meat, fills it with salt, and then sends the salty water back in, leaving the meat well seasoned and moistened throughout.

Meat brine

~

¼ cup salt
½ tablespoon sugar
water
2 bay leaves
2 whole dried chiles
1 teaspoon juniper berries
4 sprigs thyme
1 teaspoon peppercorns

Combine the salt and sugar over low heat with ¼ cup water. As soon as the salt and sugar have dissolved, take it off the heat. In the container in which you're going to brine the pork leg roast, combine everything with a few ice cubes. Mix it all well. Once it is cool, add the meat and water to cover.

Brine, before meat is added, stays good forever.

Pork roast

~

Brine a three-pound pork leg roast overnight in the refrigerator. Cover the meat with a plate that fits inside the container and weigh it down so that it doesn't float.

Heat the oven to 375 degrees. Remove the pork from the brine and pat it dry. Heat a cast-iron pan or a heavy-bottomed pot over medium heat and add 1 tablespoon olive oil. Brown each side of the meat over medium-high heat. Let each side turn caramel brown. This will take 10 to 15 minutes.

Once the pork is browned, put the pan or pot directly in the oven. Cook the meat, untouched, until it's medium-rare. In an oven, this will take about 20 minutes per pound. Pork will need an internal temperature of 165 degrees when you pull it out of the oven, and will go on cooking once you remove it. Err on the side of undercooking the meat. Check it with a meat thermometer at its thickest part until you get good at telling doneness by pressing on the meat.

Remove the meat from the pan and let it sit on a cutting board. It needs to rest for at least 20 minutes. Sliced earlier, the outside of the pork may taste salty; if there is still a bone in the cut, the meat along it will still be bloody.

Slice the meat thinly with a sharp knife. If you can avoid it, leave the serrated knife for bread and use the sharpest straight blade you have.

Serve with a big green salad.

I will happily sit by a great open fire smelling roasting meat and feeling hedonistic and alive. When it comes time for dinner, though, I'm just as glad to leave the meat and sit back humming, warming my toes in the fire's heat, and sop up the drippings from another hunter's roast. However you feel, wherever you are, do catch the drippings and eat them.

Drippings can be used as gravy for any meat that made them. Pour off any fat that's collected and save it for cooking. Warm drippings drizzled onto lettuce are delicious. Mix rice with herbs and toasted nuts, then mix drippings into that. Or eat the drippings on corn bread or biscuits. Or use them instead of bouillon cubes.

A confit of meat is cooked and stored in its fat. It's a simple method of preserving and a good way of ensuring you have access to well-raised meat. Once you cook and store meat in fat, it stays good for a few months in the refrigerator.

One of the first recipes I ever read for confit was in a cookbook by Judy Rodgers, who began making it after time spent in a region of France she calls "confit country." I like the idea of confit country, where the life of anything perishable is extended by good, lovingly applied fat. How lovely a place confit country must be.

I usually make confit of chicken thighs. For eight chicken thighs, pound together two dried bay leaves and a half teaspoon whole peppercorns in a mortar with a pestle and mix in a lot of salt. Season the meat well with the mixture. Let it sit, salted and lightly covered with wax paper, in the refrigerator overnight.

Heat an oven to 225 degrees. In an oven-safe casserole with a lid, heat enough olive oil to cover the thighs until it is just warm to the touch. Add the meat and submerge it. It can be in two layers, but must be completely covered in oil.

Carefully put the pot into the oven, and let the meat cook, covered, for three to four hours. Check for doneness by inserting a knife near a bone. The meat should be about to fall off.

Remove the pot and carefully remove each piece of meat with a slotted spoon. Let the olive oil cool. Once the meat is cool to the touch, fit it fairly closely into glass jars. Pour the cooled oil over the meat, making sure everything is completely covered, then cover and close. Strain and save any excess oil for the next time you make confit.

To serve confit, bring it up to room temperature in its fat. Remove whatever you plan to serve. Add the pieces of confit to a cold pan. A nice thing about anything having been stored in fat is that it is perfectly prepared to get crisp brown surfaces. Once the meat has browned, put the pan in the oven until the meat is warm throughout. I like eating this best with salad.

You can follow the same instructions to make confit from pork shoulder, cut into small pieces.

As to forays into the murky, hidden, tender world beneath what we consider meat, start small. The hearts and livers of chickens and kidneys and hearts of lambs are simple to cook and delicious.

These parts are called "offal," a terrible name, reminding the unconverted that organs are cast-offs and underlining suspicions that they might taste bad. They are also called the "fifth quarter." The other four quarters are two fore, two rear. This one is kept quite private, hidden inside.

If you buy them whole, chickens often come with their livers still in them, though detached. The livers can be salted, lightly seared in butter, then sliced and eaten on buttered toast, as tentatively and inquisitively as you want.

I buy chicken livers by the pound from whoever sells me my chickens and make them into pâté. It's an inexpensive way to get something quite luxurious into my house, and because I eat it in place of the meat of the animals themselves, it is not, as people always act as though it is, a great indulgence.

Chicken liver pâté

~

> 1 pound chicken livers
> salt and freshly ground black pepper
> 12 tablespoons (1½ sticks) butter
> 2 tablespoons white wine, sherry, bourbon,
>   Scotch, Cognac, or brandy
> 1 shallot, finely chopped
> ½ leek, finely sliced
> ½ clove garlic, finely chopped
> 2 tablespoons water
> a tiny, tiny pinch of ground cloves
> half that amount ground cinnamon
> ⅛ bay leaf, finely crumbled
> ¼ cup well-picked fresh thyme leaves, chopped

Clean any connective membranes from the livers and season them with salt and pepper. Melt 1 tablespoon butter in a nonstick frying pan. When the pan is hot enough to sizzle, add some of the livers. Leave a bit of space around each liver. Let each liver get browned on one side. Flip and brown them on the other side.

Take the livers out of the pan and put them on a plate. Add 1 tablespoon wine or liquor to the pan and scrape it with a wooden spoon. Pour the liquid over the livers you've cooked. Wipe the pan out with a paper towel. Repeat with the rest of the livers without adding the remaining wine or spirits.

Once all the livers are cooked and removed, add the shallot, leek, and garlic to the pan along with the rest of the liquor and 2 tablespoons water. Cook over medium heat until the vegetables are completely tender.

When they are, combine them, the dried spices, fresh thyme, the livers, and their liquid to the blender. Add 1 stick butter, cut into pieces.

Blend. Taste. If it's not acting funny, separating, or seeming milk-shaky—add more butter by the tablespoon, or leave as is. Add more salt as needed. Pour into a bowl and let cool at least a half hour.

This should be made at least a half hour in advance. Right after having been blended, it will be almost liquidy, but will cool and tighten to a smooth, spreadable consistency after a little time refrigerated. Serve it spread on little toasts, with a few leaves of fresh thyme on top. Cover the remainder with melted butter to store for up to 2 weeks.

The best small inner parts I've ever had were ones I was instructed to make by Fergus Henderson, the chef of St. John. They were for a special meal he was cooking in New York for which I happened to be in the kitchen. He wanted lamb hearts marinated with big slices of shallot, balsamic vinegar, red wine vinegar, and salt. I did that, then I sliced each one thickly, cooked it in a very hot pan, and laid the slices on a plate. They were served with leaves of lettuce that you were supposed to pick up, fill with a few pieces of bright, vinegary meat, and eat like a taco. They were delicious.

In the end, we can only guess at unknowable truths about the morality of domestication. We love tenderly and well, when we remember to. We must treat what we love kindly. We must make the most of it. The more we do, the closer we come to the old terms of meat eating, a noble exchange of good life for good life.

Fifteen

How to Fry the Littlest Fish

And really, fish look bigger than they are
before they're caught—
When the pole is bent into a bow and the slender line is taut.
—Eugene Field, "Our Biggest Fish"

There are plenty of fish in the sea as good at sharpening our minds and oiling our bones as tuna and salmon. They are not big fish, but small fish and shellfish and fish whose silvery little bodies are unfamiliar but delicious, or fish whose hard shells intimidate, but keep safe the sweetest flesh. There are plenty of freckly mackerel, meaty little sardines, delicately saline squid, and flinty-shelled clams and oysters. In New York, there are oily-fleshed blue-fish; in California, rock cod and fierce Dungeness crabs; in cold lakes and brooks and mountain farms, there are trout. Most of these fish are more affordable than environmentally troubling tuna and salmon, which makes buying them doubly responsible.

We should approach this wide variety of smaller fish with the inclusiveness of cultures that rely on fish as a staple. Their diets are not made up of one kind of fish, cooked one way, but all the fish the deeps can offer, cooked in all different ways.

On days when mackerel is the freshest, mackerel fillets will be on the table, tasting as clean and oceanic as the water they were pulled from. If bony, rocky fish are in the net, they will be simmered whole in tomato and olive oil and enjoyed because they were easy to catch and easy to cook. If clams were dug it will be clams. If eels, thick, terrifying eels it will be.

We should also cook our fish more inclusively. We act as though fish is singularly resistant to resourceful cooking. This is not because it is, but because it comes from a strange dark world, where things fall up not down and it is hard to see.

Where fish is common, it is treated like the rough-and-tumble wild animal it is, the same peasant tricks applied to it as are applied to loaves of bread. Fish is bought in its entirety. Fish that isn't freshest is kept, even though there are more like it in surrounding waters. It is salted so that it can be poached in milk, or turned into a stew with strong flavors, like chile and lime, and an amount of fish that would have fed two if fresh, or none if discarded, will feed four, and well. When there is no more fresh mackerel, there will be a few jars of it stored in olive oil, where it will stay good for months. Fillets of big fish will be smoked or cured, so that the hard work that went into catching them won't be used up in a single dinner, and another big fish simply down for the count.

Buying fish whole, on the bone, with head and tail, is a good practice. It means fish stock, and there may be nothing more elegant or subtle than a minimally made one. You can also tell the most about fish's freshness if you can press its skin, which should bounce back, and look in its eye, which should be glossy.

There is, too, something noble about serving a whole, antique-looking, picturesque fish, evoking a long tradition of handing over a fishing rod instead of a fish itself, echoing the miracle of multiplying loaves and fishes.

When you buy whole fish, ask for it to be scaled and gutted. It will arrive in your basket with its skin still on, but its hard, silvery scales removed. If it does not come scaled and gutted, take a dull knife and scrape it down the length of the fish in the direction opposite the shingling of the scales. This is a messy but fast ordeal. To remove a fish's guts is surprisingly ungalling. They're rather petite, and the only hard part is making the first cut into the fish's belly. Cut into it sharply, make a long slit, and remove everything inside. Rinse the fish and dry it.

To roast fish whole, heat an oven to 400 degrees. Make sure the fish skin is very dry, and then salt it well. Sprinkle salt inside it, a little less well, and fill the rest of the cavity with thinly sliced lemon, thyme, and rosemary. If you have none of those, count on salt and fish to collaborate, which they have done successfully until now.

Put the fish in a roasting pan, however it fits. Drizzle olive oil onto the fish skin.

Fish is best checked for doneness with your finger. It takes about fifteen minutes per inch of thickness for fish to roast. Fish takes longer to cook when it is on the bone, which makes cooking a whole one more forgiving than cooking fillets. Choose a sacrificial spot at the thickest part of the fish and poke into it as often as you need to to feel that its cooking is still under your control. It will be done when it is opaque and it flakes. If whole fish—or any fish—show signs of having been repeatedly poked at, cover your tracks with parsley.

Serve a whole fish as you would a roast chicken: gleaming and ready, on its own platter, with some acknowledgment of its silvery skin, crisp tail, single, reminding, glassy eye. Leave the head on, so that you get a chance to regard the fish as she regards you, and there's a proper ceremony to the exchange.

Serving a fish whole will also give you the rare chance to see a tiny, quirky dividing line between people who thrill at fish bones and those who shudder at them. I have rarely seen such glee in an eater's eye as when my mother is allowed to pick away at the flesh left on a fish's delicate, gelatinous bones. I only see fish skeletons as a necessary end for getting to fish soup, but to watch her seize on them with such relish gives me great pleasure.

Remove its fillets. The first may come off in a few pieces, but then you can remove the backbone, tail to head, and be left with a complete second fillet. Discard the herbs in its middle, squeeze each fillet with lemon, and drizzle it with olive oil.

Or buy fish that are small enough to oil well and stick, in their

shimmering entirety, on a hot grill. Little sardines and small mackerel, which are some of the best fish to buy anyway, just need to be
cooked whole, hot, and fast. They can be served a few per person.
They are as easy to cook as hot dogs and should be cooked the same
way: allowed to char, flipped over once, then moved onto waiting
plates.

Fish stock is treated as though it's much more careful a thing than it
needs to be. Fish stock is easy to make and free. Keep fish bones frozen until you've got a nice cache of them. Two or three pounds will
yield four cups of fish stock, which is enough to reasonably make
a meal for four people. You don't need to weigh the bones for this,
but just keep an eye out for enough to fill your boiling pot.

The best bones for making stock come from bony white fish. So
few people make stock these days that you can usually get bones
just by asking from a farmers' market stand or fish store. To use the
bones from a fish you buy whole, either remove the fillets before
cooking it, and panfry the fillets instead of roasting the whole fish,
or use the bones from a fish you've cooked. It will be a much more
subtly flavored stock, and there are disagreements about whether
it's worth doing. I think it is, because even a very light stock reminds
you to go on cooking.

Melt two tablespoons of butter in the bottom of a big pot, add a
chopped onion or leek and a half cup of chopped fennel or fennel
scraps. Break up your fish skeletons so that they fit into the pot.
Fish heads should be included, their dark, shingled gills first pulled
out through their cheeks. Salmon, mackerel, bluefish, and sardines
make stock that is too oily. Their skeletons should be picked at and
then discarded.

Add the skeletons and a quarter cup of dry white wine. Let the
wine and vegetables cook for five minutes, then add water to cover
it all by three inches. Add parsley stems, a bay leaf, a judicious pinch
of whole peppercorns, an even more judicious one of fennel seeds
and coriander seeds, and two whole canned tomatoes. Bring the pot

to a boil, then lower it to a simmer. Skim whatever murk rises to the top of the pot. Let it all cook for thirty minutes, or longer if it doesn't taste flavorful yet.

Strain the stock through a fine-mesh sieve. I smash at everything as I strain it, which extracts more flavor, unless I have special plans that require a clear fish stock.

Make stock from shrimp, crab, or lobster shells the same way, but smash all of those twice, first before you put them in the pot, and second while you are straining their stock.

Fish stock is the basis for the best fish soups. Fish soups are wonderful: fish does well in liquid, even after it has stopped swimming. While the oceans may not be thick with all fish, the world is thick with excellent fish soup recipes. If you make the recipe for risotto on page 121, or the recipe for bread soup on pages 86–87, using fish stock instead of meat stock or any other liquid, you will get a lovely fish risotto, or a lovely fish bread soup. Like all stock, fish stock can be frozen.

A fresh fillet of fish can be a wonderful thing to eat. Cook fillets on a hot grill or in a hot pan and serve them with a bowl of thick, garlicky parsley oil, or a bowl of glossy yellow aioli. Don't bother the fillets themselves with crusts of breadcrumbs or horseradish or mustard, which overwhelm the delicate flavor of fish, never mind making it hard to check for doneness by poking. You can focus, then, on learning how to season fish properly, and listen clearly to the sound of it sizzle in the pan.

Salting fish is the process by which we used to preserve all fish, and still preserve some. If you buy a fillet and don't cook it on the day you intend to, shower it with kosher salt so that it is well covered but not caked and put it in a drainer pan or colander over another pan in the refrigerator. Cover it lightly with plastic wrap.

Your salting won't preserve the fish long term, but draw liquid out, which both keeps it good and leaves it firm enough to be made into one of my favorite, and possibly the thriftiest of all fish preparations, brandade.

I served a traditional French brandade, a purée of poached salt cod, potato, and garlic, for years because it was inexpensive, sounded elegant, and could be made ahead. Then I learned about the over-fishing of Atlantic cod, which was a great disappointment, but left me a clear plan for any other white fish I didn't cook immediately.

Brandade de morue

~

> 1 pound salted white fish, such as Alaskan or California
>   halibut, croaker, pollock, rockfish, or trout
> kosher salt
> 1 quart milk
> 1 bay leaf
> 2 Idaho or other big baking potatoes, peeled and cut into large
>   cubes, or any other potatoes to equal the same volume:
>   5 new potatoes, 3 or 4 Yukon Golds
> 2 cloves garlic, ground to a paste with salt
> 1¼ cups olive oil
> freshly cracked black pepper

Remove the fish from the salt, brush off the excess, and place in a small pot with the milk and bay leaf. Cook at just below a simmer for 5 to 10 minutes until flaky, then remove and mash by hand or in a food processor, making sure to remove the bay leaf and any bones and/or skin. Reserve the milk.

Boil the potatoes until they're chalky and then press them through a potato ricer or a food mill, or mash them with a handheld masher. Whip the garlic and olive oil (which will seem like way too much) into the fish mash and then combine with the potatoes. Taste for salt and add pepper. Add a little milk if it needs loosening to your taste. Smooth into a shallow, oven-safe container, like a small glass roasting pan.

Before serving, brown under the broiler. Save the reserved milk if you're going to make another batch in the next week or so.

Once you've salted fish overnight, you can also turn it into fish confit. It will keep for months, and instead of losing what you'd hoped would be yesterday's meal, you'll have prepared part of tomorrow's.

Brush excess salt off your fish. Cut thick pieces into two-inch cubes and thin fillets into halves. In a small, deep pot, heat as much olive oil as it will take to cover the fish completely. Add two dried chiles, a bay leaf, a pinch of whole peppercorns, a whole clove of garlic, a few slices of lemon peel or orange peel, a small pinch of fennel seeds, and a few parsley stems and whole stalks of thyme.

Once the oil is just warm, place the fish into the pot. Check it for doneness after a few minutes by retrieving a piece with a slotted spoon. The fish will be done when it just flakes.

Let the fish cool in the oil off the heat, then store it in its poaching oil in glass jars in the refrigerator. Fish confit is delicious tossed with pasta, or eaten as smoked fish often is, with a few pert capers over warm boiled potatoes, or on a bagel, or in a sandwich instead of canned tuna.

Or turn aging fish into curry. This is one that I invented to temper the strong flavors in bluefish that had not only edged past its prime, but catapulted past it after I'd gone fishing and brought home thirty pounds. A freezer is only so big, regardless of how small and safely caught the fish in it. Bluefish ripens rather vehemently. If this worked with bluefish, it will work with any fish.

Very spicy curry for blue (or graying) fish

~

1½ pounds fish, strong-flavored by design or by miscalculation
juice of 1 lemon or lime
salt
2 tablespoons peanut or olive oil
6 shallots, or the white parts of 2 leeks, sliced into thin rounds
1-inch piece ginger, finely chopped
1 stalk lemongrass, finely chopped

2 tablespoons combination chopped roasted peppers and
    very spicy fresh chiles

½ teaspoon Thai or Vietnamese fish sauce

2 teaspoons grated lime zest

2 whole canned tomatoes, chopped, or 1 big fresh tomato, skin
    left on, chopped, or as many chopped medium-sized fresh
    tomatoes as it takes to get the same amount

1 cup fish stock if you have it, or some combination of beer and
    water, or vegetable stock (the tomato liquid from the can of
    tomatoes is a good stand-in)

½ can coconut milk

1 cup chopped cilantro, mint, or basil, or a mixture of all three, or
    the tops of scallions, sliced on a diagonal as finely as possible

Remove skin, if any, from the fish. Cut it into pieces about 1 to 2 inches around. Squeeze lemon or lime juice over them, sprinkle them with salt, mix it through, and let it sit until the rest of the stew is done.

    Heat a deep sauté pan or wide pot and add the oil. Add the shallots, ginger, and lemongrass. As soon as they have started to soften, add the peppers, chiles, salt, and fish sauce. Once it's all soft, but not completely tender, add the lime zest and chopped tomato. Let it cook over low heat until the tomato has collapsed. Add the fish stock, or your replacement, and coconut milk. Let it simmer for 5 minutes then add the fish, lifting it off the plate instead of tipping the plate in. Cook at a bare simmer for 4 to 5 minutes until the fish is cooked through. Turn off the heat, add the herbs, and serve it over hot white rice.

If you want to buy a big piece of a big fish, make it last. If you are going to have been plundered for, remove your hat, bow your head, and relish your plunder slowly.

    Do what salmon-loving Swedes do. Salt and pepper a big piece of salmon, blanket it with whole sprigs of dill, douse it in the strong caraway-flavored liquor called aquavit, and press it under weights for four days in the refrigerator until it is salty and tasting of dill. It will remain perfectly preserved for two weeks in the refrigerator, and each day you can eat thin slices of it on hard brown crackers, spread with butter and topped with sweet onion.

I get too much satisfaction from such things, but if you take salmon skin off its fillet before cooking, you double the number of meals you get from it. Delicately fry the skin on its own, until crisp and caramel brown, in a little olive oil in a cast-iron pan, then drain and salt it while still warm, and eat it cracked into little pieces.

To take Mark Twain's aphorism about dogfighting for a dunk: it is not the size of the fish in the fight, but the size of the fight in the fish.

Clams and mussels, with their hard little shells and tiny bodies, are among the most naturally giving of sea creatures. They carry tiny wells of seawater with them wherever they go. They might be so kind because, as Curtis Badger put it in *Clams: How to Find, Catch, and Cook Them,* clams have two goals in life—to eat and have sex. That they are dedicated wholly to those aspirations is, I imagine, why we describe happiness as clamlike.

When their shells pop open, clams and mussels release the salty soup they've brought with them. As long as you scrub them well before cooking them, you only need to get the soup started by putting a little cold butter and a splash of wine or beer at the bottom of a pot big enough to hold the mollusks. Once the pot is covered, and a fire lit under it, the little mollusks will gasp and open, and you will be left with two elements of a meal: rich broth and the things themselves, sweetly waiting to be plucked from their shells.

Clams, still in their elegantly ringed shells, can be served on their own with a little melted butter on the side for dipping, or a little garlicky parsley oil. As with any food that involves manual labor on the part of its eater, clams served in their shells provide both the small entertainment of touching what is on your plate and get messy hands, and time to get full, as you go to the trouble of removing each one.

If you want to make sure to get more than one meal out of your pot of clams, strain the broth left at its bottom before serving and set it aside to turn into soup tomorrow.

You can make a simple one with only the impression of clam left in the broth. Cook a little onion or leek in butter until tender, and warm the broth you set aside with enough chicken stock or water to make it into a proper broth. Add a few cooked beans and a big squeeze of lemon and serve it over a hot grilled crouton, topping it with parsley and garlicky mayonnaise.

Or steam the clams, set them aside, and make a big bowl of any long pasta, then warm a little of the clam broth with a little wine and a little butter, add a splash of pasta water and toss it through the pasta. Serve each bowl of pasta topped with a few whole clams, still in their shell, for the fun of removing them. This means fewer clams per person, and a still happy, clammy meal.

You will have cooked clams left for tomorrow to turn into chowder: cook a little bacon and leeks in the bottom of a soup pot and add clam broth, water, and heavy cream. Boil a few cubes of potato and add them to the broth along with the remaining clams. Serve the soup topped with oyster crackers, or butter-fried croutons, or chopped parsley floating about the pools of butter.

If you are feeling as magnanimous as a sated clam, serve clams and their broth in the same meal, with their broth in the bottom of the bowls the clams are in. Or serve the broth warm in little mugs alongside the clams to drink, like rich consommé or bouillon.

"Fish she is very small" is the motto of a Canadian sardine canning company. Sardines are some of the ocean's most prolific fish. The strangest, saddest thing about them is that we feed most of the ones we catch to the big fish we raise in farms instead of putting them on our grills or in our pans.

Thankfully, many are still put in cans, which are as little as can be. Fish are canned when they are very fresh and preserved well. You can keep cans around without worrying about salting or poaching or turning anything into curry. They are as delicious and healthy for you as any fish plucked directly from the cold blue.

This is better with canned sardines than fresh ones.

Pasta with sardines

~

2 tablespoons olive oil	salt
½ onion, sliced	1 bunch parsley, leaves picked
1 clove garlic, sliced	and roughly chopped
1 can good olive-oil-packed sardines	1 cup toasted breadcrumbs
1 pound spaghetti	optional: dried chile flakes

Heat the olive oil in a deep pan big enough to hold the pasta once it's cooked. Once the oil is warm, add the onion and garlic and cook until it's soft but not completely tender, 5 to 10 minutes. Add the sardines and their olive oil and let them fry in the pan, breaking them up with your spoon. Turn the heat off once the sardines have broken down.

Cook the pasta in well-salted water. While the pasta is cooking, chop the parsley leaves. Remove a glass of pasta water from the pasta pot just before you remove the pasta.

When the pasta is almost done, turn the heat on under the pan of sardines. Remove the pasta from its pot with tongs and drop it directly into the pan. Add ¼ cup pasta water and mix the sardines and the onions through the pasta. Add more water by the splash if it all seems dry and rigid. When the noodles and sauce seem well combined, add half the breadcrumbs and parsley and mix them through.

Serve the pasta in a big bowl, topped with the remaining breadcrumbs and parsley. A few shakes of dried chile are good here, too.

In his poem about the sweet complexities of conquests unwon, the poet Eugene Field was being metaphorical. I, however, am not.

I would not have it otherwise; 'tis better there should be
Much bigger fish than I have caught a-swimming in the sea.

Sixteen

How to Snatch Victory from
the Jaws of Defeat

A thing that has failed can, if you change its place,
be a thing that has come off.
— Robert Bresson, *Notes on the Cinematographer*

T he best lens through which to view mistakes in the kitchen
belongs to the French filmmaker Robert Bresson. It's a good
lens through which to view most situations, but particularly apt in
cooking, which is half perspective: if you change how you look at
it, what seems like a failure may be a success. (I am not the first
to apply Bresson's thoughts on filmmaking to cooking. The writer
Chip Brantley considers the director his culinary guru.)

You must sharpen strategies for turning failures into successes. It
is as essential to cooking as unraveling the small mysteries of heating a pan or boiling an egg. It is inevitable that at some time, something will go wrong, and when it does, there will be something you
can do to make it right.

You must first allow the possibility that something that happens unintentionally is not necessarily bad. Take burned vegetables. There are the most perfectly oily, charred vegetables in
Greek, Turkish, Middle Eastern, and Chinese cuisines, where

peppers and eggplants and string beans are cooked until black and wrinkled.

I like asparagus charred on the grill until it is beginning to pucker; cooking greens are wonderful when allowed to get crisp and burned in places. The same is true of roasted fish and of toast, both of which I find most delicious with bits of crisp blackening on their edges. I love an Italian dish of soft, occasionally blackened Roma beans, which are cooked in hot oil, covered, allowed to get slightly charred, and called "long cooked." There is no such thing as a burned onion.

I've read advice to bring any food that has burned outside to taste because it's easiest to be objective in fresh air, away from the smell and memory of smoke. Unless the room is filled with a billowing black cloud, you can stay inside. But let the metaphorical smoke clear before you decide you need to do any more than a slight reconsideration.

If you do, turn to a category of Bengali dishes called *charchari,* or "char-flavored." It consists of vegetables cooked in hot iron pots and left over very high heat to burn at the end of their cooking and acquire the taste of fire.

If you have time to boil rice, turn any vegetable you've charred into a *charchari*. In a small frying pan, cook a little finely diced onion and a teaspoon of Indian spices—cumin, coriander, and chile—in butter. When the onion is softened and heavily spiced, add the onion spice mixture to your vegetables. Serve on rice.

Or quickly rub the worst of the char off your vegetables and turn them into the Middle Eastern salad *baba ghanoush,* traditionally made with charred eggplant but also good with charred zucchini or tomato.

N.B. Recipes here and in the appendix of fixes at the end of the book call for a certain quantity of ingredients like "burned vegetables" or "salty rice." Make any recipe with your quantity of the offending ingredient, adjusting the rest of the ingredients accordingly.

Baba ghanoush

~

2 cups burned eggplant, zucchini, or tomatoes
½ clove garlic, pounded to paste
a few drops lemon juice
1 tablespoon olive oil
1½ tablespoons mayonnaise
optional: fresh parsley or mint leaves, chopped

Cut or wipe as much of the burn off your vegetables as you can, discarding anything that tastes charcoaly. Put all ingredients, except the chopped herbs, in a food processor or blender and blend until creamy and smooth. This is delicious at room temperature, served with warm pita or toast. It is especially good topped with chopped parsley or mint.

Or use any charred, spicy, sour, or oily vegetable as a condiment. Decide it is supposed to be unapologetically *intense,* and eat it in dabs on rice. Or substitute it for mustard or salsa on tacos and sandwiches. Save overdressed salad for the same.

The only vegetable that's categorically unpleasant burned is garlic. If garlic burns it needs to be discarded. Slice more garlic, use fresh oil, and make sure it is just warm. Add garlic, lightly salt it immediately, and cook it heaped in one corner of a pan. The salt and piling up will draw an infinitesimal amount of water out of the garlic so it softly steams as it cooks.

A great benefit of boiling vegetables is that if they get overcooked, they only end up soft, not burned. If you've forgotten a vegetable in a pot of water on the stove, scoop it out and drain it in a colander or a fine-mesh sieve. Its drying out will help, and some of its waterlogged-ness will fade. After shaking it dry, spread it out on a baking sheet. Taste it. Before trying to solve anything, discover whether you like it as is.

If a vegetable is irrefutably mushy, your direction is clear. Whatever it is, mash it. Textural reconsiderations can be your best friend.

Make this while the vegetables are still quite hot. It will help them absorb the vinegar, mustard, and herbs.

German vegetable salad

~

1 cup overboiled potatoes, turnips, or cauliflower
½ teaspoon sharp mustard
½ teaspoon white wine vinegar
2 tablespoons olive oil
a handful of parsley

While they are still warm, mix the overboiled vegetables with the other ingredients. Mix vigorously until they are all smashed together and warm and vinegary and somewhere in between salad, dip, boiled vegetable, and mash. Anything other than potatoes can be whipped in a blender instead of mixed by hand. Try adding a half clove garlic ground to a paste with salt as a variation.

Or mash overboiled vegetables with a little butter and herbs and warm them slowly in a little pot, and call it mashed turnips, or mashed potatoes, or whatever it is you've mashed. Or after mixing in butter and herbs spread it all into a buttered casserole, bake it until it starts to bubble, sprinkle the top with toasted breadcrumbs, return it to the oven until they brown, and serve it as a gratin.

If it's anything but a potato, make the English pickle piccalilli, called chow-chow in the South. This sweet, prickly pickle is delicious in sandwiches of boiled egg, cold roast chicken, or ham. Because there have been so many occasions for me to practice my strategies for dealing with mistakes, they overflowed into the appendix, beginning on page 229. There is a recipe for piccalilli in it.

Keep toast in mind when unclassifiable disasters strike: when your pickled beets end up covered in ants; when a bowl of squash mostly drops on the way to the table; when you catch the dog red pawed, face buried in the cabbage. Salvage what you can without endangering your health, chop it, make whatever other amendments suggest themselves, and put it on toast.

Mushy zucchini will want to be whipped with a little olive oil and have freshly toasted walnuts scattered over it. Burned peppers ask to be slickly vinegared and topped with quartered boiled egg or a few thin pieces of anchovy. Burned greens want ricotta, or freshly grated Parmesan.

If vegetables do the opposite and won't get cooked, I recommend this salad. I first made it not to solve the problem of undercooked vegetables, but because I'd run out of chestnuts and was trying to replicate their pleasant mealyness. Partially cooked sweet potato solved that problem and created the most interesting new one, which is that if anyone is instructed to undercook a vegetable, he will almost invariably cook it perfectly.

Apple and half-cooked-vegetable salad

~

2 tablespoons olive oil
1 green apple, cut into ½-inch dice
2 shallots, sliced
½ cup fennel, cut into ½-inch dice
1 cup undercooked squash, sweet potato,
    pumpkin, or beets, cut into ½-inch dice
1½ tablespoons red wine vinegar
salt
½ teaspoon walnut or olive oil
4 cups escarole or finely sliced kale

Heat the olive oil over medium heat. Add the apple, shallots, and fennel, and cook them until they've all begun to get tender. Add the undercooked vegetable. Cook everything together for a minute, then turn the heat up under the pan, add the vinegar and a pinch of salt. Cook for another 30 seconds to 1 minute. Remove from the heat. Mix walnut or olive oil into the warm vegetables. Arrange the greens on a plate and tip the salad onto it, piling a little as you do.

If you burn rice to a pot, you'll have made the specialty of a lot of cuisines. The crust formed where it sticks is called *tah dig* in Persian, *koge* in Japanese, *pegao* in Puerto Rican food, and *nooleung ji* in Korean, and in those countries' cooking, it's the sign of a properly cooked batch of rice. In South Korea, there is an ice cream flavored to taste like the bottom of a rice pot.

When you end up with a crust at the bottom of your rice pot, scoop the rest of the rice onto the serving dish. Melt a tablespoon of butter in a small pot, drizzle it and a few drops of water over the burned rice crust, then turn the heat up until you hear a sizzle and the water has evaporated. Scoop the crust out with a metal spoon in pieces and serve it, broken, over the top of the rice. Call it by whichever name best fits your meal.

There are good things to do with rice that comes out too hard or too soft. They are in the chapter on rice and in the appendix.

When I've asked people what goes wrong most often when they cook, many say that their food tastes dull.

If what you're cooking seems to have come together nicely, and is thick and fragrant, but doesn't taste like much of anything, add more salt. Salt is food's mouthpiece. Acid also helps food find its voice. Add a squeeze of lemon, a drizzle of white wine vinegar. Add a light pour of olive oil, or a pat of butter, whether the recipe told you to or not.

Whatever it is also needs to cook longer. Recipes are terrified of instructing you to overcook. If a soup seems thin, let it go on cooking. If tomato sauce still tastes acidic, give everyone a bowl of olives and a stern look and cook the sauce until it mellows out.

If everything is properly seasoned and has cooked enough but you need something a little peppier, do what you would to perk anything up. Quickly chop parsley, pound a little garlic, douse both in good olive oil, and spoon it on top. Or make a fast *salsa verde* or olive tapenade. Or scatter a handful of chopped toasted nuts or nicely oiled toasted breadcrumbs on top.

There's nothing so important to keep from being "a thing that has failed" as meat. If you're cooking meat in a pot and notice the bottom begin to stick, take the pot off the heat and delicately remove the ingredients. Remove the meat gently with tongs or spoons, without scraping the bottom of the pot or pan. Pour the broth into a bowl. Scoop anything else out with a wooden spoon, letting what's stuck stay stuck.

Taste the liquid, meat, and vegetables. Keep as open a mind to it as you can. It may all taste fine. If it does, switch everything to a new pot, add a tablespoon of white wine for good measure, and let it finish cooking. If the meat tastes fine but the broth a little black, put fresh meat or vegetable stock in a new pot and add the meat and let it finish cooking in it.

It may all taste stained by smoke. I burned short ribs when I was a new chef in Georgia by cooking them in ovens I knew were too hot. I was rushing and tricked myself into thinking the short ribs might also rush, which they didn't. I wasn't about to squander the cow's hard work or mine. So I sang a silent requiem and pulled off the bits of meat that weren't stuck, made a vinegary barbecue sauce, then let the meat finish cooking in it. It made delicious, smoky sandwiches.

This sauce will work well.

Vinegary barbecue sauce

~

1¼ cup apple cider vinegar
½ teaspoon ground cinnamon
½ teaspoon ground cumin
1 tablespoon ground coriander
2 tablespoons whole-grain or
   Dijon mustard

2 tablespoons Tabasco or other
   sour hot sauce, like Tapatio
2 tablespoons honey
2 cups chicken or beef stock

*Heat the vinegar and dried spices in a pot. When it is warm, add
the rest of the ingredients. Bring to a simmer, then lower the heat and
reduce the sauce by half. Pull the meat into pieces so that it looks like
pulled pork and let it soak in the warm sauce for at least half an hour
before serving.*

Or heat chicken stock or bean broth with a few cloves of whole
garlic, a little butter, a fresh bay leaf, and a few drops of hot sauce.
Pull scorched meat into shreds and simmer it in the garlicky broth
for twenty minutes. Toast a thick slice of bread per person, rub each
with a piece of garlic, drizzle it with olive oil, and ladle the warm
meat over the toast.

If a piece of quick-cooking meat, like a steak, chicken breast, pork
chop, or fillet of fish overcooks and gets dry, make the crunchy Thai
salad called *laarb*, which is spicy and salty and acidic, and in which
the texture of the meat is barely noticeable. Like most meat dishes
from Asian cuisines, it's made of as many herbs and vegetables as
pieces of meat.

Laarb makes a perfectly wonderful main course, with or without
rice, and takes only a few minutes, a few limes, and a lot of herbs.

Thai toasted rice salad (laarb)

~

1 cup dried-out meat or fish
1 tablespoon rice
*3 tablespoons any colored onion, finely chopped,
    soaked in lime juice for 10 minutes*
1 tablespoon chopped jalapeño or other spicy fresh chile
salt
1 teaspoon sugar
optional: fish sauce
1 cup roughly chopped cilantro and mint
juice from at least 1 lime

Pull the meat into thin shreds. Toast rice in a little pan on medium heat, in no oil, until the rice is just opaque and smells nutty. Grind it briefly in a mortar with a pestle or in a spice grinder.

Mix the shredded meat with the onion and chiles. Add a little salt, the sugar, and a few drops of fish sauce, if you have it. Add the toasted rice, herbs, and then more lime juice and fish sauce as you need to for it all to taste very bold and juicy.

Serve cabbage or lettuce leaves on a plate alongside to fold around the laarb *into little packets. Cold raw radishes, cucumbers, or carrots are good accompaniments.*

Robert Bresson was uncannily right about handling overseasoning. He wrote a note to himself that said: "Unbalance so as to rebalance." Too much salt needs to be counteracted with acid or cream or butter. Unbalance your way back to balance with intrepid squeezes of lemon or drizzles of red or white wine vinegar and pats of butter or splashes of fat.

The seasoning should quiet. If it does, in exchange for the dish tasting acidic or rich, add the adjectives "lemony" or "buttery," which will quiet the critical audience, as well.

Fat also cools spice. Use a little cream to mollify any Italian or French dish that tastes agitated. Indian food that tastes salty or too spicy should be taken off the heat and have a big spoonful of cold yogurt added. Or leave the dish itself as is and serve a bowl of cold yogurt alongside.

Put a potato in a pot of soup or sauce to soak up unwanted salt. They are like sponges. Whenever I reach for one to desalinate a dish, I picture grandmothers the world over standing by their own traitorously salty pots, dropping cubes of potato into them, then returning to their knitting.

Peel a potato and cut it into big pieces. If you are feeling rich in potatoes, add it to whatever tastes salty after turning the burner under the pot off, let it sit for half an hour, then remove it. If you're feeling potato poor and it's a stew that won't be hurt by a little potato, cut yours into nice little pieces and cook them into the fin-ished dish.

If you've oversalted something between whose injuriously salty fibers a potato won't fit, bring a pot of unsalted water to a boil, add a freshly cut potato or two, cook it, then smash the unsalted potato with too-salted meat or fish and bake the mixture in a little buttered dish.

If you end up with salty beans, turn the contents of the bean pot into two meals. Strain beans from their liquid, keeping the liquid. Put them in new water or broth and butter to flush out salt, and simmer them until the flavor has evened out. Tonight, eat the beans in their new, plainer, buttery broth or purée them into a creamy soup. Tomorrow, sauté chopped onion or leek and garlic in butter, then add dried lentils or barley and your salty liquid, some water, and a lot of herbs, and make lentil or barley soup.

Although he bluffs about it, defeat does not have a sweet tooth. I have looked for solutions to blundered desserts and have found that they are best served as they are. If you've tried to make homemade ice cream and it hasn't come together, serve it in glasses and call it milkshakes. Undercooked cake should be called "pudding cake," or "molten."

If cake is too dry, make a sugar syrup by cooking a cup of sugar in a cup of simmering water and add a big splash of rum. Pour it over the cake, and let it sit and soak it up, and think of it as *rum baba* or boozy baklava.

When I've asked bakers what to do about broken cake they have told me, unhelpfully, that I should always make an extra cake. Eas-ier to make extra frosting and use it to piece what you can together, or layer your pieces of cake in tall glasses with whipped cream, top them with fruit, and call them trifle.

And then there is the art of letting go. Being moved to surrender is an act of grace. Be glad today's failure is behind you. Know that the next time, whether because you've learned how to avoid it or just to look at it differently, it won't be as bad.

Here is a good recipe for grilled cheese sandwiches. Perhaps deciding you'll still have a delicious meal, burned, salty, spicy, oily, broken, undercooked plan be damned, will be your victory today.

Grilled cheese sandwiches

~

thick-crusted bread, sliced, or baguette, cut into 4-inch
    lengths, split, bready middles removed and saved for
    breadcrumbs
olive oil
a handful of fresh parsley, basil, or mint leaves, arugula,
    or a handful of roughly chopped cooked greens
pickled chiles or cornichons, cut into thin rounds
thickly sliced mozzarella, spoonfuls of soft ricotta,
    or Taleggio or Robiola
olive tapenade or salsa verde

For each sandwich, drizzle one half of the bread heavily with olive oil, then add the herbs or greens, then a few of the pickled chiles or cornichons. Top with the cheese, then top that with a few more chiles or cornichons. Spread the other half of the bread thickly with tapenade or salsa verde. Close the sandwiches.

Heat a cast-iron or grill pan. Lightly oil it. Add the sandwiches and put a second heavy pan on top with a heavy weight inside it. Press against it so that the sandwiches get thin and crisp.

Seventeen

How to Weather a Storm

Winds whistle shrill,
Icy and chill,
Little care we:
Little we fear
Weather without,
Sheltered about the Mahogany Tree.

— W. M. Thackeray, "The Mahogany Tree"

If there are no onions or cabbage or celery and no stale bread and no chance of getting any, the odds of eating well seem bleak. So head directly to the canned aisle of your grocery store, or climb up on your counter and look into the backmost corner of your topmost shelf, and collect whatever cans and jars you find.

Then get your hands on a bottle of olive oil, a stick of butter, vinegar, and some salt. Find half bags of pasta or rice you've stuffed into drawers, look for single potatoes and ends of bags of nuts. Get out a pot and a pan, and decide that no matter how hard the wind is whipping at the windows, you will be well fed through the storm.

One of the most consoling dishes to make from a can is roasted tomatoes. If canned tomatoes aren't in your pantry already, they're easy to find in most stores. A nine-inch pie dish is the right size for tomatoes from a large can, but anything oven safe and similar will work perfectly.

Heat your oven to 400 degrees and drain the tomatoes over a bowl. Save the liquid for minestrone, and be one ingredient closer to that comforting soup. If you have any garlic, scatter a few peeled cloves in the bottom of the pan. Lay whole tomatoes tightly side by side over the garlic or the bare pan, coat them well with olive oil, salt them lightly, and roast them, uncovered, until they're glossy and jamlike and completely collapsed, about forty minutes. Eat them as a side dish, or on toast or rice, or toss them with pasta.

Store away whatever you don't eat, and when things brighten up, buy some rosemary or thyme and add a few sprigs to the jar. Once you've eaten all of the tomatoes, you'll be left with a fragrant, herby, tomato-infused olive oil to use in a vinaigrette, or to marinate goat cheese in, or just for general drizzling.

I find that canned beans need a good long simmer and olive oil before they become really likable. Once they've gotten both, they make wonderful soups. If you have an onion, finely dice half of it, and if you have garlic, slice three cloves. Cook them in a good amount of olive oil in a big soup pot, along with a healthy sprinkle of cinnamon, a tiny pinch of sugar, and a big pinch of salt. Drain a big can of chickpeas through a colander, rinse them well, and add them to the pot once the onions and garlic are tender. Cover them completely with chicken stock or water and cook until the chickpeas are very soft, about thirty minutes.

Purée the soup in batches or with a handheld blender, adding another long pour of olive oil to the pot just before you do. If you had cooked them from dried, the chickpeas' broth would already be thick and fragrant with oil. These ones need help. Leave a few ladlefuls unblended so that the finished soup is only mostly smooth. Add a big squeeze of lemon to the whole pot of soup when you're done. This is delicious topped with croutons or just drizzled with more olive oil.

If you have only the chickpeas, or any other canned bean, and no onion or garlic, simmer them in well-salted water or broth, to which you should add a bay leaf if you find one in your foraging, until they're very soft, and purée them with a lot, lot of olive oil. It seems a cheap trick, but it works.

If you have dried pasta and a can of chickpeas you can make chickpea pasta, which is solace in a bowl. I've had some very bad versions of chickpea pasta. It has never been because of mediocre pasta or generic chickpeas, which are often all that's available—I once made a good one with pasta I rescued from a box of macaroni and cheese—but because the chickpeas have been unceremoniously drained out of their can and poured into waiting pasta, instead of being introduced via liaisons of heat and fat and time. You must dote on these chickpeas carefully. They must become both good beans and good sauce.

Chickpea pasta

~

one 30-ounce can chickpeas
5 tablespoons olive oil
optional: 2 cloves garlic, sliced or chopped. This tastes better
    with the garlic, I think, but I am so proud of the union of
    just the pasta, water, oil, and canned beans that I can't say
    without reservation
salt
freshly ground black pepper
1 pound small shaped pasta such as orecchiette, penne, farfalle,
    elbow macaroni

Drain the chickpeas through a colander and rinse them for a minute. Heat a small, deep pot and add the olive oil. When it begins to shimmer, add the garlic, if using. Cook over very low heat until soft. Add the chickpeas, a pinch of salt, and water to cover by 1 inch.

Cook the beans for 30 to 45 minutes before you begin tasting them for doneness. Add small pours of water to the pot, keeping them short of what looks wet. This will leave you with a creamy sauce that sticks to your noodles. Taste five beans when you think they're done. If any bean is not totally velvety, let them go on cooking. When five taste completely creamy, lower the heat to almost off and add freshly cracked black pepper.

Cook the pasta in well-salted boiling water. Just before you drain it, remove a small glass of pasta water and stir a quarter of it into your pot of chickpeas. If they are still on low heat, the liquid should become integrated fairly quickly. Combine the pasta and chickpea sauce in a big bowl and mix well. If it seems dry, or the chickpeas are separate from the pasta instead of completely devoted to it, add a little more of the starchy pasta water and stir through.

If you have a can of already-made bean soup, improve it. Add a few drops of vinegar or sherry as you warm the soup up, or put a Parmesan cheese rind in the pot of soup for ten minutes to add richness. If you don't have a Parmesan rind, look for ends of other cheeses, which you can cut or scrape into little pieces and put in the bottom of your soup bowl, so that as you eat, you get an occasional bite of warm, melted cheese. Or fry a little dried cumin in a tablespoon of olive oil in a pan, then, when your soup is warm and ready to eat, drizzle the cumin oil on top.

If your pantry doesn't already contain a dusty, unopened jar of sauerkraut, you can surely find some at a corner store or the nearest gas station, where it will be sitting unruffled next to the engine coolant.

In France, Germany, and Austria, where hot dogs are eaten bunless, in just their snappy skins, on platters of sausages, sauerkraut is eaten as a side dish. It is simmered in hot goose fat with a smattering of whole toasted caraway or fennel seeds or cloves or other aromatic spices. There may be sweet onions sautéed in the fat until golden, or no onions, but a sprinkling of white raisins, plumped in wine. There may be little red potatoes, sliced and cooked in the pot.

Make a similar dish. Drain and rinse two cups of sauerkraut. Put any pan drippings or stored bacon fat you have, or a half cup of unsalted butter, in a small pot. If you have an onion, slice it thinly and cook it in the fat until it begins to brown. Add the sauerkraut, a big splash of white wine, and a few whole cloves, and cook it at a low simmer for half an hour, until it tastes rich and less piquant than usual. A little spoonful of toasted cumin or caraway is a good addition. Eat this as you would any side dish.

If you have stale bread, bowls, spoons, a lot of black pepper, and good appetites, turn this whole rigmarole into a soup. Add as much chicken or beef stock as you need to make it soupy, toast stale bread, put a piece in every bowl, and ladle the soup on top.

Canned foods had their heyday in the 1950s. There was a lot of ducking and covering in those years, and I imagine a fragile comfort born of faith that if above- and belowground pantries were stocked similarly, life beneath could bear a reasonable resemblance to life on top.

A lot of popular canned ingredients from the era taste as though they've been embalmed. If canned asparagus, canned peas, canned spinach, canned corn, or canned carrots are your only options, resuscitate them. Drain any well, put it in a pot, add a quarter as much butter as vegetable, let it simmer for fifteen minutes, then pulse it in a food processor and eat it on toast or crackers.

Canned green beans, though, can be made into a very convincing, wonderful, warm, spicy salad.

This is something like the green beans you sometimes get at Chinese restaurants, softened, crinkly, and pleasantly charred. I think it is quite delicious.

Spicy green beans

~

one 15-ounce can whole green beans
1 clove garlic
½ cup almonds, toasted
1 tablespoon olive oil
2 teaspoons dried chile flakes
2 teaspoons red wine vinegar
½ teaspoon salt

Drain and rinse the beans. In a food processor or with a mortar and pestle, pound the garlic to a paste, then pound the almonds in with it. This doesn't need to be smooth, and there can be different-sized pieces of nut and bits of garlic.

Heat the oil to smoking in a wok or big frying pan. Add the beans in a single layer. Let them cook over high heat, without turning, for 30 to 60 seconds, until you see char begin to creep up their sides. Use a sharp spoon or spatula to firmly turn the beans over once. Add the chile flakes. Keep the beans in a single layer and move them as little as possible.

When their second sides have browned and begun to blister, turn off the heat and add the nuts and garlic. Mix it through, still being frugal with your movement, then add the vinegar, sprinkling it over the surface. Mix it through once and taste for salt.

Serve on hot white rice.

Canned sardines and canned mackerel and canned wild salmon have fed me better through all different kinds of storm than any other ingredient I can think of. In the days of the bomb shelter pantry, little pancakes made from canned fish were more common than fish. While now as unfashionable as bomb shelters, fish cakes remain a sturdy, steadying meal.

This recipe cheats, imagining that somehow in the absence of onions and celery you can still get lemongrass, chiles, and ginger. It is also good without them.

Fish cakes

~

1 cup canned wild-caught salmon or mackerel,
    packed in water, well drained
½ cup frozen peas, thawed
¼ cup smashed cooked chickpeas or mashed potatoes
1 tablespoon chopped fresh cilantro or mint
½ teaspoon finely chopped fresh ginger
    or ¼ teaspoon dried ginger
½ teaspoon finely chopped lemongrass
¼ teaspoon finely chopped fresh chile, or ⅛ teaspoon chile flakes

1 egg
¼ cup fine breadcrumbs, fresh or toasted
½ teaspoon red wine vinegar
olive or peanut oil for frying

In a bowl, combine all the ingredients except the oil. These need to be cooked before they taste like themselves, so wait to judge the mixture for salt or vinegar until the first one is done. Heat a tablespoon olive or peanut oil in a nonstick pan until it sizzles when you let an edge of a cake or a bit of mixture touch it. Form the first little cake and fry it to see if it will hold together. Each one should be only a few inches around. Taste it for seasoning and piquancy. Add more breadcrumbs or salt or vinegar if it needs it.

Form into little round cakes and put them on a plate. Cook as many as you can per pan without them running into each other. Cook them just until their first sides are golden brown. Flip them over as confidently as you can and brown the second side. Keep them on a plate covered with a paper towel while you cook the rest.

Make a dipping sauce by combining ½ teaspoon sugar, ¼ cup white vinegar, 1 teaspoon fish sauce, and finely chopped chiles in a bowl.

Canned foods seem antithetical to the idea of salad. I made this salad, though, once, from ingredients I'd unearthed in a chef's earthquake kit and found it quite revitalizing.

A salad for a natural disaster

~

1 can bamboo shoots, well drained
* and cut into rounds*
1 can artichoke hearts, well drained
* and quartered*
1 teaspoon Dijon mustard
1½ teaspoons red wine vinegar

1 teaspoon jarred horseradish,
* drained*
1 teaspoon ground black pepper
2 tablespoons olive oil
salt to taste

Mix well and hope for the best.

There are certain stormy days when a sensible meal of chickpea soup won't do. That is when I turn to a secret cache of cans I keep, even though they are frivolous, for the strange weather that needs them.

Tins and jars of exotic foods are my vice. I can resist expensive oils and salts, but I fall under the spell of little tins of cuttlefish packed in their own ink; Italian figs plumped with honey and wine; monkfish liver terrine; pin-sized baby eels. I have a red oval tin of Italian sardines, marked with their vintage. I have an alluringly inconspicuous elliptical French can that lists as its contents goose neck, black truffles, and pâté. I have bought more caviar than I will admit.

It is as wise to be prepared for an impractical meal as for a practical one. If something so good or so bad has happened that only buttered toast and cuttlefish, or delicately whipped liver, or goose neck, or pâté are appropriate, as long as you keep your pantry stocked with a few lovely, uncommon things, you can open it and be as well set up to celebrate as to survive.

Eighteen

How to Have Your Day

Our fear of death is like our fear that summer
will be short. But when we have had our swing of
pleasure, our fill of fruit, and our swelter of heat,
we say we have had our day.
— Ralph Waldo Emerson, *Journals*, Volume 8

People who grew up in households where pickles were fermented recall, shiny-eyed, the sound of the lids of ceramic crocks clattering all night long as cucumbers and green tomatoes made their way from vegetable to pickle. The same oldsters say they can still see their grandmothers stirring bubbling pots and smell the sweetness of caramelizing fruit.

Preserving food used to be a necessity of eating. When it was, a day would be chosen, vegetables and fruits picked, crocks and jars washed. A little ramshackle cottage industry of trimming and scrubbing and salting and brining and boiling would be engineered, and food for the winter would be, as they used to say, "put up."

Since we've stopped preserving as a regular practice, we've come to associate the processes themselves—salting or steeping things in vinegar, or stewing fruit before it rotted, or filling jars with ripe vegetables to keep on our shelves—with a kind of cooking of obligation that's needless today.

But knowing how to do the simplest sorts of preserving still accomplishes the same goals and can be done on a less urgent schedule and on a less urgent scale.

Though we can have vegetables year-round now, we can't have our own vegetables, or our neighbor's, or ones grown nearby year-round unless we remember how easy it is to make a pot of vinegar brine, quickly cut vegetables up, and stick them in it. They're less romantic than clattering crocks, but vinegar pickles are simple and immediate. The easiest ones are just vegetables doused in hot vinegar and salt, and stored in the refrigerator.

I couldn't live as happily without pickled chiles. I buy fresh chiles when I see them. Then if I'm feeling rushed and in the mood to have them available but not to really *make* them, I quickly slice them into rounds, pack them into a glass jar, heat plain white vinegar in a pot, and pour it over them.

They can be plain jalapeños, or they can be a combination of different sizes and colors and shapes of chiles. Rinse them and slice all but the spiciest, like Scotch bonnet peppers or Thai bird's-eye chiles, whose unflagging heat can be a terror to get off your hands, into rounds. Pack the rounds tightly in a transparent jar; when you see them, brightly colored and waiting for you, they'll beckon, and you'll begin to think about making rice, or cooking an egg, or warming beans to put them on.

These are legitimate pickles and they have pickles' true spirit: pickles aren't just this season's vegetable, but the vegetable recharged by vinegar, bright and vivifying, spicy and acidic, able to get anything to hop to. The vinegar in a jar of pickled chiles does wonders for newly roasted vegetables or sautéed greens, used as the "pepper vinegar" found on Southern tables is there, or added secretly to a bowl of pasta with onions or cabbage.

If you have a few more minutes, or have brought home any vegetable other than chiles, make a quick pickle brine.

Add one and a half times as much white vinegar as water to a pot and bring it to a boil. For every four cups of liquid, add a quarter cup salt and a quarter cup raw sugar, and simmer until they dissolve. Or don't measure anything and add salt and sugar until the brine tastes like you want the vegetable you've preserved in it to: potent, salty, and just barely sweet.

Pickle brine is also the best place, other than cocktails, to put leftover brine from jars of capers and other pickles. If you have any, either add them to your own brine, or simply heat them all together, taste them, then add salt or sugar or water or straight vinegar until it tastes good.

If you make brine, pickle onions in the jar with your chiles. Thinly slice one onion per two jars of chiles and fit the slices amid the little rounds of chile. Pour the brine over the chiles and onion. After a few days in the jar, the onions will be perfectly peppery and hot and you can use them the same way as the chiles. You can keep using one bottomless jar of pickled chiles for a year. Top off the chiles or brine as either runs low. Keep doing this until the vinegar gets murky or impossibly spicy.

There are vegetables I think taste better pickled than they do fresh. If creation had had any pretensions of being perfect, okra and green beans would have both grown from seed to fruit full of vinegar and salt. In summer, when I see small okra or stout green beans, I buy extra of each and take them home to do what nature would have if it hadn't had so much on its plate.

Sometimes I pickle slices of radishes, or green tomatoes, or a small, sweet-looking cabbage, or a bunch of celery, or stems of cooking greens. Radishes and green tomatoes get wedged, the others cut into thin slices that will fit tightly in jars. If it's any of those, add a teaspoon of fennel seeds, a half teaspoon of coriander seeds, a bay leaf, and a few fresh or dried chiles. I add a whole peeled clove of garlic, too, because it is nice to have a clove of pickled garlic in a Bloody Mary.

Pour hot brine directly over the vegetables, in glass jars, and seal the jars tightly. Stored in the refrigerator, these stay good for a few months. If you want them to sit on a shelf, follow the instructions for canning jars of tomatoes on pages 211–12.

—————

I have never tried to make a jelly because it involves the perplexing extra step of suspending fruit in a bag. I will, however, make a compote of anything that crosses my path.

My favorite one is very much like marmalade. It is both bitter and sweet, and because it asks for more peel than jams and jellies, you get to use the parts that get ignored.

Bittersweet compote

~

about 3½ pounds any combination　2 cups water
blood oranges, navel oranges,　1 cup sugar
and grapefruits

Wash the citrus and remove the peels from half with a vegetable peeler. Cut the peels into very thin, fine strips and add to a small pot with the water and sugar. Bring to a boil, then lower to a simmer. Cook for half an hour, until a spoonful of the liquid drizzled onto a plate seems syruplike. Turn off the heat. Remove the peels and all the bitter white pith from the remaining citrus. Cut the fruit free from their membranes with a sharp knife. This will be a messy affair. When you have sectioned all of the fruit, gently mix them with the citrus syrup.

The only preserving I'm serious about is canning tomatoes.

I can tomatoes like a grandmother staking her hopes on fermenting vegetables and pots of boiling fruit. I can enough to eat tomatoes grown nearby all through the icy northeastern winter, and give a jar to anyone who shows up looking peaked. I do it as though my doing it will stop the summer from ending, and in a way it does.

To can tomatoes, buy local tomatoes at your farmers' market when they're very ripe, toward the end of the season. Buy them by the case. They may be less expensive. Two cases of tomatoes fill twelve to fifteen quart-sized jars. Any tomato with a high flesh-to-seed ratio is good. I like Roma tomatoes and the perfectly round ones called Early Girls.

Then invite a lot of people over and tell them to bring beer and bread and cheese and jars.

Boil two big pots of water, one for jars and one for tomatoes. Sterilize the jars by running them through a detergent-free dishwasher or in one of the pots at just below a simmer, lowering jars a few at a time into the water and leaving them in for about ten seconds each. Remove them with tongs to a clean dry towel. Do the same with tops and sealing rings. Leave all the sterilized jars and lids in one area and leave the pot simmering.

Put a big container of ice water and a big bowl next to the second boiling pot. Add the tomatoes to the boiling water in batches of three to five. Let them cook for thirty seconds, just long enough for their skins to start to crack. The tomatoes don't need to cook at all, just to loosen from their skins. Scoop them out and drop them in the ice water.

Have someone stationed at the ice water, plucking skins off and putting the peeled tomatoes in the waiting bowl. If you are planning to slow-cook any meat or make vegetable stock in the next few days, save some tomato skins. Add them to either one when you add the rest of the vegetables.

Fill your jars tightly with tomatoes. I often add a sprig of basil and a whole clove of garlic to each. There's some bacterial danger to this. I can only recommend it from the perspective of taste—they're delicious—and luck—so far, so good. Pack the tomatoes in well, without smashing them, with a clean spatula. Leave an inch of space between tomatoes and lid, wipe it with a towel, put on the top, and seal the ring around it.

Lower the jars carefully into the simmering water. The contents of the jars and the temperature of the water should be close to matching. The hotter the tomatoes, the closer the water can be to boiling when you add them. If a jar is just barely warm, the water should be just barely simmering, then brought slowly back to a boil with the jars in it.

If a jar shatters once it's lowered into water, the water was hotter than the jar's contents. Remove the other jars in the pot. Scoop out the glass. Clean the pot, refill it, and heat it up again. I lose at least one per season. It happens to everyone. When it happens to you, soldier on.

There are canning racks designed to fit into the bottom of canning pots that keep them from rattling around. If yours rattle, and you don't have a rack, a few kitchen towels jammed inside in the pot will help.

Bring the water to a slow boil with the jars in it and let them cook for forty minutes. Remove them carefully with tongs and let them cool on a cloth towel on your counter.

They take hours to fully seal. They will do it on their own schedule. As they do, you will hear small pops. If you can tomatoes in the evening, go to bed with your door open. You will hear the sound of the last bits of air escaping jars and quiet, settling popping all night long.

If any jars haven't sealed by the next day—which you'll know by pressing on their lids, which should be firmly sunken in—refrigerate them and eat the tomatoes in the following week.

If you want to make vinegar pickles to keep on your shelf, treat them similarly: pickle them directly in sterilized jars, lower them into water the same temperature as the pickles, and cook the jars in the water for twenty to thirty minutes.

Pickles and tomatoes canned like this stay good for ages, and better if they're stored out of the light. If you want to display them, do it somewhere dark, like a bookshelf.

Pickles you make yourself will taste familiar. Tomatoes stored in glass will be a revelation. They retain a delicate freshness. Use them to make tomato sauce for pasta, cooked for a shorter time. Roast the tomatoes in a hot oven with salt, olive oil, and a few sprigs of fresh rosemary and eat them as a side dish. Cook sliced garlic and Indian spices in butter, add a jar of your own tomatoes and roughly chopped leaves and stems of cilantro, then a half jar of coconut milk, and have tomato curry.

What you preserve is the cheeriest memento mori. It is a way to say and mean: of everything that passes, this is what I choose to keep. It is a clear reminder, there for the tasting, of where and when and how you have lived.

Nineteen

How to Drink to Saints

No feast day of the church passed unnoticed:
we drank to every saint and never went to mass.
— Bill Neal, *Bill Neal's Southern Cooking*

We're anxious about serving, but the simple, blessed fact is that no one ever comes to dinner for what you're cooking. We are all hungry and thirsty and happy that someone's predicted we would be and made arrangements for dealing with it. We come for the opportunity to look up from our plates and say "thank you." It is for recognition of our common hungers that we come when we are asked.

My father could not boil water for tea, or toast bread, but he had a reputation as a great host because he fed anyone who stayed longer than the mailman. (And even the mailman could be found, of an afternoon, munching thoughtfully on an Egyptian olive.)

Offer something small to eat as soon as anyone enters your house. It needn't be sophisticated. Serve little halved radishes, chilled in the refrigerator, a dish of salt, and another filled with softened sweet butter. Let everyone spread the radishes with a smear of butter and sprinkle them with salt. Or serve a plate of fennel, cut into thin wedges. Or cut carrots and celery into pretty sticks and quickly pickle them and serve them with butter and crackers.

215

If you have olives, customize them. Drain them of their brine and put them in a small pot with a few wide pieces of orange or lemon peel, a teaspoon of chile flakes, a few fennel seeds, and a little good olive oil. Serve them warm.

Or serve small pieces of stale bread quickly toasted and drizzled with herby oil, or toasted nuts, or halved soft-boiled eggs sprinkled with salt or topped with slivered anchovy.

You will have provided the greatest hospitality you can, acknowledging the quiet gurglings we all have and never bother to tell anyone about: we're *supposed* to be hungry three times a day. When you insist whoever crosses your threshold is hungry for an olive all of the time, you permit hungers outside the thrice daily ones prescribed.

The wise men of Proverbs say that a crust eaten in peace is better than a banquet partaken in anxiety. It may be fairly easy when there are only two of you sitting down to eat for you to cook your specialty of delicate pink lamb chops with roasted potatoes, which must be served hot, and a small pile of lightly wilted spinach. But if you are serving eight, and eight lamb chops don't fit in the pan at once, you will be standing nervously at your stove, cooking chops in rounds, hoping the earliest ones stay delicate and pink, and rushing the last ones, so that you can be done already, and you will be lightly wilting spinach while everyone is eating their crisp vegetables and olives.

One of the calmest and most pleasant dinners I remember attending was at the house of a very accomplished cook who'd plated our entire dinners: braised short ribs, haricots verts, and potato purée, and left them sitting on the dining room table for an hour while we drank wine and ate prosciutto in the living room.

Because everything, down to the trouble of transferring dinner from pot to plate, had been done in advance, our hostess was utterly serene. She sat smoothly with us while we slowly lubricated our tongues and warmed our appetites. One of the guests spilled an entire glass of red wine on our hostess's fox throw blanket, at which our hostess laughed, before moving the blanket to another room.

It doesn't need to be on the table chilling, but serve something best cooked in advance. It will sit calmly, as everyone settles into the evening, and let you sit calmly with them rather than standing worriedly in another room.

Slow-cooked meat is perfect. It will wait in the oven until you eat, and looks appealing cut into pieces and placed rustically on polenta, or puréed sweet potatoes, or mashed turnips or potatoes, all of which can be cooked and sit in their pots on the back of the stove, ready to be warmed when you need them.

This slow-cooked meat dish must be one of the most delicious things ever made from any of the ingredients in it. The cooked milk separates into golden curds, which look strange and taste divine.

Pork shoulder braised in milk with garlic, sage, and lemon

~

1 boneless pork shoulder from a happily raised pig, about 5 pounds	2 sprigs savory
tons of salt	2 sprigs sage
2 tablespoons extra virgin olive oil	1 bay leaf
3 tablespoons butter	strips of lemon peel from 4 lemons
6 garlic cloves, peeled	3 cups whole milk

The pork shoulder will probably come tied. Leave it tied for cooking. The day before you plan to cook it, salt the roast five times as heavily as you want.

Heat the oven to 325 degrees.

Heat a deep oven-safe pot, then add the olive oil and half the butter. When the butter stops foaming, add the pork and let it get brown on all sides. It can take up to 5 minutes per side.

Remove the pork from the pan. Warm the garlic, savory, sage, bay leaf, and lemon zest in the remaining butter in the same pot for a few minutes. Return the pork to the pan, add 1½ cups milk, and bring to a boil. Reduce it to a simmer, partially cover, and put the pot in the oven. Check the pork every half hour, turning it occasionally.

As the milk evaporates, add more by the ladleful. As the pork cooks and the milk reduces, the milk will start to caramelize into golden curds. Let it cook for 4 to 5 hours until it is tender and the liquid is a golden tan, reduced juice.

Unimaginable amounts of fat will rise to the top of this while it cooks—there is fat in the pig and fat in the milk. Skim it off if you're eating this immediately. If you're cooking it ahead, cool the pork in the refrigerator covered with the layer of fat until the day you want to serve it, then remove the fat in pieces.

Reheat the pork at 300 degrees until warm. If the curds of milk aren't richly brown, remove the pork and set it aside, then let the milk continue cooking over low heat on the stove, letting the curds caramelize further. Turn off the heat and return the pork to the pot.

To serve, cut the strings off the pork and slice it against the grain into thick pieces. Serve in its golden sauce on polenta or smashed or puréed vegetables.

Or roast or boil chickens, which you can do ahead of time. If they're roasted, let them sit out, happy and browned, or if boiled in an uncovered pot, in their broth, while your guests eye them and get hungry.

I like either at room temperature. If you want to serve chicken hot, cut it into pieces after cooking, then put pieces of roast chicken in a roasting pan, skin side up, and pour in the pan drippings and a little chicken stock, or return boiled chicken to its broth. Let either warm up in the oven or on the stove before you sit down to eat.

Even if every dish is done, cooked and waiting, and you've had a moment to sit down and smooth your hair, leave small, simple tasks unfinished. Leave parsley and mint to be picked off their stems. If you expecting a guest who likes to cook, hand over a whisk and vinaigrette you've started, and instructions to add olive oil. I only ever open the first bottle of wine and otherwise hand bottle opener and bottle to someone else. I do the same with the bread knife, tasking someone else with slicing the bread. People enjoy having their hands busied. Especially if it's a guest who doesn't often cook, she will enjoy her exchange with parsley as much as she will enjoy eating what you scatter it over.

There's great value in being able to say "yes" when people ask if there is anything they can do. By letting people pick herbs or slice bread instead of bringing a salad, you make your kitchen a universe in which you can give completely and ask for help. The more environments with that atmospheric makeup we can find or create, the better.

When it comes to presentation, I care what things look like, but not too much. I'm practical. If the rims of bowls are smeared, I clean them. Nothing will be stacked, because I don't want to fear a tumble. I rarely put individual meals on plates in the kitchen, then deliver them, because serving and eating are a single activity, and when I separate them at the last moment, becoming a person who rushes around making plates look perfect, I steal myself away from the meal at the moment when it needs me most.

I believe what I serve must look beautiful, but only according to my tastes and priorities.

There are herbs scattered over everything I serve (especially if I had to cut into the chicken three times to see if it was cooked). I don't worry about slices of meat or vegetable lying in perfect fans, because nothing in my house ever does. I move things around: I arrange a wrinkled ribbon of kale somewhere, or make sure a few toasted nuts peek out of the rice. My favorite platters of food will be recognizable by their looking like their ingredients tumbled, in medias res, out of bed onto them.

I like to serve food family style. It's pleasurable to spoon a potato onto a fellow diner's plate. It binds you to her, for the duration of the dinner at least, in a way that makes conversation easy and the atmosphere good.

You, of course, are not I, and it must be from someplace in you, not this book, that you serve. If you like symmetry, you must line things up. If you feel most satisfied composing plates away from your table, do it happily, for it will be genuine and full of what is yours to offer. Only remember what is plainly and always true: the act of serving fulfills itself. It doesn't matter what you serve.

Twenty

How to End

What are you seeking
finishes at a start, and with ending, begins.
—Rainer Maria Rilke, "The Sonnets to Orpheus," part two, XII

What we eat at the end of a meal marks its passage. If we have eaten well, our hearts and bellies full, the occasion will be bittersweet. Conversation will have slowed, the night's slope tilted. What seemed like it would last forever now seems certain to be nearly done.

I am always grateful for a little more time at the table; the meal must pass somehow, and I am better consoled with one more taste than with the rather less voluptuary sound of a gong.

But, if it has been a good meal I think, listening to the rattle of a whisk in a bowl of cream, that I would forgo the golden slice of cake, the pretty figs, the cold whipped cream if it meant I could stay sitting there, where and when and with whom I am. If the meal would last, and I wouldn't have to put that tiny, deft, certain dot at the end of it that says, "This one, my dear, is done."

If a meal cannot go on forever I ask only that its passage be not too jarring.

I ask dessert to leave room for the flavors and smells before it, to let them linger faint, and not erased, in its margins. I prefer not to clear my mental slate. I ask dessert to look kindly on my current condition: what tastes have been on my tongue, how much I have eaten, and of what.

A good dessert does not obligate its creator to great effort. The famous eighteenth-century chef Marie-Antoine Carême called the art of dessert the "principle branch of architecture."

The desserts I bake are as like the architecturally accomplished cakes and pastries to which he referred as my bookshelves, made of wine crates, are like the grand New York Public Library. Both hold books, both support my reading, neither does me better than the other, except that my shaky shelves are close at hand.

If you want to bake dessert, choose an easy one. Easy baking exists, and if you are not trying to pummel a meal's savor out of memory with sugar and cream, but to usher it to a graceful close, the simplest cakes and cookies are often the best.

I like this cake, because it's not so sweet that I'm quietly sad that the salad has left the table. There are no layers or frosting; nothing to crack or leak. The olive oil in the batter is forgiving of hasty measuring and doesn't mind the temperature at which it's mixed.

Tomorrow, warmed in an oven, a slice of this cake, spread with jam, makes a consummate breakfast.

Rosemary cake

(adapted from Cooking by Hand, *by Paul Bertolli)*

~

8 *eggs*
1½ *cups raw sugar*
1⅔ *cups olive oil*
4 *tablespoons finely chopped fresh rosemary*
3 *cups flour*
2 *tablespoons baking powder*
1 *teaspoon kosher salt*

Heat the oven to 325 degrees.

Coat a bundt pan first with butter, then with flour, tapping out the excess flour.

Beat the eggs for 30 seconds with a handheld beater. Slowly add the sugar and continue to beat until the mixture is very foamy and pale. Still mixing, slowly drizzle in the olive oil. Using a spatula, fold in the rosemary.

In a separate bowl, whisk together the flour, baking powder, and salt. Keeping the mixer on low speed, gradually add the dry ingredients to the egg mixture. Pour the batter into the bundt pan.

Bake for 45 to 50 minutes, rotating the pan halfway through. The cake is done when it is golden brown and springs back when touched, or when a skewer inserted in the center comes out clean. Allow the cake to cool briefly in the pan and then tip it out onto a rack to continue cooling.

This is delicious on its own, or accompanied by freshly whipped unsweetened cream, or the wonderfully rich, soft Italian cream cheese called mascarpone.

Italian cookies called *brutti ma buoni* ("ugly but good") are worth keeping in your quiver, first because most disappointment or satisfaction has its origin in expectations, and here you have made your intentions very clear; second, because they are truly not ugly, but simply plain, and additionally light and delicious.

Brutti ma buoni

～

6 egg whites
3½ cups combined toasted hazelnuts and almonds,
    very finely chopped in a food processor
1⅔ cups powdered sugar
2 drops vanilla extract
a small pinch each ground cinnamon and ground coriander

Heat the oven to 325 degrees. Beat the egg whites to stiff peaks and carefully fold in the remaining ingredients. Put parchment paper on a cookie sheet. Drop the batter in walnut-sized pieces onto the sheet, well spaced. Bake for 30 minutes for a chewy cookie, or 40 minutes for a crunchy one. Let cool completely on the pan. These are very good with dessert wine.

If you want something chocolate, make these brownies, which my mother did while I was growing up, often deciding to do so as we began to clear the table.

Amy's brownies

~

4 ounces unsweetened chocolate   *2 teaspoons vanilla*
1 cup (2 sticks) butter   *1 cup flour*
3 eggs   *chocolate chips or walnuts*
2 cups sugar

Heat the oven to 350 degrees. Grease a 13- x 9-inch baking pan. Melt the chocolate and butter in a mixing bowl placed over a small pot of boiling water. Remove from the heat and allow to cool for 5 minutes. Beat in 1 egg at a time. Add the sugar and vanilla and beat until combined, then add the flour. Spread in the pan and top with chocolate chips or walnuts or anything else you like. Check them after 20 minutes. They should be done by 25 to 30.

One of the best desserts is fruit. Fruit is a chance for cook and eater to make a final pact to end a meal together. Serve fruit whole. Let people choose to use their hands or a knife. Give everyone an opportunity to feel the meal's energy vibrate, to feel and smell something raw, and to be both feeding themselves and being fed.

If it is spring, pile ripe apricots in a big bowl, or bright red cherries, which I like at room temperature. If it's summer serve peaches or plums, or figs, figs, figs. Or slice melons into fat wedges.

Make a bowl of fruit abundant. Whatever isn't eaten tonight will be eaten tomorrow, and filling a bowl with enough that everyone can have more makes it look opulent, and keeps people from feeling as though they have each been assigned a fruit.

If it is winter, slowly warm dried figs or prunes with a little sugar and a cinnamon stick in sweet wine, like port or brandy. Once the wine has heated, leave the fruit in it for an hour, on very low heat, or off the burner completely, until it plumps up. Remove the fruit and let the wine reduce for ten minutes to sweet, thick syrup. Serve it in little bowls or teacups, dolloped with mascarpone, or serve the heady compote, once it has chilled, over vanilla ice cream.

Or serve little pieces of the same bread you had at dinner, flattened in a hot cast-iron pan with another pressed on top of it, or made very hot on a griddle, then topped with a heaping spoonful of fresh ricotta cheese and a big handful of roughly chopped toasted almonds or hazelnuts, all of it drizzled with honey.

Or press and heat pieces of baguette, then make them into little sandwiches filled with squares of barely sweet dark chocolate, as severe and gratifying as coffee. First spread one side of the sandwich with cold butter, then scatter a few grains of flaky salt over it, then add the square of chocolate and the second little piece of bread, and press down with the second pan.

Or dispense with any heating and combining and buy a few dark chocolate bars. Break them into big squares and serve them in a tumble on a plate, with a glass of Scotch per person, which will make each appetite feel listened to, and provide a tiny anesthetic to the pain of letting go.

There's an old British tradition of serving something savory at the end of a meal. It is designed as a shield against dessert's taunt. What if, a savory bite asks, the wisp of sadness at a meal's close were swept away with a riddle? It is a tradition I like. Serve little bites of strong cheddar cheese melted with beer alongside dark toasts, or tins of caviar and buttered bread. Then, more wine may be opened and the night can march on . . .

———————

I ate the best dessert of my life almost a decade ago in a town called Praiano, seven miles down the winding road that leads from the cliffside town of Positano toward the sea.

At the bottom of the road there is a tiny harbor where a man named Armandino runs a restaurant with his daughter. I ate lunch there, outside by the pier on a clear blue spring day.

I was with the man I loved, and we ate. We ate tuna preserved in olive oil, with little black olives and slivers of onion. Then pasta with baby clams, still in their shells.

Then there was a plate of seafood: baby octopus, no bigger than the pad of my thumb; pin-sized white bait; whole little anchovies; a single, whole red mullet, just longer from his head to tail than my hand. Each had been dipped in batter and fried and served with lemon. After lunch we had hard nut cookies and a kind of half-frozen pudding. And then small dark coffees. After coffee, there was *limoncello,* made from the lemons that grow up and down the cliffs.

When we finished our liqueur we sat, dazzled by the meal, the bright water, and the birds picking fish off rocks and letting them fall again, boats dropping in and out of the nearby harbors, which were sunk too deep into the cliffs' mouths for us to watch them dock.

Then Armandino came to our table carrying a bowl of dark, wet walnuts, still in their shells, and two half glasses of red wine. We explained that we were too full and had a distance still to drive that day. Armandino pressed the wineglasses down and cleared a space between them for the bowl of walnuts, and another for their shells. It would be better, he said, if we left lunch with the tastes of the next meal already in our mouths.

Cookies and lemon liqueur said nothing of dinner, but half sweet walnuts and wine began to whisper. Something of another hunger, another meal, of again finding a place to sit together, again finding something good to eat.

We nodded, understanding then, and began to crack and peel the nuts, still wet inside their shells.

We stopped talking and just peeled, watching thin filaments of walnut skin coming off when either of us hit on spots with good focus. We sipped our wine slowly and remained there, peeling and sipping, getting no drunker but more ready, until the sky began to darken, and it made sense for us to go.

Appendix

~

Further Fixes

Dried-out pork chops, chicken breasts, or steak can be turned into little lardons, a little like the pork or duck you get in pearl-sized pieces in fried rice at Chinese restaurants.

Crispy lardons

~

Cut overcooked meat into small pieces. Heat 1 tablespoon butter and 2 tablespoons olive oil in a broad, shallow pan. When the fat is almost smoking, add the pieces of meat, making sure not to crowd them. You may have to cook them in batches. Start each batch with a little new butter.

Let the meat sizzle on one side. Once a side is properly browned, the pieces will move easily. Turn them once. Remove them with a slotted spoon or spatula and let them drain on a dish towel on a plate.

To use as lardons, put the meat while still warm on a salad of hardy greens, tossed with vinaigrette. Top with a poached egg.

To make these into fried rice, fry rice according to the instructions on page 123. Add the meat when you add cucumbers.

Or turn them into a big, hearty hash. This is a good solution for oversalted meat as well.

Meat and vegetable hash

~

¼ *cup butter, or a little less*
2 *cups finely diced dry or oversalted meat*
⅓ *cup very thinly sliced onion, any color*
1 *cup finely diced cooked potatoes*
¾ *cup finely diced other cooked vegetables, such as roasted beets,*
     roasted root vegetables, or roasted cauliflower or broccoli
salt
1 *tablespoon chopped fresh parsley*
optional: 1 *teaspoon chopped fresh rosemary*
1 *teaspoon red wine vinegar or the juice of* ¼ *lemon*
optional: ⅛ *teaspoon cayenne pepper*

Heat half the butter in a broad, shallow pan. Cook the meat into lardons.

Remove the meat from the pan with a slotted spoon.

In the same pan, melt the rest of the butter. Making sure it's not so hot that the onion will burn, add the onion. Once it's just barely sizzling, spread the onion out and cook it, stirring often, until it's begun to soften. This should take a minute or two.

Add the vegetables and spread them out over the surface of the pan. Smash and mix well. Once it's all begun to cook and the pan is sizzling, add the meat and spread it all out again. Let it cook over medium-high heat for a minute. With a metal spatula, scrape the bottom of the pan, turn it all over, and let it cook.

Do this a few times, chopping at things a bit with the side of the spatula, then respreading. When it starts to look like you think a hash is meant to, lower the heat and taste it for salt. Then add the herbs, vinegar or lemon juice, and cayenne pepper, and let it cook undisturbed for 30 seconds. This is good topped with an egg or any creamy cheese, like goat cheese, and next to a salad.

Undercooked meat should be removed from its bones, then put in a pot with a little butter, a bay leaf, and enough chicken stock to just cover the meat. Let it cook over low heat until cooked through. While the meat finishes cooking, make a big pot of buttered noodles. Ladle the warm, brothy meat over, top it all with chopped fresh herbs, and call it "buttered noodles with ragout."

Burned vegetables that you didn't turn into baba ghanoush can become this salad, which is closer to a Middle Eastern chutney.

Smoky vegetable salad

~

> 2 cups burned eggplant or zucchini or peppers
> olive oil
> 2 cloves garlic, sliced
> 2½ tablespoons tomato paste
> 2 tablespoons water
> 2 tablespoons red wine vinegar
> 1 tablespoon yellow or brown raisins
> salt

Chop the vegetable into small pieces and put it in a small mixing bowl. If you've burned it in a sauté pan, wipe the pan clean of whatever's stuck to it and let it cool.

Add 1 teaspoon olive oil and cook the garlic on low heat until it's just softened. Add the tomato paste and the water and cook until the tomato darkens and begins to caramelize and thicken. Scrape it into the bowl with your vegetable.

Combine the vinegar and raisins in a small pot. Bring to a simmer, turn the heat off, and let the raisins rehydrate in the vinegar for 5 minutes. Remove the raisins and roughly chop them. Save the vinegar. Mix the raisins and vinegar into the vegetable mixture. Salt to taste. For a variation, add a few drained capers or olives.

Burned onions and leeks are not an obstacle so much as a lucky mistake. If yours get too charred to eat as you'd planned, make one of these delicious sandwich condiments.

Onion sauce I

~

Chop burned leeks or onions finely. Combine 1 cup with ¾ cup mayonnaise, ¼ cup chopped cornichons or other cucumber pickles, and any herbs you have chopped.

Onion sauce II

~

Make a sachet of 2 cloves smashed garlic, 1 bay leaf, and 1 small sprig rosemary. Reduce 2 cups cream by one-third, with the sachet in it. Remove the sachet and add 2 cups chopped burned leeks to the cream. Finish with chopped fresh tarragon, parsley, and chives.

Too spicy or too sour vegetable soup or stew should be treated as curry concentrate. The word *curry* means so many things that whatever you're beginning with is bound to be traditional somewhere. I've had curries with raisins and bananas in them, and curries with nuts, and tomatoes and tuna, and summer squash.

Adaptable curry

~

½ cup finely diced onion or scallions
½ cup thinly sliced fennel, if you have it
1 clove garlic, thinly sliced
1 chile, thinly sliced (unless the problem is spiciness)
1 tablespoon peanut oil
scant ⅛ tablespoon cinnamon, if the dish contains fruit
*   or nuts*
1 to 2 cups overseasoned ingredient
1 can coconut milk
salt to taste (unless the problem is saltiness)
¼ cup lime juice (unless the problem is sourness)

Cook the onion, fennel, garlic, and chile, if using, over low heat in the peanut oil until tender. Add your overseasoned vegetable, stir through, then add the coconut milk. Cook it over low heat until it's combined. Taste for salt. Add lime juice if using. Serve topped with fresh mint or basil if you have any, on rice.

Salty eggplant, green beans, tomatoes, peppers, onions, cauliflower, fennel, broccoli, or zucchini should be marinated in olive oil, garlic, and anchovy. They will become a perfect version of Italian vegetables *sott'olio,* or "under oil." This is a lovely appetizer laid over hot toast.

Vegetables sott'olio

~

oversalted vegetables   4 anchovy fillets
1 clove garlic   olive oil to cover

Cut the vegetables into pieces of even size. Put them in a jar with the garlic, anchovy fillets, and olive oil to cover it all well by ½ inch. Let it sit together for a day before tasting. This is also good on sandwiches, or for topping soft-boiled eggs.

Salty kale, collard greens, or Swiss chard make good pesto.

Cooking greens pesto

~

3 cups oversalted cooked greens, cooled and finely chopped
½ clove garlic
¼ cup ground toasted pine nuts, walnuts, or pecans
1 cup freshly grated Parmesan cheese
enough olive oil to turn it into a thick paste

Combine the first four in a food processor, drizzling in the oil while processing.

Mushy carrots, green beans, or broccoli become a delicious sandwich condiment, especially for cold meat. This is also good on its own served on crackers or toast.

Carrot or green bean or broccoli piccalilli or chow-chow

~

2 cups carrots or green beans or broccoli
1 scant tablespoon grainy or smooth Dijon mustard
1 scant tablespoon pickled onions or chiles
1 scant tablespoon of chopped cornichons
½ clove garlic, pounded to a paste
ground black pepper
½ tablespoon red wine vinegar
a squeeze of lemon
a drizzle of honey
2 tablespoons chopped roasted peppers
1 to 2 tablespoons olive oil

Chop the vegetables up. Combine with the other ingredients. Store in a jar in the refrigerator and eat in sandwiches.

Beets or potatoes too crunchy to be a side dish make good relish.

Eastern European beet or potato relish

~

Finely dice half as much onion as you have undercooked vegetable. Soak the onion in equal parts mustard and white vinegar. Let it sit for 15 minutes. Mix the beet or potato with the onion, and add a big handful of chopped herbs and 1 tablespoon chopped pickles. Serve it spooned over the fish or chicken the vegetable was supposed to accompany. For a variation, add 1 tablespoon sour cream, yogurt, or mayonnaise. Adjust the seasoning accordingly.

Undercooked rice should be turned into elegant little rice crispies. These are a poor consolation at dinnertime but a nice soup garnish. Fry a small handful in a few inches of hot grapeseed or peanut oil. Let them drain, then freeze them and use them on puréed soups.

Overcooked rice becomes this delicious pudding. Should you undercook rice, then try to amend it by cooking it further and end up with overcooked rice, turn here, too.

Savory rice pudding

~

¼ cup finely diced white or yellow onion
1 tablespoon butter
1 tablespoon rice wine vinegar or white wine
1 cup overcooked rice
1 to 2 cups chicken stock
¼ cup frozen English peas, or rings of shallot quickly fried in
*   hot oil, or thinly sliced scallions tossed with roasted peanuts*
*   and a sprinkle of vinegar*
1 teaspoon soy sauce and ⅛ teaspoon sugar, or ½ cup grated
*   Parmesan cheese*
chopped fresh parsley or other herb

Sauté the onions in the butter until tender. If you want this to seem Asian, add rice vinegar; if Italian, white wine. Add the rice. Add enough stock to make the rice soupy. Thaw the peas under warm running water or fry the shallots or slice the scallions, and so on. Taste the savory pudding for salt. If it is to be Asian, combine the soy sauce and sugar and mix it into the pudding. If it is to be Italian, mix in the cheese, parsley, and peas. Serve in hot bowls, garnished, with more soy sauce or cheese for adding to each bowl. If you have the fried shallots, scatter them on the Asian pudding.

Overcooked rice or lentils should be turned into little pancakes and panfried. This is a truly delicious solution.

Rice or lentil pancakes

~

Press out any excess liquid by putting mushy rice or lentils in a colander and pressing down with your hands or a kitchen towel. Taste them for salt. Heat a little olive oil in a nonstick frying pan. Once the oil is hot, use your hands to form pancakes about 2 to 3 inches around and carefully place them into the hot pan. Adjust the heat to keep them cooking well and sizzling, but not burning.

Let the pancakes cook on their first side until you see a browned surface begin to spread up their sides. Try not to move them around or prod them too much. Turn each one over quickly and cook it on its second side until it's nicely browned.

If the mixture doesn't stay together when you press it into cakes, add a little beaten egg. This also works with gluey mashed potatoes: dust them lightly first in flour, then dip them in beaten egg, then coat them in breadcrumbs before frying as above.

These are wonderful topped with a little spoonful of crème fraîche or sour cream and a few chopped chives. I had a bad rice moment a few years ago and got into the habit of keeping American paddlefish caviar, which is inexpensive and environmentally friendly, in the house. It is a spectacular accompaniment.

Overcooked beans should be turned into pancakes as above, or mashed further with a little good olive oil and called bean purée.

Oversalted rice should be saved for using in small amounts in soup. If you're not making soup soon, freeze it, labeled "oversalted." Undersalt the next soup you make, thaw the rice, and add it to the soup as it warms.

Oversalted grits or polenta should be made into fries.

> *Pour salty grits or polenta onto a baking sheet or cutting board and let them cool. Cut them into pieces good for picking up. Put out one plate each of flour, beaten egg, and breadcrumbs. Dip pieces of grits or polenta into first flour, then egg, then breadcrumbs, and lay them on wax paper. Heat a shallow layer of peanut or olive oil in a skillet and panfry the pieces on each side until they're golden. Serve them with plain yogurt mixed with a little garlic pounded to a paste, or undersalted* salsa verde.

Oversalted pasta should be saved, mixed with unsalted butter and a lot of fresh herbs, like parsley, rosemary, and marjoram, and made into a pasta frittata, using the recipe on page 30. Remember not to salt the eggs.

Undercooked boiled eggs can only be discovered once you've peeled one. If one in a batch is clearly wobbly, the others are, too. My two strategies, depending on time and circumstance, have always been to either serve them anyway, with a bowl of salt and a spoon, in egg cups, or to put the ones I haven't peeled back into simmering water for a minute. If you've peeled them all, you can put them on a cookie sheet in a toaster oven or regular oven and bake them until they have, as a friend put it, "more integrity." They will emerge with interesting browning in places.

Overboiled eggs should be turned into egg salad. If the yolks are unpleasantly chalky or the white rubbery, separate the two parts from each other, finely chop each, then put them in a bowl. Add a heaping spoonful mayonnaise, homemade if you have time, a teaspoon chopped drained capers, and a finely chopped anchovy per two overcooked eggs. Salt and pepper to taste and eat the egg salad on buttered toast.

Broken aioli: Set aside two cups. Cook a pound of any pasta in well-seasoned water. Once you drain it, add a quarter cup of pasta water, the broken aioli, a cup toasted, chopped walnuts, and a half cup of chopped fresh parsley. This is very rich, and good compensation for the eggs' and oil's rebelliousness. It is even better if you top each bowl with a half cup of toasted breadcrumbs.

Acknowledgments

~

Thank you to everyone who started the wheels turning in the strange, creaky process of getting this book written and published: Katrina Heron, without whom I never would have started; Roger Hodge, who has been a mentor and role model for a decade; Michael Pollan, who was unstinting with support and feedback; Alice Waters, who gave me inspiration and confidence to speak in my voice; Beth Wareham, who thought writing it a good idea; Kara Watson, who agreed, and helped me create a book I liked, even when it made her job harder, and then harder yet; Heather Schroder, who loves food and words and giving advice, and is a formidable ally.

My deepest thanks to everyone who read various versions of these pages: Gabriel Kahane, Gabriel Boylan, Ilmi Granoff, Ben Pauker, Ethan Devine, Pankaj Venugopal, Keith Sharman, Marcia Posner, and Marissa Guggiana.

Thank you to everyone who hosted me during this book's writing: Andrew Beahrs, Dan Holton-Roth, Kit Crosby, and Dan Tepfer.

I couldn't have written it without having been taught to cook. Thank you to Gabrielle Hamilton, Olivia Sargeant, the staff of Farm 255, Dan Barber, Michael Anthony, and Cal Peternell for teaching me.

Thank you to everyone who put up with me while I was writing, whether by staying close or staying away. Many of your names are above. If yours isn't and this sounds familiar, it is addressed to you.

The wonderful thing about the village it takes to write a book is that everyone has more than one job. My recipe testers are among the people I've thanked above, as are people who've helped me work through ideas and eaten the results. Thank you all again for assuming the secondary duty of cooking and eating on my behalf.

I have dedicated this book to my mother and my brother, and the dedication is not enough. They have done all of the above: started wheels turning and hosted and read and tested recipes and stayed close and stayed away. They've taught me to taste and cook and eat and love. I have dedicated it to amateurs, for whom I wrote it and to whom I am indebted. I have dedicated it to my father also, and I thank him again, too, for having shown me grace.

Index

~

adaptable curry, 232–33
Adler, Tamar, xi–xiii
aioli, 31–34, 179
   broken, 238
anchovies, 17, 50, 101, 129–31,
   132, 134, 135, 137, 138, 148,
   149
   bagna cauda, 131
   in oil, 130
   paste made from, 130
   storing of, 130
animals, treatment of, 155–56
Apicius, 137
apple and half-cooked-vegetable
   salad, 191
arancini, 122
artichokes, 56–57, 96
arugula, 73
asparagus, 80

baba ghanoush, 188
bacon, 156, 168
bagna cauda, 131
barley, 127, 196
basic vinaigrette, 100

basil, 70, 71, 72–73, 211
   pesto, 72–73
bay leaf, 107, 153, 159, 178, 180,
   181
beans, 105–15, 135
   broth of, 107, 108–9, 114,
     117–18, 194
   canned, 200
   cassoulet, 110
   cooking of, 108
   dried vs. fresh, 114
   as economical, 109
   eggs and, 110
   meat and, 110–11
   minestrone, 111–13
   overcooked, 236
   salty, 196
   soaking of, 106
   soup of, 111–13, 135, 202
   storing of, 109
   testing doneness of, 108
   see also specific beans
béchamel sauce, 36, 49–50
beef stew, 60
beer, 92, 159, 183, 225

beet(s), 36, 38, 39, 41, 46, 47
  leaves of, 41–42
  relish, Eastern European, 234
  soup of, 48
bigoli in salsa, 132, 148–49
bittersweet compote, 210
Bloody Mary, 136, 209
bluefish, 178
boiling water, 5–17, 21, 23
  adding salt to, 7, 8
  beans and, 108, 110
  covering, 6
  eggs in, 6, 21–22
  fish in, 179
  leeks in, 150
  in making preserves, 211–12
  meat in, 11–17
  olive oil in, 6
  pasta in, 6, 7, 10
  reusing, 11
  rice in, 118–19
  tasting of, 6–7
  use of cold vs. hot water for, 6
  vegetables in, 6, 8, 9–10, 11
bollito misto, 11, 12
Bolognese sauce, 164–65
bones, 165–67, 168, 177, 178
bouille, 12
Brantley, Chip, 187
bread, 79–82, 84–88, 92, 225
  croutons, 88
  Jim Lahey's no-knead, 81–82
  olive toasts, 135
  seasonal recipes for, 80
  stale, 84–85, 86, 87, 105, 148
  storing of, 88
breadcrumbs, 88

bread salad, 87
bread soup, 85–87
  ribollita, 85–86, 87, 90
Bresson, Robert, 187, 195
Brillat-Savarin, Jean Anthelme,
  167
brine, 136–37
  meat, 169
  pickle, 208–9
  vinegar, 208
broccoli, 8–9, 36, 38–39, 45, 47,
  234
  hot, toasty, 50–51
  soup of, 48
broth, 15, 59, 166, 184
  bean, 107, 108–9, 114, 117–18,
  194
  poached eggs in, 24
  rice in, 117–18
  seasonal recipes for, 15
  see also stock
brownies, Amy's, 224
brutti ma buoni, 223–24
butter, 73, 76, 120, 122, 125, 131,
  148, 152, 168, 172, 178, 183,
  217
  clarified, 26, 72
  herb, 73
  maître d'hôtel, 73
butter lettuce, 99–100
buttermilk, 108
butternut squash, 36, 39–40, 80

cabbage, 96, 131
  boiling of, 8, 10, 153
  roasting of, 153
calçots, 52

canned food, 199–206
capers, 17, 94, 97, 129, 134, 135,
  138, 139
  brined vs. salt-packed, 136
Capon, Robert Farrar, 69,
  156–57, 158
carbonara, 24–25
Carême, Marie-Antoine, 222
carrot(s), 215
  piccalilli (chow-chow), 234
cassoulet, 110
cauliflower, 8–9, 36, 38, 40, 45,
  47, 190
  hot, toasty, 50–51
  soup of, 48
celery, 85, 86, 131, 151, 162, 215
  with lemon, 152
celery root, 39, 95
charchari, 188
cheese, 10, 22, 47, 89–92, 122, 202
  grilled, sandwiches, 197
  making of, 90
  sotto cielo, 90
  see also specific cheeses
cherries, 224
Chez Panisse, xi, 65, 97
chicken, 134, 143
  boiling of, 13–15, 218
  boneless breasts of, 157–58
  checking for doneness of,
    14–15
  confit of, 170
  cutting of, 16
  feet, 13
  livers of, 171–73
  roasting, 158, 218
  stock of, 126, 194, 200, 218

chickpea(s), 56, 135, 200
  pasta, 201–2
  soup, 206
Child, Julia, 6, 34
chile, 123, 169, 181, 208, 209
chives, 153
chops, 157–58
chow-chow (piccalilli), 190, 234
chowder, 184
chuck eye, 158
cilantro, 71
cinnamon, 14, 124
citrus fruits, 97
  peels of, 58
  syrup of, 58
clams, 183–84
clarified butter, 26, 72
collard greens, 86
compote, 210
cooking, 1–4
  balance in, 195
  economical, xi
  falling in love with, 141–45
  learning while, 63–67
  with scraps, xi
  senses used during, 64
  turning failures into successes
    in, 187–97
  using tail ends in, 57–61, 87,
    99, 107, 151, 159, 165, 166,
    178
  utensils used for, 64–67
Cook's Oracle, The (Kitchiner), 12
coriander seeds, 178
corn, ground, *see* grits; polenta
cornichons (gherkins), 94, 129,
  137, 138, 139

creamy vinaigrette, 108
crispy lardons, 229
Crock-Pot, 66
croûte au pot, 85
croutons, 88
curry, 181
   adaptable, 232–33
   end-of-the-week vegetable,
     51–52
   very spicy, for bluefish, 181

dandelions, 102
David, Elizabeth, 93, 96, 102, 122
desserts, 221–27
dill, 182
dough, olive oil tart, 83–84, 149

eggplant, 80, 189, 231
eggs, xii, 19–34, 131
   beans and, 110
   boiling of, 6, 21–22, 237
   duck, 25
   frittatas, 29, 30
   frying of, 24–25
   mayonnaise and, 31–34
   meat and, 167
   oeufs en restes, 24
   oeufs mayonnaise, 34
   olive oil and, 25, 26
   overboiled, 237
   pickles and, 137
   pies, 29–30
   poached, 22–24, 126, 150
   sauce gribiche, 138
   scrambling of, 24–25
   served cold, 29
   in stew, 24
   on toast, 22

tortilla española, 29–30
undercooked boiled, 237
yolks of, 19–20
see also omelets
English peas, 53, 80

farro, 127
fat, 71–72, 136, 156, 166, 167,
   195
   meat stored in, 170
   saving of, 15
fava beans, 55
Fearnley-Whittingstall, Hugh,
   155, 156, 158
fennel, 178, 181, 215
figs, 224
fish, 175–85
   bones of, 177, 178
   brandade de morue, 180
   buying, 176
   cakes, 204–5
   canned, 204
   cleaning of, 176–77
   confit of, 181
   cost of, 175
   curing of, 176
   fillet of, 179
   freshness of, 176
   poaching of, 176, 181
   roasting of, 177
   salting of, 179–80, 181
   smoking of, 176
   soup of, 177, 179
   spicy curry for, 181
   stock of, 176, 178, 182
   testing for doneness of, 177
   using tail ends of, 178, 183
   see also shellfish; *specific fish*

Fisher, M. F. K., xii, 1, 3, 5, 19, 79, 89, 129
food:
  memories of, 142
  preservation of, 207–13
  rationing of, 1
frittatas, 29, 30
fruit, 96–97, 224
  dried, 134
  see also citrus fruits; *specific fruits*

garlic(ky), 17, 32, 81, 85, 100, 101, 108, 112, 123, 125, 126, 131, 134, 135, 154, 162, 163, 180, 181, 185, 189, 200, 201, 203, 211, 217, 231
  leaf, stem, and core pesto, 43
German vegetable salad, 190
ghee, 72
gherkins (cornichons), 94, 129, 137, 138, 139
giblets, chicken, 13
goat cheese, 91
gratin, 36, 49–50, 111, 190
gravy, 170
green bean(s), 209, 234
  spicy, 203–4
greens, 37, 41–42, 86, 125
  boiling of, 6
  on bread, 80
  cooking greens pesto, 233
  gratin, 49–50
grilled cheese sandwiches, 197
grits, 124–26
  oversalted, 237

ham (pork leg), 156, 168
Hamilton, Gabrielle, 27

heavy cream, 108, 124
Henderson, Fergus, 9, 173
herbs, 69–77, 138
  butter flavored with, 73
  butter or oil with, 72, 73–74
  frying of, 74, 76
  minestra di herbe passate, 75–76
  oils flavored with, 71–72
  omelet made with, 75, 79
  storing of, 71
  see also specific herbs
Hesser, Amanda, 34, 164
homemade soda, 58
How to Cook a Wolf (Fisher), 1, 5, 79

juniper berries, 169

kalamata olives, 132
kale, 125
kohlrabi, 36

laarb, 194–95
laitue au jus, 102
lamb:
  heart of, 173
  leg of, 156
leeks, 86, 150, 178, 184
  burned, 231
leftovers, xii
  meat, 161
  oeufs en restes, 24
  risotto, 122
lemon, 100, 108, 181
  celery with, 152
  juice of, 32, 101, 135, 139
  peel of, 134, 181

lentil(s), 97, 109, 196
  overcooked, 236
  pancakes, 236
  salad, 97–98
lettuce, 93, 98–100, 108
  butter, 99–100
  and rice soup, 120–21
  served hot, 102
  storing of, 99
lovage, 137
lucques olives, 133

McGee, Harold, 107–8
mackerel, 175, 178, 204
maître d'hôtel butter, 73
marinated goat cheese, 91
marjoram, 72
marmalade, 210
mayonnaise, 31–34, 73, 74, 95,
    108, 139
meat, 155–73, 193
  beans and, 110–11, 112
  boiling of, 11–17
  bones of, 165–67, 168
  braised, 159–60
  braising liquid from, 162–63
  brine, 169
  buying, 158
  confit of, 170
  crispy lardons, 229
  dried out, 229
  drippings from, 170
  eggs and, 167
  fried, 163
  ground, 163–64
  morality of eating, 155, 173
  "offal," 171–73

reheating of, 157
roasting of, 167–68
slow-cooked, 157, 159, 160,
    217
slow-cooked, summer veg-
    etables and, 162
stock of, 166, 168
terrines of, 165
undercooked, 230–31
and vegetable hash, 230
white Bolognese sauce, 164–65
see also specific meats
meat loaf, 165
melons, 224
minestrone, 111–13, 114
mirotons, 161
mortar and pestle, 65
mussels, 183
mustard, 32, 100, 101, 135, 138

nasturtiums, 137
niçoise olives, 132, 139, 149
nutmeg, 124
nuts, 44, 45, 72, 73, 97
  walnuts, 226–27

okra, 209
olive(s), 125, 129, 132–35, 137,
    216
  kalamata, 132
  lucques, 133
  niçoise, 132, 139, 149
  paste made from, 134–35
  picholine, 133
  pitting of, 133, 139
  seasoned, 132
  toast, 135

olive oil, 17, 23, 28, 32–33, 73, 87, 88, 92, 93, 94, 113, 126, 135, 138, 139, 148, 149, 153, 162, 180, 181, 200, 203, 217
  with beans, 107, 111
  on bread, 80, 81
  eggs and, 25, 26
  meat stored in, 171
  in salad dressing, 95, 100, 101, 108, 135
  tart dough, 83–84
omelets, 2, 26–28, 60, 149
  fillings for, 27–28
  flat, 28
  herb, 75
onion(s), 29, 44, 45, 84, 85, 86, 120, 147–48, 149, 154, 163, 178, 184, 200, 209
  burned, 231
  sauces, 232
  soup, 148
oregano, 97
osso buco, 156
oysters, 145

Parmesan cheese, 16, 22, 25, 30, 43, 49, 72, 73, 86, 87, 109, 121, 125–26, 191, 202
parsley, 17, 69–70, 74, 87, 94, 120, 126, 135
  leaves of, 139
  oil of, 72, 179
  salad, 94–95
  stems of, 57, 70, 107, 178, 181
pasta, 6, 7, 10, 17, 25, 30, 43, 114, 148, 184
  bigoli in salsa, 148–49

chickpea, 201–2
  oversalted, 237
  pasta e fagioli, 109
  with sardines, 185
  sauce for, 10, 134, 163
pâté, chicken liver, 172–73
peanut oil, 123, 181
peas, 7
  English, 53, 80
  soup of, 53–54
Pecorino cheese, 22
peppercorns, 169, 178, 181
peppers, 162, 182, 231
pesto, 43, 72–73
  basil, 72–73
  cooking greens, 233
picholine olives, 133
pickle brine, 208–9
pickles, 137, 207, 212
  cornichons (gherkins), 94, 129, 137, 138, 139
  eggs and, 137
  relish, 137
plums, 224
polenta, 22, 124–26, 217
  oversalted, 237
  polenta Bolognese, 125
polentina, 126–27
pork:
  belly, 168
  ham (pork leg), 156, 168
  roast, 169–70
  shoulder braised in milk with garlic, sage, and lemon, 217–18
potato(es), 29, 75, 131, 153, 161, 162, 163, 180, 190, 217

potato(es) (*continued*)
  boiling of, 6, 10, 14
  roasting of, 153
  as salt sponges, 195–96
  sweet, *see* sweet potato(es)
pot-au-feu, 11, 12
pots and pans, 65
Prune Restaurant, 27, 94
pudding:
  rice, 123–24
  savory rice, 235
purée, 48–49, 200
puttanesca sauce, 134

quinoa, 127

radishes, 215
raisins, 124
ribollita, 85–86, 87, 90
rice, 22, 97, 98, 110, 117–21, 123,
    127, 188
  burned, 192
  fried, 122–23
  and lettuce soup, 120–21
  overcooked, 119, 235, 236
  oversalted, 236
  pancakes, 236
  pudding, 129–30
  pudding, savory, 235
  salad, 97–98
  sticky, 143
  Thai fried, 123
  undercooked, 235
ricotta, 84, 89, 91–92, 191
  savory baked, 92
risotto, 49, 120–22, 166
  Bolognese, 121

leftover, 122
Milanese, 121
risotto in cantina, 122
root vegetable(s), 38, 39–41,
    95–96, 163
rémoulade, 95–96
rosé, 32
rosemary, 71, 74, 84, 87, 135
  cake, 222–23

saag paneer, 60
sage, 72, 74
salad, 93–103, 151
  cold-weather, 95–96
  composed, 98
  dressing for, 106–9
  fruit in, 96–97
  German vegetable, 190
  of grains and beans, 97–98
  for a natural disaster, 205
  parsley, 94–95
  rice or lentil, 97–98
  root vegetable rémoulade,
    95–96
  salade niçoise, 98
  smoky vegetable, 231
  Thai toasted rice, 194–95
  vegetable, 45, 93–94, 188–90
salami, 125, 126
salmon, 175, 178, 204
salsa verde, 16, 19, 27–28, 71, 151
salt, xii, 13, 17, 23, 107, 136, 169,
    180, 181, 192
  anchovies packed in, 129, 130
  for boiling water, 7, 8
sandwiches, 46–47, 60, 161
  grilled cheese, 197

sardines, 178, 184, 204
  pasta with, 185
satsumaimo, 46
sauce gribiche, 138
sauerkraut, 202
scallions, 150
Serve It Forth (Fisher), 3
shakshouka, 24
shallots, 17, 94, 100, 123, 149,
    172, 181, 191
  vinegar roasted, 149–50
shellfish:
  clams, 183–84
  lobster, 178
  mussels, 183
  oysters, 145
  shrimp, 132, 137, 179
  see also fish
soda, homemade, 58
sotto cielo, 90
soup, 15–16, 47–48, 59, 163, 166,
    183, 184, 195, 196, 203
  bean, 111–13, 141, 202
  bread, 85–87
  fish, 177, 179
  meat, 165
  minestrone, 111–13
  onion, 148
  rice and lettuce, 120–21
  seasonal, 112
  tail ends in, 99
squash, 38, 40–41, 125
star anise, 14
stock, 8, 120, 126, 148, 151, 159,
    162, 164, 166, 168, 176, 178,
    182, 194, 200

summer vegetables and slow-
    cooked meat, 162
Supper of the Lamb, The (Capon),
    156
sweet potato(es), 37, 41, 46, 51,
    217
  salad, Peruvian, 46
  soup of, 48
Swiss chard, 37, 58–59

tacos, 161
tapas, 44
tapenade, 135
tarragon, 71
tart(s), 87–89
  dough, olive oil, 83–84, 149
  seasonal recipes for, 84
  vegetables in, 84
tartar sauce, 138–39
terrine, 165
thyme, 71, 84, 107, 149, 169, 181
tomatoes, 80, 86, 176, 189
  canned, 178, 182, 199–200
  canning of, 210–12
tomato paste, 162, 163, 231
tuna, 175
turnips, 37, 190, 217

vanilla, 124
vegetable(s):
  baba ghanoush, 189
  boiling of, 6, 8, 9–10, 11, 189
  burned, 187–88, 231
  cooking of, ahead of time, 35
  crunchy, 234
  curry, end-of-the-week, 51–52
  frying of, 56

vegetable(s) (*continued*)
  German vegetable salad, 190
  meat and vegetable hash, 230
  mushy, 234
  oversalted, 233
  pickling of, 208–9
  poached eggs in, 22
  roasting of, 35, 36, 37–38, 40,
    151, 153
  salad, smoky, 231
  salad of, 45, 93–94, 188–90,
    231
  in sandwiches, 46–47
  "shocking" of, 9
  sott'olio, 233
  summer, and slow-cooked
    meat, 162
  in tarts, 84
  undercooking of, 9, 191
  using tail ends of, 58–59, 99,
    107, 151, 159, 166
  see also root vegetable(s); *specific*
    vegetables

vinaigrette, 44, 100–101, 135
  basic, 100
  creamy, 108
  dogged, 101
vinegar(y), 17, 23, 32, 41, 45, 93,
    95, 100, 101, 108, 125–26,
    135, 138, 139, 149, 173, 191,
    203, 231
  barbecue sauce, 193–94
  brine, 208, 212
  roasted shallots, 149–50

walnuts, 226–27
water, boiling of, *see* boiling water
Waters, Alice, xi–xiii
white Bolognese sauce, 164–65
wine, 92, 113, 159, 162, 172, 183,
    184, 217, 225, 226–27

yogurt, 73, 74

zucchini, 80, 96, 162, 189, 191,
    231